stepfamilies

stepfamilies

Love, Marriage, and Parenting in the First Decade

Dr. James H. Bray

and John Kelly

Broadway Books New York

BROADWAY

A hardcover edition of this book was published in 1998 by Broadway Books.

STEPFAMILIES. Copyright © 1998 by Dr. James H. Bray and John Kelly. All rights reserved. Printed in the United States of America. No part of this book may be reproduced or transmitted in any form or by any means, electronic or mechanical, including photocopying, recording, or by any information storage and retrieval system, without written permission from the publisher. For information, address Broadway Books, a division of Random House, Inc., 1540 Broadway, New York, NY 10036.

Broadway Books titles may be purchased for business or promotional use or for special sales. For information, please write to: Special Markets Department, Random House, Inc., 1540 Broadway, New York, NY 10036.

BROADWAY BOOKS and its logo, a letter B bisected on the diagonal, are trademarks of Broadway Books, a division of Random House, Inc.

First trade paperback edition published 1999.

Designed by Songhee Kim

The Library of Congress has catalogued the hardcover edition as:
Bray, James H.
    StepFamilies : love, marriage, and parenting in the first decade / by James H. Bray and John Kelly. —1st ed.
        p.   cm.
    ISBN 0-7679-0102-9 (hardcover)
    1. Stepfamilies.   2. Remarriage.   3. Stepparents.   4. Stepchildren.
I. Kelly, John, 1945-   .   II. Title.
HQ759.92.B73   1998
306.874—dc21   98-3543
                                                                           CIP

ISBN 0-7679-0103-7

04   05   06   13   12   11   10   9   8   7

This book is dedicated to my family for their love and support, which has enriched my life in finite ways.
This book is especially dedicated to my children:

TO LINDSEY, I say thank you for your sweetness, tenacity, and love. You have brought great joy and happiness to me.

TO JESSICA, I say thank you for your special smile, your love and kindness, and your creative spirit, which impacts all whom you touch.

TO MATTHEW, I say thank you for your love of life— playing full out—your fearlessness, and your special tenderness and love that is ever present.

You have added many dimensions to my life and have inspired me to make a difference, as you are all doing.

This project could not have been completed without the hard work and dedication of a large number of people. I first became interested in studying stepfamilies through an invitation from Dr. Carol Brady, a psychologist, and Joyce Ambler, a social worker, who noticed that children from divorced families and stepfamilies were overrepresented in our clinic. We decided to submit a grant proposal to develop and evaluate a treatment program to help stepfamilies cope with their particular stresses and problems. While this grant application was not funded, it eventually led me to create the Developmental Issues in StepFamilies (DIS) Research Project.

I owe a really special debt of gratitude to Sandra Berger, a social worker, who was my collaborator throughout the project. Sandra made invaluable contributions all around. It has been an extraordinary pleasure to work with her. She is a first-rate scholar, a great collaborator, and a wonderful person. Joyce Ambler helped at the beginning of the DIS Project to get it going, but she had to leave during the first year.

There were numerous graduate and undergraduate students who contributed to the project, interviewed the families, and analyzed the data. These include Tom Mann, Brad Michael, Alan Silverblatt, Sarah Milford, Carol Boethel, Susan Gershenhorn, Josue Maymi, Jovana Cowart, Lynne Higgenbotham, Kathy Pacey, Sarah Pollack, Odett McGowan, Alixandre Bennett, Liz Mercier, Jadine Hoefker, Susan Scott, Gina Touch, Jeffrey Parsons, and Dianne Kraft. I am proud to say that they completed their degrees, and many of them are now practicing psychologists and therapists, often helping stepfamilies in our communities. Carol Boethel deserves special thanks for continuing to help me after the project was over.

Lynn Corazao, Deborah Harper, and Ellen Fadigan served as our able support staff. Through a cooperative arrangement with the University of Houston Psychology Department, we also had many undergraduate psychology majors help us analyze and code the videotapes of the families. Their help was also invaluable for completing the project.

Dr. E. Mavis Hetherington and her staff (especially Anne Hollier, Margaret Hagan, and Marlene Eisenberg) at the University of Virginia served as our consultants throughout the project. Mavis has become a great friend and colleague, whom I can't thank enough. I will always appreciate her for setting high standards of excellence to emulate.

This research was supported by National Institutes of Health grants, RO1 HD 18025 and RO1 HD 22642, from the National Institute of Child Health and Human Development. Dr. Josephine Arasteh was our grants officer and she provided outstanding technical help and support for our project. Dr. Teresa Levitin was the head of the review panel that made valuable suggestions for improving the project. The first grant was awarded while I was on the faculty in the Department of Psychology at Texas Woman's University-Houston Center. I completed the second grant while I was on the faculty in the Department of Family Medicine at Baylor College of Medicine.

I also appreciate the small grant from the Kempner Foundation of Galveston, which helped us get the project started. Katherine Oerting of Eisaman, Johns & Laws Advertising, Inc., developed and donated a poster for our project to help us recruit families. Jane Hargis of Kwik Koopy Greenway Plaza donated the printing for the poster.

I also acknowledge and thank the many scholars and clinicians who discussed their ideas about divorce and remarriage with us over the years. Emily and John Visher are real pioneers in this area, and their early publications helped me get going. Many others also contributed: Connie Ahrons, Scott Browning, Marilyn Coleman, Charlene Depner, Mark Hine, Larry Ganong, Janet Johnston, Joan Kelly, Larry Kurdek, Kay Pasley, Patricia Papernow, Cliff Sager, Judith Wallerstein, and Nick Zill.

I also appreciate the love of my former wife, Juneau N. Shepherd, during the project.

My parents, Jamie and Joveda Bray, have always been a source of love and support for me. I thank them for this and for providing "The Barn" to have fun parties for the StepFamily Project staff.

I also want to thank John Eddie Williams, Jr., for his support and encouragement and my former chairman, Dr. Bob Rakel, and John Eddie for their continual urging to do this book. I thank Colleen and Bernadette for their support and help in beginning this book. I am especially grateful to Louise for her encouragement and words of wisdom in completing the book.

It has been a pleasure to get to know and work with Sheila Weller. Sheila helped us interview several of the families for the book and contributed her outstanding writing and editing skills.

The editors and staff at Broadway Books have been wonderful to work with. Janet Goldstein's, Charlie Conrad's, and Ted Sammons's comments and encouragement have helped guide this project from a proposal into the reality of a book that we are proud of. Trigg Robinson and Debbie Stier have been wonderful to work with in arranging for the publicity for the book.

Finally, I want to thank the two hundred plus families who participated in the study and who entrusted their families to my professional help. They contributed the essential information that will be useful to the people who read this book. I acknowledge their dedication and support of this project and appreciate the difference they have made in the lives of others who are touched by sharing their lives with us.

There is an old Texas saying, "Blessed is he who has nothing to say and gives no verbal proof of the fact." After reading this book I think you will find that we have a lot of valuable things to say. Fifteen years later I believe we now have many good answers to the question of what's "regular" and unique for stepfamilies. You will find these answers in the pages of this book.

March 1998
James H. Bray
Houston, Texas

Contents

stepfamilies

The videotape opens with a shot of the wedding guests. About a hundred of them are gathered on the lawn in front of Temple Beth-El on what looks like a perfect spring day. The Texas sky above the temple is a flawless blue, except for a single cloud over the head of a woman in an extravagant red hat. As the synagogue doors open, a cheer goes up. The crowd can see what the camera cannot yet: a man and a woman about to emerge onto the steps. There they are now. The man is in his late thirties, tall, balding, thickly eyebrowed, and serious-looking. He has the face of a professor or a professional man—a doctor or lawyer, perhaps. But even on this happy occasion, there is something reserved, formal about him. One would guess that he takes himself very seriously.

The woman next to him is about thirty-three or thirty-four, short and slim with dark, closely cropped hair. She is not pretty, not by Texas standards, but her face—animated, lively, intelligent—is attractive and something more. Confident isn't quite the right word, but there is a quality in the face that suggests grace, ease, centeredness.

The woman bends down and whispers something to the curly-haired girl beside her. The little girl smiles and nods; she takes the bouquet of flowers from the woman and throws it out into the crowd.

The videotape ends with another shot of the child, whose name is Naomi. In this frame the seven-year-old stands on the sidewalk waving to a departing black Lexus. The bumper sticker on the back of the car, "Just Married," surprises. It seems out of character for the couple, particularly for the austere-looking man.

When the videotape is over, I am almost tempted to ask Jeffrey Goldsmith about the bumper sticker. But I decide to reserve my curiosity for another time. He and his wife, Sarah, are eager to talk about their stepfamily tonight. The wedding video, I gather, is intended to be the first page of the story. Jeffrey and Sarah will show me how happy they were on their wedding day, then tell me everything that has gone wrong in the six months since.

As in most marriages, the Goldsmiths have two different versions of what has gone wrong and why. In Jeffrey's version, Naomi, Sarah's daughter and the little girl in the video, bears a major responsibility for the past months of unhappiness. Jeffrey complains that Naomi is distant and cold. Often, he says, she behaves in ways that divide the Goldsmith home, turn it into warring camps. "I live in one camp," Jeffrey declares, "Naomi and Sarah live in the other."

Jeffrey tells me he has made attempts to bridge the chasm. "I've tried to befriend Naomi," he says. "Sarah knows how hard I've tried. But all I get is sullenness."

Sarah's response to Jeffrey's criticism is to provide her own version of the Goldsmiths' decline and fall. It has two villains. The first is Barbara, Jeffrey's former wife. "She calls incessantly," Sarah says, "and thoughtful Jeffrey here always takes her calls." Sarah looks over at her husband. "If Barbara says jump, you say how high."

Sarah says Barbara is a constant drain on the Goldsmiths' finances and "crazy to boot—pathological even. She scares me sometimes." Jeffrey's younger son, Aaron, also is a "big problem," according to Sarah. Aaron is rebellious and rude, she says, rude to her and rude to Naomi.

"He's still adjusting to the divorce," Jeffrey declares, but Sarah dismisses the remark with an impatient wave of the hand.

"I thought we agreed to stop making excuses for our kids," she says.

The more the Goldsmiths talk, the clearer two things become to me. Despite the mutual recriminations, Jeffrey and Sarah still love one another, and, like so many new recruits to stepfamily life, they are confused and frightened. Only six months ago, standing on the steps of Temple Beth-El on that perfect spring day, it had all looked so simple. How could two mature, sensitive, intelligent people *not* succeed at stepfamily life? Yet here the Goldsmiths are now, together not even a year and already angry and alienated.

How could their shiny dream of a life together tarnish so quickly?

The Goldsmiths' story of hope and disillusionment is perhaps the most common story of stepfamily life. And, more than half the time, it is a story that ends in divorce. Up to 60 percent of stepfamily-based second marriages do not succeed. The amount of human suffering caused by these failures is incalculable: hopes and dreams dashed, second chances destroyed, lives permanently cast adrift. But the suffering of the adults caught in the wreckage of destroyed families is nothing compared to the suffering of the children. When a second family and a second marriage dissolve, the children internalize the lessons that marriage is not permanent, that a home is never stable, and that you cannot trust the people you love.

What makes the modern stepfamily—the family formed from divorce, not death—so vulnerable?

Much of the instability is the result of recent cultural changes that are affecting all marriages. Thirty years of profound and continuous social change have frayed—and, in some places, torn—the intricate web of custom, tradition, law, and economic interdependence that in earlier times bound a marriage and family together. Also badly frayed is the marital ethos of familial self-sacrifice and devotion that used to help carry a couple and a family through troubled times. Increasingly, modern marriage is an existential creation, an institution whose primary purpose is to serve as a vehicle for self-realization and self-fulfillment.

Changing gender roles, although generally beneficial, also have contributed to marital instability by creating confusion about the roles men and women are supposed to play in a marriage and in a family.

THE UNIQUENESS OF THE STEPFAMILY MARRIAGE

In the context of these common marital challenges, stepfamily-based marriages face special pressures. An example is the Ghost at the Table phenomenon. No one enters stepfamily life unencumbered. Children are bound to absent parents, adults to past lives and past marriages. These invisible psychological bonds are the Ghosts at the Table, and because they play on the most elemental emotions—emotions like love and loyalty and guilt and fear—they have the power to tear a marriage and a stepfamily apart.

A stepfamily also is assaulted on all sides by difficult and often divisive questions. How much control should a stepparent have over a stepchild? How much authority should a nonresidential parent exert over a child? How should a difficult former spouse be handled? How does an "ours" baby change the emotional dynamic in a stepfamily? Why is marital satisfaction so low during the first years of stepfamily life?

Additionally, stepfamilies labor under knowledge gaps. Most people do not know what to expect from stepfamily life because most people grew up in a nuclear family, and often ignorance works against them. For example, we now know that in the first two years of stepfamily life, turmoil and conflict are normal—even for families who later become very happy. But since no map of stepfamily life exists, couples like the Goldsmiths have no way to put their conflicts into perspective—no way to understand what the conflicts do and do not signify.

I do not think it mere coincidence that divorce is most common in the first two years of stepfamily life.

Other important knowledge gaps include the nature of the stepfamily marriage and the stepparent-stepchild relationship. Should the marriage feel the same as a nuclear-family marriage or different? What is a normal parent-child relationship in a stepfamily, and what is abnormal? Does the stepfamily have its own special cycles, its own special rules, or does it follow nuclear-family patterns?

The purpose of *StepFamilies* is to answer all the important questions of stepfamily life—to fill in the knowledge gaps that undermine so many stepfamilies today.

Most of the material in the book, including the stories of the couples who appear in its pages, is drawn from the files of the Developmental Issues in StepFamilies Research Project (DIS). One of the largest and longest studies of stepfamily life conducted, the project grew out of two complementary desires: the desire of the National Institute of Child Health and Human Development to learn more about the operation of the modern stepfamily and my wish to strengthen the stepfamily— particularly for its youngest members, its children.

In translating project data into practical strategies for readers, I also have drawn on my experience as a clinical psychologist who has worked with stepfamilies for two decades.

THE TEARS OF A MOTHER: THE ORIGIN OF THE DIS PROJECT

Sometimes academic research originates out of a personal experience. A chance encounter strikes a chord or raises a question about a phenomenon, or one wonders about the possibility of uncovering something unknown. My interest in stepfamilies grew out of such an encounter— or rather a series of them—at a time when we didn't know much about stepfamilies.

Jennifer Sampson was bright, vivacious, recently remarried, and, on the sunny December morning in 1979 when I met her for the first time, very worried. Matthew and Polly, her two children, were not adapting well to stepfamily life. "I thought that with time the kids would settle down," Jennifer told me. "But after last week, I'm not so sure anymore."

I asked her what happened last week.

"A fight," Jennifer replied, "an awful, ugly fight."

I noticed that she had stopped looking at me. She was staring down at the floor. "Tom—my new husband—asked Matthew to clear the table after dinner. Matthew refused. Tom told him he had to, then Matthew lost it. He shouted, 'I don't have to do anything you say, you're not my daddy.' Then he ran into his room in tears.

"Tom's a wonderful man," Jennifer said. "He's been a saint with Matthew. I'm beginning to think *I'm* the one who's the problem. I don't know if I should have remarried. The divorce was hard on the kids. Now this. I don't want to ruin their lives with my bad choices."

I asked Jennifer if she thought a stepfamily was a bad choice for a child.

"You tell me," she said, "you're the expert."

In 1979 I was anything but an expert. I was a doctoral candidate at the University of Houston working at the Houston Child Guidance Center where Jennifer had come for help. Nonetheless, I wanted to help her if I could. Jennifer's pain, almost palpable that morning, touched me deeply.

The next day I reviewed the literature on stepfamilies. I was surprised at how skimpy it was. There were very few studies, and none of them had much to say about the modern stepfamily—the stepfamilies formed by divorce, not death—or how to help its members. So when Jennifer reappeared at the clinic a week later with her children in tow, I decided to treat the Sampsons as I would a nuclear family. And for a while the strategy seemed to work.

As therapy progressed, Jennifer's confidence returned—or at least, it appeared to—and there were no repeats of the ugly dinnertime confrontation between nine-year-old Matthew and Tom Sampson. Tom, I thought, also should be participating in our sessions, but when I suggested it, the message he sent via Jennifer was "This is *her* problem and *her* kids and she has to take care of it." Jennifer occasionally brought up issues between her ex-husband and the children. I usually brushed over these incidents to focus on the "real problems" in her new family. After Jennifer left therapy in August 1979, I did not hear from her again for nearly a year. Then one morning in April 1980 she called me at the clinic and asked if I "could make some time for her tomorrow."

"Of course," I said. As I hung up, I wondered whether Matthew and Tom were fighting again. Jennifer had sounded unsettled on the phone.

They were, but the Sampson stepfamily also had a new problem. Now Jennifer and husband Tom were not getting along either. Jennifer blamed this new round of conflict on the reappearance of her former spouse. Her ex-husband had dropped out of Matthew's and Polly's lives after the divorce, but now he was seeing the children again, and, according to Jennifer, his visits were having a pinball effect. Tom was mad at her—how could this intruder, this interloper, just walk in and disrupt their lives? Polly and Matthew were confused—two dads were even harder to figure out than the new math; and, she, Jennifer, was guilt-ridden and full of self-recrimination.

"I brought this on everyone," she said. "It's all my fault. I wanted to make everyone happy and I've made them miserable instead. Stupid, selfish me." Then she began to cry softly.

A few days later I began to compile a list of questions I thought the research would need to answer before we could begin to help stepfamilies like the Sampsons. They were:

- How does life in a stepfamily affect such personal markers as self-esteem, social and emotional adjustment, and cognitive development?
- What does a normal stepfamily look like, and how does it operate? How is it different from a nuclear family?
- How do marriage and parenting interact in a stepfamily—the same way they do in a nuclear family or differently?

- What does a normal stepparent-stepchild relationship look like?
- How long does it take for relationships to develop in a stepfamily?
- How do extended family relationships in stepfamilies function?
- What factors determine whether a stepfamily succeeds or fails?

In early 1982, during a visit to the National Institute of Child Health and Human Development, I presented my list of questions to agency officials. I also pointed out that due to the spike in the divorce rate during the 1970s, stepfamilies were becoming much more common. "Perhaps it was time we did a study of its developmental effects," I said. On my return to Houston, I submitted a proposal for such a study.

Six months later the NICHHD responded to my proposal with a number of suggestions. New demographic projections were showing that by the year 2000, more Americans would be living in stepfamilies than in nuclear families. To prepare for this change, the NICHHD wanted an extensive picture of the stepfamily phenomenon and how it impacted children. Would I be interested in expanding my study to look at broader and long-term issues for stepfamilies?

I realized that a study that would address these broad issues would have the potential to help millions of men, women, and children like the Sampsons. I agreed to the expansion and thus proceeded with what became the Developmental Issues in StepFamilies (DIS) Research Project.

WHAT THE DIS PROJECT FOUND

Most academic research runs for a year or two and involves thirty to fifty study participants. But I realized that to draw a truly comprehensive map of stepfamily life, hundreds of families would need to be recruited, and each family would have to be followed for an extended time. I also realized that, in order to take a comprehensive psychological snapshot of the stepfamily phenomenon, many different kinds of assessment tools would have to be employed: in-home interviews, questionnaires, psychological tests, and videotapes of families interacting. I also realized that I could not run a large-scale study alone. I would need a large staff to help me.

In early 1984 our team of professionals and graduate students launched what ultimately would grow into a nine-year study of two hundred families—one hundred stepfamilies and one hundred nuclear families. To keep data collection manageable, we decided to focus on a single child in each study family. This "target child" would provide us with information about the developmental effects of the stepfamily. Adult participants would provide information about marriage, parenting, and family life.

In April 1984 the study was officially launched with an initial distribution of three thousand recruitment letters. My staff and I cast such a wide net because we wanted a diverse subject population in terms of occupation, income, and education (though a high school degree was a minimum requirement for project participation). We also wanted many different kinds of people with many different kinds of backgrounds in the study. We wanted professionals like the Goldsmiths and couples of more modest means like the Lawtons, whom you will meet later, although our study base was all white and middle class. Our participants also shared another commonality. Because most stepfamilies are stepfather families—families in whose household the children are only biologically linked to the mother—with young children, we decided to focus our efforts on this form of stepfamily.

We were astonished at the response our letters elicited. Within weeks the project office received several hundred inquiries. I think the reason why so many families expressed an interest in our study was our positive approach. We focused on the things that made stepfamilies and marriages work.

Originally the project was designated to end in 1988. But when my staff and I began to analyze study data in 1987, we discovered that our findings raised as many questions as they answered. A case in point is the Other Side of the Coin, a syndrome first described to me by Betty Ann Toomey, a project wife with a wry sense of humor, particularly about her taste in men.

"You know," Betty Ann said to me one day, "I'm so smart I'm dumb."

I told her I did not understand what she meant.

"Well," Betty Ann said, "John, my first husband, was an Ice King. He never talked, he never touched—half the time, I don't think he even ran a pulse. I thought Dick [Betty's current husband] was totally different. When I met him I said to myself, 'Oh, Lord, finally a nice, warm, open man. I better grab him before someone else does.' But three years later, Dick turns out to be John with a different haircut. He has just as many problems with getting close; his just take a different form. Instead of being cold and distant, Dick gets all clingy and needy."

I heard a dozen different versions of Betty Ann's story during the project, and all had the same unhappy ending. The more eager an individual was to avoid a spousal trait that produced unhappiness in a first marriage, the more likely she was to encounter the opposite side of that trait in a second marriage. The helter-skelter incidence of the syndrome was particularly puzzling. Why did it occur in some project families and not others? Was the syndrome a reflection of a personal idiosyncrasy? Something that only happened to people like Betty Ann? Or did it play a part in some larger pattern of stepfamily life that we had missed?

The Good Father syndrome raised the same kind of troubling questions. A number of project stepfathers were biological parents; they were sensitive, understanding, empathic, and enthusiastic. In short, they possessed all the qualities parenting experts describe as essential to winning the heart of a child. Yet we found that very few of these men won any hearts in their stepfamilies. More often than not, they ended up being ignored or rejected by a stepchild.

In 1988, eager to unravel mysteries like the Good Father syndrome, the National Institute of Child Health and Human Development decided to fund an extension of the project. The second phase of the study ran from 1988 to 1992 and involved the same two hundred stepfamilies and nuclear families. Taken together, the two phases of the project provided a comprehensive look at all of the major areas of stepfamily life.

Among the project's most important findings:

- *A stepfamily has its own natural lifecycle.* Stepfamily life has three major transition points, and two of the three transition points throw a family into temporary crisis.
- *A stepfamily takes several years to develop into a family unit.* The academics suggested that a stepfamily begins to coalesce in six months to a year. We found that the settling-in process takes much longer. In our study, families did not start to think and act like a family until the end of the second or third year.
- *A stepfamily is at greatest risk during the first two years.* Nearly a quarter of stepfamilies fail in this period. This finding also has a corollary, and it is noteworthy because it illustrates the danger of applying a nuclear-family map to stepfamily life. Typically, in a first marriage, marital satisfaction begins high, then declines. In a stepfamily marriage, the opposite flow occurs: Marital satisfaction starts at a medium level, then climbs. There is little or no "honeymoon effect."
- *A stepfamily ultimately coalesces into one of three basic forms.* Eventually, nearly all families acquire the characteristics of a Neotraditional, a Romantic, or a Matriarchal stepfamily. These are the three basic archetypes of stepfamily life. One of these three types succeeds nearly all of the time; the second type succeeds most of the time; and the third type is at a great risk for divorce.
- *A stepfamily must solve four basic tasks in order to succeed.* The tasks are: integrating the stepfather into the child's life, creating a satisfying second marriage and separating it from the first (the Ghosts at the Table phenomenon), managing change,

and developing workable rules for dealing with nonresidential parents and former spouses.

- *A stepfamily can heal the scars of divorce.* For the past decade, conventional wisdom has held that divorce permanently scars a child. Our data, however, paint a somewhat more complex picture. The data affirm the work of investigators like Dr. Judith Wallerstein, who believe that a child is profoundly affected by family dissolution. But we found that a loving, well-functioning stepfamily can help restore a youngster's sense of emotional and psychological well-being.

We also found something else: A strong, stable stepfamily is as capable of nurturing healthy development as a nuclear family. It can imbue values, affirm limits and boundaries, and provide a structure in which rules for living a moral and productive life are made, transmitted, tested, rebelled against, and ultimately affirmed.

STEPFAMILIES: HOW AMERICA LIVES NOW

The project began with a simple aim: to learn about stepfamily life and its effects on children. But it quickly became apparent to me—and to other project staff—that you cannot learn about the stepfamily without also learning about the impact of cultural, social, and economic change.

The problems America talks about and worries about are evident in the modern stepfamily. You can see children traumatized by divorce, children confused and angry and displaced; you can see two-worker families struggling to get by; and you can see people fleeing from terrible pasts, from betrayals and infidelities, from partners with destructive drug and alcohol problems.

But you can see other things as well. You can see the resiliency of the human spirit, the ability of people to overcome the past, no matter how terrible it has been. You can see the power of hope, and, I think, you also can see the beginnings of an important new social development, a development that has implications not just for the stepfamily but for all of us who live in families. As I visited with project participants, talked to them, watched them struggle with the pressures of modern marriage and modern family life, I sensed that our subjects—and stepfamilies generally—are forging a new social paradigm, a paradigm that combines the best of the old values (such as honoring traditional values like family and parenting) with the best of contemporary values (such as self-expression and self-fulfillment).

Watching project participants, I also learned something else about the modern American stepfamily, something that surprised me just as much. It possesses a unique ability to nurture and affirm its members. "I didn't marry a wife, I married a *life*," a project participant named Joseph Fletcher said to me one day shortly after the project began. Since Joseph, a refinery worker, was also an aspiring country-western singer, at first I thought he was testing out a new song lyric on me.

I told Joseph I wasn't sure what he meant.

His long, leathery face broke into a smile. He said that when he married his wife Alice, he knew as much about her life as he did about his own.

Back then I understood what Joseph meant, but I still did not understand why that knowledge would please him.

Today I do.

Joseph was trying to explain one of the most important ways a stepfamily nurtures its members—through affirmation and acceptance.

In a nuclear family, each spouse brings a past to the marriage, but in a stepfamily, a husband and wife bring their past *into* the marriage. The reason is simple: children. The presence of children requires near-total personal disclosure, and near-total personal disclosure promotes an unusual degree of emotional closeness. During another visit to the Fletchers, Alice, a schoolteacher, described the process to me thusly. "Joe and I don't keep secrets," she said. "My life is all open to him. My life before I met him, his before he met me. It's all here. Joe has bonded with the child I had with Rudy [Alice's first husband], and I have bonded with the child he had with Tiffany [Joseph's first wife]. Our links to each other run deep."

The stepfamily's unique nurturing power also is reflected in its ability to validate what otherwise might be construed as past mistakes, as a reckless youth. As a project mother named Becky Thurgeson, who entered an ill-considered first marriage at twenty, put it, "Neil [her second husband] has come to love Samantha, and when I see the two of them coloring or playing Nintendo together, I realize I was wrong to berate myself for the years with David [her first husband]. They led to Sam, and Sam gives Neil as much joy as she gives me."

Over the course of the project, we also found that when a marriage works in a stepfamily, it often works especially well. Initially we thought that this curve of marital happiness might be a facet of comparison. All remarried couples bring bad marriages to a stepfamily; otherwise they would not be in a stepfamily. Perhaps, we thought, this standard of comparison makes even a reasonably good second marriage seem blissfully happy. But gradually it became clear to us that the explanation was more complicated. Recent research shows that every marriage—every *good* marriage—is built on a thousand small acts of self-sacrifice. Gym nights are given up, lunches are "brown-bagged" to save money, household chores like laundry and cleaning are shared. Such gestures may sound trivial and unimportant, but each involves a sacrifice of "me" to "us," to the marriage. And as the frequency of these acts grow, they draw the husband and wife closer together. As we looked more closely at our couples, we realized that a stepfamily provides more opportunities for such acts. Wary children have to be understood, former spouses managed—a dozen situations each day give one partner an opportunity to show the other in deed as well as in word how much the marriage and the stepfamily mean to him or her.

The goal of *StepFamilies* is to show readers how to take advantage of these opportunities, how to use all the tools we discovered during the project to build a strong, secure, stable, happy stepfamily.

The best place to see these tools in operation are in the archetypes of stepfamily life: Neotraditional, Matriarchal, and Romantic. So we begin our exploration of stepfamily life with them.

part one

The Families

Most popular books and articles about stepfamily life contain a singular peculiarity. They talk about *the stepfamily* as if there were only one kind, as if all the tens of millions of men, women, and children in all the millions of stepfamilies across the United States were the same, as if these families and everyone in them were shaped by the same set of emotional, psychological, and developmental factors.

At the start of the project, I knew that this one-size-fits-all view of the stepfamily was oversimplified. I had sensed real differences among the stepfamilies I worked with in my clinical practice, and I expected that project data would bear out my anecdotal impressions. That is to say, I expected that I and my coworkers would find several different types of stepfamilies. But I also expected that these types would be shaped by such traditional social science variables as socioeconomic status, educational level, and upbringing. I expected upper-middle-class stepfamilies to behave one way and working-class stepfamilies, another.

I turned out to be right in my first expectation and wrong in my second.

There are indeed different stepfamily types. But traditional social science variables like socioeconomic status play only a small role in their formation. The key variable in determining stepfamily type are the choices a couple makes about the four basic tasks of stepfamily life: parenting, managing change, separating a second marriage from a first, and dealing with the nonresidential parent. Husbands and wives who choose one way on these tasks develop into Neotraditional stepfamilies, husbands and wives who choose another way into Romantic stepfamilies, and couples who choose a third way, into Matriarchal stepfamilies.

These are the names we gave to the three stepfamily archetypes we identified during the project. And of the three, the first, Neotraditional, probably comes closest to conforming to the popular image of the happy stepfamily. The Neotraditional family is a kind of contemporary version of the 1950s white-picket-fence family; it is close-knit, loving, and works very well for a couple with compatible values. At the end of our study, we found that, on average, our Neotraditional couples scored very high on such important markers of success as marital satisfaction and conflict resolution; the children in our Neotraditional families also had a lower incidence of behavior problems.

Our two other stepfamily types represent more of a departure from the media ideal, although, on occasion, glimpses of the Romantic stepfamily can be found in the popular literature. Romantics expect everything from stepfamily life that Neotraditionalists do, but unlike Neotraditionalists, Romantics expect everything *immediately*. They expect feelings of love and harmony and closeness to begin flowing as soon as the couple and the children officially become a stepfamily.

We found that the early conflict-prone period of the stepfamily cycle is particularly difficult for Romantic stepfamilies. Indeed, Romantics had the highest family breakup rate in the project.

Matriarchal, our third archetype, is rarely, if ever, mentioned in the popular literature. But anyone familiar with stepfamily life will recognize the type instantly. The chief characteristic of the Matriarchal family is the dominant role of the wife. Matriarchal women usually have powerful personalities, a high degree of domestic competence, and a strong desire to be the family leader. This stepfamily, which accounted for about 25 percent of our study sample, is frequently successful if the Matriarchal woman is married to a man with compatible values.

These three archetypes form the heart of the talks I give from time to time on stepfamily life. Invariably, after I have finished describing these types, a hand is raised in the audience. "My family has features of a Neotraditional type," the questioner will say, "but in other ways, Dr. Bray, we sound more like a Romantic stepfamily."

Life—life as it is lived in the everyday world—is rarely as neat and tidy as a researcher's categories. Many stepfamilies do indeed share characteristics of other stepfamily forms. I encountered this crossover phenomenon dozens of times during the project. But on the whole, most stepfamilies conform to one of our three archetypes, in the sense that they possess most of the characteristics of one particular form.

The chapters that follow explore the characteristics of each archetype through the experiences and choices of three project families. As you follow these families, as you watch how each grows and changes, you also will be introduced to other important project discoveries, including the distinct cycles of stepfamily life and the subtle but critically important interactions between parenting and marriage in such families.

To further illuminate project findings, I have included the stories of other stepfamilies as well; some participated in the project; I worked with others in my capacity as a clinical psychologist. I hope and believe that what you learn from these families will help your stepfamily succeed.

chapter one

The Neotraditionalist Stepfamily:

Sarah and Jeffrey Goldsmith

Sarah and Jeffrey Goldsmith met through a mutual friend.

One Saturday afternoon, about a year after his divorce, Jeffrey was leaving a movie theater near the Galleria in southwest Houston when he ran into an old college friend.

Jeffrey acted delighted to see the woman, but in truth he was anxious to get away, to get back to his car. It had rained earlier—a sultry, early-summer delta rain—and now the sky looked threatening again. An ominous cloud cover was rolling up from Galveston, and Jeffrey, always the worrier, was sure it was going to start pouring again. Uncharacteristically, he—Jeffrey, the careful planner, the anticipator—had forgotten his umbrella. It was sitting on the front seat of his car in a parking lot on the other side of the Galleria.

Jeffrey was also anxious to get away for a reason entirely separate from the weather. He knew that if he and the woman talked for any length of time, eventually she would ask about his wife, Barbara. Then, when he mentioned that he and Barbara were divorced, the friend would want to know what had happened, and Jeffrey was tired of telling people what had happened to that marriage.

Then—and most dreaded to Jeffrey—the friend would almost certainly tell him that she knew someone he "ought to meet."

It did not rain, but all of Jeffrey's other fears came true. The friend did ask about the divorce, and after Jeffrey gave her a Disney-rated version of what had been, in truth, a very ugly breakup, the friend did tell him she knew "someone." The someone's name was Sarah Kahn. She was thirty-one, an interior decorator, attractive, and, like Jeffrey, divorced. Jeffrey listened unenthusiastically. Well-meaning friends had arranged dozens of fix-ups for him since the divorce, and none had worked out. The women were always pleasant enough, attractive and sociable, but they were not interested in the things that Jeffrey was interested in. And in truth, they were usually not very interested in Jeffrey either. Women, at least the kind he met on blind dates, seemed to want a different type of man: someone who was a little less inhibited, who did not worry so much; someone who was more exciting, better at small talk, more playful, smoother.

Often, Jeffrey thought, he was too serious for his own good.

At the end of the conversation, the friend said she was having a dinner party. Why didn't Jeffrey come? Maybe because he had not evidenced much interest when she mentioned Sarah, the friend did not tell him the "someone" would be there too.

There were two other women at the dinner party, but Jeffrey's eye went to Sarah immediately. She was standing in the living room talking to another man when he walked in. She was absolutely lovely: dark and slender and fine-featured with a dazzling smile—the most dazzling smile Jeffrey had ever seen. When he got an opportunity to talk to her, he also discovered that Sarah was intelligent and funny in a nicely cutting way, and, surprise of surprises, she liked the things that he liked: classical music, art, and theater. Possibly best of all, Sarah did not seem to think it odd or pretentious that a wholesaler in kitchen supplies should have such tastes.

In the weeks that followed, Jeffrey found other things to like about Sarah. There was her competence. Sarah was one of those people who was competent not just at one or two things but at life itself. She always seemed to know what to say to a troubled friend, whom to call for last-minute theater tickets, and how to find the cheapest air fares. Jeffrey also liked Sarah's confidence and centeredness. She knew who she was and what she liked and what she did not like. Once or twice Jeffrey did notice an edginess about Sarah, a slightly off-kilter quality. But he liked that too; it gave her a mysterious air. Within a month of the dinner party, Jeffrey was in love.

Sarah's feelings for Jeffrey took a good while longer to percolate. "I found him a little stiff and awkward at first," she told me later. And contrary to what Jeffrey thought, initially Sarah did find him if not exactly pretentious, then a bit pompous. Jeffrey's interests had nothing to do with this judgment. Sarah thought the conjunction of classical music, art, and wholesale kitchen supplies "wonderfully offbeat." It was Jeffrey's *behavior* that led her to judge him as pompous—specifically, his reaction when Sarah made the mistake of calling him "Jeff."

"He looked absolutely horrified," Sarah said later. "He threw back his head, puffed out his chest, and said, 'If you don't mind, I prefer to be called Jeffrey.'" Sarah's imitation of her husband's deep baritone was flawless.

Within a month or two, however, Sarah began to change her mind about Jeffrey. What appeared to be pomposity at first now began to look like gravitas. Unexciting Jeffrey might be, but he had character. He was deliberate, thoughtful, and responsible—very responsible. He did not run from problems; just the opposite, in fact. When a problem arose, Jeffrey would pick it up, turn it over; he would examine it from this angle, then from that angle, and then from a half-dozen angles that Sarah had not even thought of.

Sometimes this thorough scrutiny of every little blip in their relationship exhausted Sarah. Other times she thought it masked a need to control. But it was also refreshing to be with a man who was not afraid to examine difficulties. Sarah's first husband would not even acknowledge that they had marital problems, not until the day she asked him for a divorce.

One day, about six months after the Goldsmiths met, Jeffrey's former wife moved herself and Jeffrey's two sons to New Hampshire and a new job. Every relationship has a watershed moment, and the move became one for Jeffrey—and even more a watershed for Sarah, who had, until then, remained ambivalent about Jeffrey. Their relationship promised security, stability, and affluence but not much in the way of excitement or romance, and Sarah was not sure she could live without at least an occasional taste of the latter two qualities.

The night his sons moved, Jeffrey was preparing to leave Sarah's house—he already had his coat on—when he suddenly sat down on the couch and announced that he did not want to go home, *could* not go home: could not face an empty bed that night. Jeffrey—stoic, super-controlled Jeffrey—had never done anything like this before, and it touched Sarah. He always worked so hard to appear in command, and now there he was unraveling on her couch.

Sarah, always very good in emergencies, was very good in this emergency. She suggested that Jeffrey stay and help her bake a cake. So instead of going home to an empty apartment and an empty bed, Jeffrey—and Sarah—stayed up most of the night baking an Italian cream cake.

Later, when I asked Sarah how this incident changed her feelings about Jeffrey, she smiled an ironic smile and said, "Before I was just sort of being a nice person to Jeffrey. After you could say I was more of a nice, *committed* person."

I met the Goldsmiths six months after their marriage—the point at which new stepfamilies entered the study—and, like most of our other recently married couples, they were experiencing a lot of conflict.

Jeffrey was angry at Sarah, Sarah was angry at Jeffrey; and Naomi, I think, was angry at both of them: at Jeffrey for being stern and gruff and at Sarah for marrying a man who was stern and gruff.

Apart from the biographical and family data I collected during the visit, this was all I knew about the Goldsmiths for the next year or so.

In the meantime, though, I did learn something new about stepfamilies. By the end of the project's first year, about 40 percent of our participants were beginning to form into units that looked and acted like a traditional nuclear family. The emergence of this group surprised us. The then-current thinking among family scholars was that stepfamilies not only started out operating differently from nuclear families but that the differences remained as the years went by—the differences were *permanent*. A stepfamily always looked like a stepfamily, a nuclear family like a nuclear family.

The experience of our Neotraditional stepfamilies invalidated this theory. Not only did these stepfamilies experience much change over time; they also, ultimately, converged with profiles like nuclear families. Eventually the families in our Neotraditional group began to acquire many of the characteristics of the traditional nuclear family, including a fairly high degree of emotional cohesiveness: Family members were bound closely to one another and to the stepfamily; there was a close parent-child bond; and at the heart of the family, there lay a very stable, satisfying marriage.

During the first year of the project, I also learned something else about stepfamilies, something that helped explain and contextualize the anger and hostility I encountered from the Goldsmiths during my first visit. Stepfamily life runs in cycles, and the first cycle—the cycle Jeffrey and Sarah were in when I met them—is tumultuous for everyone. During the first twenty-four months (the duration of the first cycle), anger, conflict, and unhappiness are the rule, even in stepfamilies that later become very harmonious and loving, like the Goldsmiths, who eventually formed a Neotraditional family, the first and most successful of our three family archetypes.

CHARACTERISTICS OF A
NEOTRADITIONAL STEPFAMILY

Dozens of studies, including our own, have shown that the principal challenge of stepfamily life is building an emotionally satisfying marriage.

What makes this *the* paramount challenge for couples like the Goldsmiths is the changing nature of marriage—or, perhaps more accurately, the change in the reasons that people marry. Unlike men and women in earlier generations—who married for a variety of practical reasons, chiefly financial security—today people marry out of a desire for personal fulfillment: for happiness. This motivation is as active for men and women entering a second marriage as it is for those entering a first, and it accounts for a correlation we saw again and again in the study.

Marital satisfaction almost always determines stepfamily stability. If satisfaction is high, tolerance for the normal tumult and conflict of stepfamily life is correspondingly high. If satisfaction is low, tolerance for conflict is so low that often the stepfamily dissolves in divorce.

In a recent book, psychologist and family therapist Patricia Popenow describes the qualities that make a marriage satisfying. Her list includes shared values, shared rituals and gestures, a common problem-solving style, a similar way of looking at the world, and also the small daily acts of self-sacrifice that signal an individual's willingness to put "we" above "me." Dr. Popenow calls this group of characteristics the *middle ground* of a marriage, and she finds that this middle ground operates on two levels, both of which enrich the husband and wife.

On a practical level, a middle ground works like an instruction manual. Without consulting one another, the couple knows what should be done about a child, a bill, an annoying relative, or the guest list for Thanksgiving dinner. On an emotional level, the middle ground is the cement that holds a marriage together, makes it cohesive. The middle ground is the place where the husband and wife exist not as "you" and "I" but as "us."

New studies have supported Dr. Popenow's viewpoint. A thick, rich middle ground of shared values, beliefs, and personal styles is indeed what makes a marriage a successful, practical, and emotional partnership.

One reason for this is pride of joint authorship. Writer Pat Conroy once observed that every marriage constitutes its own unique civilization; the shared values and feelings, the similar way of looking at things, and the small acts of sacrifice that make up the marital middle ground are the symbols, language, and currency of Conroy's marital civilization. Thus, the couple that creates them is creating something truly unique, something distinctive to them and them alone—something that no two other people in the world could have created.

Additionally, a middle ground functions as a zone of comfort. It is the place in the marriage where each partner can go for companionship, understanding, solace, and laughter; the place where each partner can escape the constraints of individualism, can be something larger—something more important and meaningful—than simply "me."

The middle ground plays one other vital role in a marriage—it acts as a stabilizer. The enormous investment of time, effort, and personal commitment needed to construct a middle ground makes a couple think twice and then a third time before proceeding to a divorce court.

Typically, in a nuclear family, the middle ground of a marriage—shared habits, feelings, and outlook—is created in the leisurely, relatively stress-free period between wedding and parenthood. Thus, when the baby arrives, husband and wife already have in place an anchor—an incentive—to keep them together: something that makes the disruptions and dislocations created by the new child worth enduring. During the dating period, people like Sarah and Jeffrey are able to do some construction work on their eventual middle ground. But a marital middle ground is so called because most of its construction must take place after—and inside—the marriage. And typically, in a stepfamily, the only interval between marriage and parenthood is the minute it takes the brand-new bride and groom to turn around and receive the congratulations of their children.

What distinguishes Neotraditional couples from the two other stepfamily types is the way they use the four tasks of stepfamily creation to build a marital middle ground. In the course of developing an appropriate parenting role for the stepfather, separating a second marriage from a first marriage for the spouses who were previously married, managing change, and dealing with a nonresidential parent, Neotraditionalists forge shared values and a shared worldview—a clear "us."

THE CONNECTION BETWEEN
MARRIAGE AND PARENTING

Sarah frowns.

"You're early, James."

I look at my watch. I am ten minutes early.

This happens frequently with the Goldsmiths. The problem is proximity. My office at Texas Women's University College is on the eastern edge of the Rice campus, so only three football fields, a track, and a few buildings separate me from Jeffrey and Sarah, who live on the northern edge of the campus. Usually Sarah does not mind if I'm early. But today, clearly, she does. She looks cross. Not only have I arrived too early, I have arrived at an inopportune moment.

A discussion—a fight, really—is in progress, and its subject is Jerome Goldsmith.

Jeffrey's feelings about his father are ambivalent. I think Jeffrey blames Jerome, founder of the family's very successful kitchen supply business, for thwarting him. With another father, a father less overwhelming and powerful, Jeffrey's life, he believes, would have taken a different direction. Today he would be a doctor or a professor; he would not be running a wholesale kitchen supply business from a large warehouse in southeast Houston.

Anger and love, however, are not mutually exclusive emotions, especially when the object of the emotions is a parent. One of the first stories Jeffrey told me about himself was really a story about him and his father, about a trip they took to New York to visit relatives when Jeffrey was eleven. As he described the visit, and especially his father's tour of Manhattan, Jeffrey did something uncharacteristic. He began to smile. When I pointed this out to him, he shook his head and laughed ruefully.

"The old man is impossible," he said, "but he's a real life force. I've never met anyone with so much goddamn energy."

The conflict I intruded upon is about Jerome's seventy-fifth birthday party and whether Naomi would attend or not. The birthday party is intended to be something of a homage to Jerome. Goldsmiths will be flying to Houston from all over the country: a younger brother and two nephews from New York; an older sister and her daughters with their husbands and children from Boston.

Naomi's attendance at the party is important to Jeffrey, and in the way that men sometimes do, he automatically had assumed that she was going. But about five minutes before my arrival, Naomi had announced from her chair in front of the living-room television set that she did not want to go. This announcement was prompted by Sarah's suggestion that Naomi might want to buy a new party dress. "Do I have to go?" Naomi said, then quickly amended that question to a statement: "I'm not going to go."

Sarah came to the door directly from a kitchen huddle with a hurt and aroused Jeffrey—a huddle, I learned later, that had involved a certain amount of finger-pointing and shouting. Indeed, it is some measure of the distress that Naomi's announcement caused the Goldsmiths that Jeffrey brought it up again in my presence.

"I don't think it's fair—to me *or* to my father," he says, after Naomi has gone upstairs.

Sarah is sympathetic but unyielding. "She's seven, Jeffrey . . . and she doesn't know your relatives. All those strange people. She's afraid of feeling overwhelmed. You can't blame her." Sarah mentions Naomi's age again.

"I really would like her to come, Sarah, out of respect . . ." The use of the charged word "respect" considerably increases the emotional stakes of the conversation.

"What will everyone think if the two of us arrive without her?" The more Jeffrey talks, the more insulted he looks.

Sarah, however, remains unbending. "I know you're disappointed, but I can't make her go. It wouldn't be fair."

Jeffrey frowns. "Jesus, Sarah, he's my father. What's he going to think? What would you think if you were him?"

"I'm sorry, Jeffrey. I truly am. But I won't make her go."

One key finding to emerge from our study was about the connection between the parenting task and the state of the marriage in a step-family. To put it baldly: Unless a couple succeeds at the parenting task—unless they find a comfortable parenting role for the stepfather— the marriage, and thus their stepfamily, is likely to falter. Moreover, the reason for the connection highlights a key difference between nuclear and stepfamilies.

In a nuclear family, a troubled child has relatively little impact on a marriage, but a troubled marriage greatly affects a child, usually because marital problems interfere with good parenting, making a parent less sensitive to the youngster's needs. While a troubled child has less impact on the marriage, in a stepfamily, the interaction between marriage and parenting flows in the opposite direction. The state of the marriage has relatively little effect on a child because children generally have a limited emotional investment in a parent's second marriage. However, the child's emotional state has an enormous impact on the emotional state of a stepfamily marriage. The reason: Children who are unhappy misbehave, act out, are rude and surly; not only does such behavior makes life unpleasant for everyone, but eventually the unhappy child begins to divide the stepparent, who is discomfited and increasingly critical of the child, from the biological parent, who is defensive and increasingly annoyed at her spouse's criticisms of her child.

Among the steps a couple must take to solve the parenting task, two are particularly critical, and the failure of a couple to take them places their new marriage at risk. Indeed, in looking closely at the couples who divorced during the course of the project, we found that a full 50 percent of them had mishandled one or both of these steps.

The first step is really a decision: when to integrate the new stepfather into the child's life. We found that many of our men, usually with a wife's encouragement, assumed an active parenting role too early in the marriage and thus fell into the trap of presuming an intimacy and authority that was still unearned.

This is the Good Father syndrome, and often its victims are left understandably baffled and hurt. Here they are, truly behaving like a good parent: giving a child time and attention, direction and guidance; yet all they receive for their efforts is a spectrum of behaviors that increase in unpleasantness from reticence, to surliness, to outright rejection, with the rejection stage usually being characterized by slamming doors, loud shouting, and painful insults.

Initially my colleagues and I also were baffled by the Good Father syndrome. We routinely videotaped our stepparents and stepchildren interacting. During the first phase of the study I remember my growing dismay as I screened these tapes. I was seeing some remarkable examples of sensitive parenting, examples that, according to all the parenting texts, should have evoked delight and interest and engagement in a child. Yet, clearly, the stepchildren I was watching were reluctant and itchy.

Eventually the riddle of these children's unresponsiveness was solved. The answer lay in the child's initial wariness of intimacy—an inbuilt go-slow mechanism. We discovered that, during the first year or two of stepfamily life, the amount of intimacy or authority a child is psychologically prepared to accept from a stepfather is akin to the amount of intimacy or authority a child is prepared to accept from a coach, or camp counselor, or other friendly adult.

Fairly early in the project we noticed that Neotraditional families were more successful than our other families in integrating a new step-father into the child's life. But, as with the Good Father syndrome, it took us a while to understand why. The answer was, in large part, realism. Neotraditional men were realistic enough to intuit what we social scientists needed months of study to discover: The child *does not want* a new parent.

In Neotraditional homes, the decision on how soon to integrate the man was always a mutual one—the result of a discussion where spousal differences were aired and resolved through compromise and conces-sion. As we shall see in a moment, Neotraditionalists usually opted to foster an intimate father-child bond, the kind characteristic of a well-functioning nuclear family. But, being realists, Neotraditional men rec-ognized that such a bond would not develop until the stepchild's trust and affection had been won. They also recognized that winning over the child would take time and that the wooing process would be com-plicated. Youngsters would have to learn not only how to love the stepfather; they would also have to learn how to love him in a way that did not make them feel they were being disloyal to a biological father.

The way Neotraditional men—and women—dealt with this com-plex situation was by introducing the stepfather's role into the family slowly. During the first few years of stepfamily life, Neotraditional men maintained a distance, a distance always short enough for children to walk across when they wished to but large enough to preserve their sense of privacy. Also, Neotraditional men did not fall into the trap of presumption. They did not presume a love or affection, or an authority, still unearned. When necessary, they also were willing to sacrifice an individual's interests to the greater good of the family. The rest of Jeffrey's and Sarah's exchange about the birthday party provides an example of the latter point.

Jeffrey pressed Sarah one last time. He told her his father would be hurt if Naomi did not come to the birthday party. "I'll be hurt too," he added. But when Sarah said no again, Jeffrey sighed a final sigh of resignation and relented.

"All right," he told her, "I won't insist. Naomi can stay home if she doesn't want to come."

"Thank you, Jeffrey," Sarah said, very softly.

The cohesive, intimate stepfather-stepchild relationships that developed in many of our Neotraditional homes illustrate that, eventually, youngsters do reward a stepparent for respecting their self-imposed boundaries. The solid marriages we found in these homes illustrate another related point. Unsurprisingly, successfully resolving the parenting task helps to eliminate a potentially very disruptive marital stress—an unhappy child. But it also has another salutary and more subtle effect on a marriage. The process of give-and-take requires a man and woman to make the kind of sacrifices that I saw Jeffrey make. And sacrifices that say "we—this family—are more important than me" are the foundation of a solid marital middle ground.

THE STEPPARENT-STEPCHILD RELATIONSHIP

"Dan changed after we moved here. He changed in ways I did not like and I did not understand."

"Dan" is Dan Fugelman, Sarah's first husband, and on this visit, I am at the Goldsmiths' to obtain more background information. During my first visit I collected dates and ages and birthplaces, the details of personal history. I learned that Sarah was thirty-three and Jeffrey thirty-eight. I learned that Sarah was born in Boston and grew up in New York City, Jeffrey in Houston. I also learned that Sarah has a B.A. from American University; Jeffrey a B.S. from the University of Texas. I learned, finally, that each had been divorced for three years before remarrying.

This afternoon, my second visit to the Goldsmiths, I am collecting information about their first marriages. Sarah is telling me about hers now.

She says that she met Dan Fugelman during her senior year at American University and married him the summer after she graduated. Sarah also says that Dan, like Jeffrey, was a small businessman, but more entrepreneurial, which is why the Fugelmans moved from Washington to Texas in the late 1970s. Houston was still in the middle of an oil boom then, and fast-talking, charming Dan wanted to take advantage of it.

However, according to Sarah, Houston did not bring out the best in Dan. "He was too eager to fit in here," she says. The new friends he met overly impressed him. Dan liked their style, their self-confidence, their swagger; he wanted to be like them; and, according to Sarah, this desire slowly gave birth to wish: Dan began to wish he were someone else. More specifically, she says, he began to wish he was not a Jew. "Dan never lied about who he was, but he became—" Here Sarah stops for a moment to search for the right word; she settles for "embarrassed."

"Dan became embarrassed," she says, and as his embarrassment grew, she says, "he began to hide his Jewishness." There were no more visits to temple, no more Passover seders; the last year of the Fugelmans' marriage, a Christmas tree was put up in the living room. Sarah frowns after disclosing this last detail. "I didn't want to be with a man who was so confused about who he was," she says.

Dan's new friends also changed him in another way that Sarah disliked. "Family is very important to me," she says. "I grew up in a house where everyone was very close. My father, my mother, me. The three of us did everything together. I wanted to re-create that closeness in my own marriage, in my own family, and when Dan and I were living in Washington I had some of it. Dan was attentive to Naomi; I have to give him credit for that. During the time we were in Washington, he was a wonderful father. But after we moved here, Dan was too busy with his new friends to have time for Naomi anymore."

Sarah says the first thing she noticed about Jeffrey was that he would be a wonderful father. Then, suddenly, she pauses.

I look up from my notebook.

Sarah is squinting and shaking her head, as if catching herself in a misperception.

"Actually, James, that's not true. That was the *second* thing I noticed about Jeffrey." A faint ironic smile appears on her face. "The *first* thing I noticed was how anal he was."

Sarah smooths down a fold in her dress, then returns to the second observation about her husband. "At first, my sense about Jeffrey as a father was based mostly on instinct. He seemed very responsible, very conscientious, and I was struck—taken really—by the way he talked about his boys. Oh, after they left, after Barbara dragged them off to New Hampshire, Jeffrey was in terrible pain, James. It broke my heart listening to him sometimes.

"The first time I saw him with his boys, I knew my instincts were right. I knew Jeffrey would be a wonderful father to Naomi."

The second step a couple must take to resolve the parenting task also involves a decision. The husband and wife must decide what kind of stepfather-stepchild relationship they want to nurture within the stepfamily. Do the husband and wife want to promote a close, intimate bond, or just a friendship?

One of the things that surprised me and my project colleagues is how little attention our couples gave to this question. Most seemed to opt for what might be called a feet-first policy. After the wedding, the couple took the children home; then everyone took a deep breath, closed their eyes, clasped hands, and jumped into the pool feet first. Sometimes the policy worked, sometimes not. In the thrust and parry of day-to-day life, some families established a very intimate stepfather-stepchild relationship—a relationship that comfortably fit the man, child, and family. But in feet-first homes, failure was more common. These homes experienced a great deal of conflict because the players in the stepparent-stepchild relationship—the stepfather, stepchild, and biological parent—had conflicting ideas about how the relationship ought to work. And, very often, as the conflicts deepened and grew bitter, coalitions and factions began to develop.

The Gillis family provides a particularly graphic example. The Gillises were not a project family. Delores Gillis was a stepmother, and entrance to the study was limited to stepfather families. I met Delores, her husband, Alan, the Gillises' son, William, and Alan's three teenage daughters from his first marriage in my capacity as a clinical psychologist.

At our first meeting, the Gillises were divided into three warring factions: a sister faction, headed by the oldest Gillis daughter, Trisha; a Delores faction, headed by Delores and including the Gillises' four-year-old son, William; and an Alan faction, which consisted of Alan alone. Not surprisingly, each camp had its own theory about how the family had arrived at its current unhappy and contentious state. According to Trisha Gillis, the problem was Delores; she was cold, unfeeling, and authoritarian. According to Delores, the Gillis girls were a disruptive force; they had not been brought up well.

"I know that sounds harsh," Delores said to me one day. "I'm sure Helen was a good woman"—Helen Gillis, the girls' mother, had died of breast cancer five years earlier at the tragically young age of thirty-seven—"but she did not do a good job with those girls. They are ill-mannered and unruly."

Alan's explanation for the factionalism was, like Alan himself, befuddled. But it seemed to boil down to the fact that altogether too many women were living in his house.

The real reason for the factionalism, however, lay in the adult Gillises' failure to address the stepparent-definition task.

Delores wanted to be "a real mother" to the girls. This is an extremely ambitious goal under the best of circumstances, but whatever chance Delores had of achieving her wish was undercut by Alan's indecisiveness. He was unable to make up his mind about what level of maternal authority he would support.

Alan did not overrule all of Delores's pronouncements about curfew hours, chores, and dress codes, but he did overrule enough to alienate his wife, who took William and angrily retreated to one side of the family. The Gillis girls also withdrew. Concluding that their father was an unreliable source of support and understanding, they banded together and retreated to the opposite side of the family. This left the unsupported and befuddled Alan in the middle of the family taking fire from both sides.

The Gillis stepfamily managed to survive its factionalism but, like most balkanized families, not happily. A few years after the last of the Gillis daughters left home, a bitter Delores stopped speaking to her stepchildren. "It just happened out of the blue," Alan said when I ran into him at a charity function a few years later. "One Christmas Day the girls came over for dinner, and Delores refused to speak to any of them."

The factionalism also took its toll on the Gillis marriage. Alan felt that Delores's behavior had turned his daughters against him, and he couldn't quite bring himself to forgive her for that. "Delores did not handle the girls well," he told me during our talk. "And I'm the one who had to pay the price. I'm still angry at her for that."

Coalitions and conflicts were less likely in Neotraditional homes, because the defintion task was usually not ignored. The stepparent-stepchild relationship usually was defined before the man joined the family or during the early months after remarriage. More often than not, the relationship Neotraditional couples settled on was a close one; the man and woman decided that the man should develop close ties with the child. But it should be noted that a stepchild-stepparent relationship does not have to be close to be workable.

Aside from avoiding factionalism, the definition task is also critical for another reason. As a couple negotiates, compromises, and discusses—as they struggle toward a mutually agreed-upon definition of the stepparent-stepchild relationship—they begin to forge the shared vision and shared values, the mutual identity that is essential to form a successful stepfamily.

AVOIDING THE GHOSTS OF MARRIAGES PAST

"God, James, it was awful. I've never seen Jeffrey lose his temper like that. Even for dealing with his ex-wife, he was furious. Furious, furious."

It is six months after Jerome Goldsmith's birthday party, and Sarah and I are sitting on the flagstone patio behind the Goldsmiths' kitchen. On the way out, Sarah opened the French doors to let the cool night air into the house. Now, as we talk, sounds begin to float into the backyard: harsh, loud sounds. They are coming from the Rice campus on the other side of the elm-shaded street. It takes me a while to identify them. They are shouts—the deep, hoarse shouts of young men practicing a football drill.

On this autumn evening, the voices hold the promise of the season to come.

Sarah takes a sip of her ice tea and tells me: "Barbara is impossible."

"Barbara" is Barbara Weller, Jeffrey's former wife.

However, this latest "Barbara emergency," as Sarah describes the periodic thunderbolts that descend on the Goldsmiths from New Hampshire, is about money. Two days earlier Barbara presented Jeffrey with an ultimatum: Unless she received three months' child support in advance, the Goldsmith boys, Aaron and Mark, would not be coming to Houston next Friday for a visit before school started.

"Barbara says she's broke. What else is new?" Sarah pauses and takes another sip of her ice tea. "Jeffrey was so angry I thought he was going to jump into the phone, come out the other end, and strangle her."

I ask Sarah what she did when Jeffrey hung up.

"Well, James, one thing I did *not* do was interrogate him. You know, ask him what Barbara said. Jeffrey was upset enough; he didn't need me drilling him. I wanted to keep things diffused. I just told him it sounded like a tough call. The next day, after he calmed down, I asked what Barbara said.

"I also told him he should not talk to Barbara so much. It upsets him. It's bad for him."

A second task of stepfamily creation is the task of separation from another, earlier family. Couples in a first marriage face a similar challenge, but in their case the separation is from a family of origin, from well-meaning but often intrusive mothers and fathers, sisters and brothers; from habits and attitudes formed in childhood and adolescence. In a second marriage, the separation is from a first marriage and a first spouse. These are the Ghosts at the Table in every stepfamily home.

The ghosts can manifest themselves in money difficulties, in legal conflicts, in the behavior of a child toward a new stepfamily and stepfather, in habits of heart and mind, and in fears and defenses formed in the old dead civilization of the first marriage. At the start of the project, we hypothesized that ghostbusting would represent a major challenge in a second marriage, and our hypothesis was proved correct. Men and women who could not free themselves from the influence of a first marriage usually ended up destroying a second. We also found that, like the other three tasks of stepfamily creation, the task of separation involves a number of discrete steps, among them the ability to actively listen to their partners.

This may sound like a simple thing to do, but a surprisingly large number of our participants had difficulty with the step—among them, a young executive named William Bledsoe.

Soon after his marriage, William received a major promotion. His company, a large oil-rigging firm, elevated him to international marketing director. Two months later William arrived home with what was supposed to be a wonderful surprise. He had been house-hunting secretly since the promotion, and on this day at lunch, William had found what he had been looking for, the house of his and, he thought, his wife, Sheila's, dreams: a lovely four-bedroom neocolonial on a half acre of land in one of Houston's loveliest neighborhoods.

At first, Sheila's very subdued reaction to the good news puzzled William. She seemed anxious—almost fearful—as he described the house. Later that night, hurt replaced confusion; William felt unappreciated. Here he was being selfless, trying to build a better life for his wife and stepdaughter—and his reward? Anxious interrogation and sulking.

The next morning at breakfast, when Sheila spurned an offer to see his wonderful house, William made a final emotional turn; he went from hurt to anger.

"What is the matter with you?" he shouted. "Why are you behaving this way? Are you that ungrateful? Are you that small and mean and ungrateful?"

William knew that there had been some financial problems in Sheila's first marriage. He was vaguely aware of the enormous credit card debts and bad checks of her first husband, Roy. But William did not know the central thing, the thing that would have made Sheila's fear and anxiety about the house comprehensible, even touching: how the experience of Roy's indebtedness had traumatized her, had made her associate debt of any kind—even debt as benign and legitimate as a mortgage—with garnished wages, with humiliating Sunday morning "reminder" calls from collection agencies, with the whole awful threadbare panoply of impoverishment. He did not know this because he hadn't really listened to Sheila.

Poor listening is cited as a common problem in marital communication. But discussions of listening usually revolve around failures of technique. The listener does not fully comprehend an experience because he interrupts too often or is not really listening; he is thinking of what he is going to say, or he is distracted by the television, the children, or the memory of something his boss said that morning. But in stepfamilies, and particularly Romantic stepfamilies like the Bledsoes, we found another deeper cause of listening breakdowns. Romantics do not want to hear anything that undermines their Romantic view of family life, so often they tend to exercise a kind of emotional and historical censorship with each other.

This attitude can cause problems in a first marriage, but it is particularly problematic in a second because there are important first-marriage experiences that need to be disclosed. In the Bledsoes' case, I know that William especially did not want to hear about the financially irresponsible Roy, whom he once described to me as "trailer-park trash." I think William did not like to be reminded that he (a rising young executive) and "trailer-park" Roy had a wife in common.

Roy was never officially declared an off-limits topic in the Bledsoes' marriage—none of our participants ever resorted to outright censorship. But a lot of them did do what William did. Through impatience and pointed inattention, through obvious changing of the subject— through winks and nods, as it were—he made it clear to Sheila that he did not want to hear much about Roy or the marriage, and that what he *did* hear had better be cleaned up enough to earn a PG-13 rating.

Dealing with old ghosts was also a challenge for our couples, including Neotraditionals. But in their homes, an open, nonjudgmental marital environment encouraged frank disclosures, disclosures that made it possible for one spouse to understand the meaning an old ghost held for the other spouse.

In the early years of the marriage, a source of discreet but palpable tension between the Goldsmiths was Jeffrey's frequent phone calls to his former wife, Barbara.

"Maintenance of a crazy person" is how Jeffrey explained the two to three calls he made to New Hampshire each week. The calls, he claimed, were a necessity, the only way he could ensure that his former wife was fulfilling her maternal responsibilities to his sons, Aaron and Mark.

Sarah, however, objected to the frequency of the calls. She said talking to Barbara so often was bad for Jeffrey. It got him upset, made him lose his temper, agitated him, caused his blood pressure to rise. But once, during a visit, Sarah did say something that suggested she might object to the calls for another reason.

At the end of the interview, I was getting ready to leave when she told me to wait a minute and vanished into the kitchen. A moment later she reappeared with a photo.

"Has Jeffrey ever shown you a picture of his first family?" Sarah asked.

"No," I said. "Never."

Sarah handed me the photograph. "See if you can guess which one is Barbara."

The photo had been taken on a beach—a beach somewhere on the East Coast, from the look of the gray-and-brown shingled houses in the background. The Goldsmith boys were in the picture; they were standing on the beach between two women: one light haired, one dark haired. I pointed to the more attractive of the two women—a tall, willowy, somewhat hard-looking blonde in a two-piece bathing suit—and asked, "Barbara?"

Sarah nodded. "Right. Great figure, huh."

I did not respond, and Sarah did not ask any more questions. She sensed my surprise at her flutter of insecurity and was embarrassed. In the mythology of the Goldsmith marriage, Jeffrey, not Sarah, was the one who was supposed to be subject to such flutters. Now here was Sarah undercutting that mythology. She removed the photo from my hand, placed it facedown on a table, and escorted me to the door.

Several years later, Jeffrey told me something about Dan Fugelman that Sarah had not mentioned.

"Dan ran around," Jeffrey said one afternoon when we happened to find ourselves alone. "The last year of the marriage, he had a girlfriend in Dallas. He used to fly over to see her on weekends. Sarah was mortified. You know how proud she is. And here was Dan—someone she didn't even respect, didn't even like any more, for Christ's sake—making a fool of her."

This disclosure came in the context of another discussion. Jeffrey had been describing his new "Barbara policy" to me. He said he had told Barbara that henceforth he would *only* take her calls at the office.

"The calls upset Sarah," he said. "She finally admitted it to me. They make her a little jealous. I think that's understandable, you know, after the Dan thing."

I was rather touched by Jeffrey's sensitivity, but I was not entirely surprised by it.

An open, accepting marital environment encourages the kind of uninhibited disclosures that reveal not only the fact of a former spouse's infidelities, for example, but also the meaning the fact holds for the person disclosing it.

If there are winners and losers in stepfamily life, Neotraditionalists would have to be accounted among the winners. Couples like the Goldsmiths scored high on most of the markers we used to assesses stepfamily function, including marital satisfaction, personal happiness (of each spouse), and the psychological and emotional development of the child. But, to a large degree, the success of Neotraditionalist stepfamilies can be explained in terms of compatible values and beliefs. Like Sarah and Jeffrey, most Neotraditional men and women want to create a modern version of the traditional nuclear family.

For couples with a different set of values and beliefs (and personalities)—for couple Andrew and Ellen Lawton, whom we will meet next—the Neotraditional stepfamily would not work at all.

POINTS TO KEEP IN MIND

- Neotraditional stepfamilies begin to look more like first-marriage families over time; they develop emotional cohesiveness and close (step)parent-child and marital bonds.
- Forming a strong marital bond is a key developmental task for all stepfamilies. It serves as the foundation for the step-

family and greatly facilitates other aspects of stepfamily life, such as parenting and the development of family rules and roles.

- A strong stepfamily marriage has three foundations. First, the husband and wife have to attend to their adult needs—to nurture their relationship. Second, they need to develop a shared vision of marriage and family life. And third, they have to develop a consensus on parenting and other child-related issues. This consensus may vary depending on the type of stepfamily that the couple forms, but the *bottom line is they have to agree on how to deal with the child.*

- Marital happiness affects children differently in step- and nuclear families. In nuclear families, there is a strong connection between how happy a couple are and how well their child does, while in stepfamilies, the opposite is true. In the early years especially, marital satisfaction has little effect on a child's adjustment. Also, in stepfamilies, happy children contribute to a happy marriage.

- The *two* critical issues of early stepfamily life are parenting and stepparenting. The family has to develop a method for integrating the stepparent into the family. It is also best to limit the stepparent's role during the early period of stepfamily life. A stepparent needs to develop a relationship with his stepchild before he tries to start parenting the child.

chapter two

The Matriarchal Stepfamily:
Andrew and Ellen Lawton

Andrew and Ellen Lawton met at a wake. *Andrew's* wake.

On the night of his first skydive, Andrew invited a select group of friends to his home for a night of mourning, music, and whiskey. A small-print paragraph at the bottom of Andrew's crepe-bordered invitations noted that should Mr. Lawton unexpectedly survive his first skydive, the wake would be redesignated a party.

Ellen did not receive one of the invitations. She barely knew Andrew. From time to time she would see him in the cafeteria of the hospital where they both worked. But the only things Ellen knew about Andrew, outside of his name and his preference for eating alone by a window, was that he worked in the social services department on the third floor and that he was very good looking. Andrew had what Ellen's mother used to call "a fine southern face": high cheekbones, deep-set eyes, a long jaw, and thick brown-black hair.

Ellen was shown Andrew's invitation by another nurse on the oncology floor.

The other nurse tittered at the drawing of the little parachutist on the front of the invitation, but Ellen thought the drawing (the parachutist was inside a casket), the invitation—the whole idea of giving yourself a wake—prankish and adolescent. She would have expected something better—something more elevated—from a man with such a sensitive face.

Still, when the other nurse asked if she wanted to go to the party, Ellen said yes, although not very enthusiastically.

Ellen was at a point in life where everything felt frozen—stuck. Her children, Todd, five, and Caroline, nine, would always be too young to do anything without her. The family, the three of them, would always live in a small cinder-block house with a chain-link fence in front. Ellen would always work fifty-hour weeks. There would never be enough money to pay the bills on time. The sink in the bathroom would always leak, the next-door neighbors would always turn on the stereo as Ellen was getting ready to go to bed. Peanut, the family cat, and Tom, Ellen's former husband, would always be around to torment her.

Ellen was wrong about things never changing—or, rather, half wrong.

Her life was about to change completely, although, in a strange way, nothing—or almost nothing—was to change at all for a very long while.

Ellen and Andrew agree: Ellen was the first to fall in love. She left Andrew's apartment after the party already in love. And while it is impossible to explain why people fall in love when they do, analytical-minded Ellen feels compelled to explain why she did. Partly, she says, it was loneliness. Only later, in retrospect, did she realize how fraught, how primed for love she was by the need for companionship, the need for a sane adult to talk to. But loneliness by itself would not have been enough, Ellen insists. Something else was necessary: Andrew had to redeem himself, had to show that he was better than those silly invitations.

Unknowingly, Andrew did this when he and another guest got into a discussion about jazz in front of Ellen and her friend. Charlie Mingus, Charlie Parker, Miles Davis—all the names in the conversation were new to Ellen. But that did not matter. Andrew made the musicians sound exciting, interesting; Ellen couldn't wait to hear their music. She also liked listening to Andrew talk, to the sound of his voice. It was deep and sandpapery, but somehow soft and gentle—sensitive. Leaving the party, Ellen thought she could listen to a voice like that forever.

Andrew's love for Ellen, like Andrew himself, took its time. It meandered, it wandered and dallied; it stopped here to admire the view and there to talk to a friend. And on arriving, Andrew's love did not announce itself in a single, startling flourish. It unfolded slowly in a dozen small moments and in a dozen small things: Andrew was entranced by the way Ellen moved—he thought her walk incredibly sensual—by her lazy, lopsided grin, and, most of all, by her skill at managing her busy, crowded, demanding life.

Ellen was different from the other single mothers Andrew had known. Those women, all brave to a fault, seemed a little sad and adrift, a little beaten down. They—and their families—seemed to float aimlessly from day to day in a miasma of unpicked-up socks and unwashed dishes. Ellen was decisive, crisp, commanding. Her children, Caroline and Todd, were disciplined and well behaved; the little house on Melton Street was neat and clean, and family life there was orderly and purposeful. Everyone had chores—"little jobs," Ellen called them. In the small cinder-block house on Melton Street, no one wasted much time in front of the television.

Self-improvement, getting ahead, was a major passion in Ellen's life. At first Andrew found the passion naive, silly. "Why are you wasting your time with this stuff?" he asked one day when he found Ellen reading a book on how to build more brain power. "If you're going to read, read something worthwhile." But gradually Ellen's little library of financial and personal self-help books—her books on how to be an effective speaker, on how to budget your time, on how to cash in on the coming boom in stocks—began to seem touching, endearing, and then, finally, *admirable* to Andrew. The little library became a symbol of everything that Andrew liked—loved—about Ellen: her pluck, her earnestness, and her dogged determination to make a better life for herself and her family. At a certain point in the relationship, it also occurred to Andrew (who is rather shrewd about himself) that Ellen would make a good mate—maybe even a good antidote—to a man like himself.

I think that we, the DIS StepFamily Project, were one of Ellen's self-improvement projects. She has a great faith in the power of understanding and knowledge. So when she saw one of our recruiting posters, she wrote down our number; the next day she called the project office.

Two weeks later an assistant and I drove out to the Lawtons to conduct a first interview. Caroline, in a Houston Oilers T-shirt, answered the door. A moment later a tall, willowy blonde, with a face more sensual than pretty, appeared behind her. This was Ellen. She led us into the living room where Andrew was waiting for us. I exchanged pleasantries with the Lawtons for a few minutes, then explained the purpose of the study. There were some questions, as there always are on such occasions. When I finished answering them, my assistant and I began to collect background information on the family.

The Lawtons looked at one another, then Andrew nudged Ellen. "Why don't you go first?"

Ellen said she was twenty-nine, had grown up in Kingsville, an oil and ranching town in South Texas, and married Tom Dietrich, her first husband, two weeks after high school graduation. Six months later her first child, Caroline, was born. Shortly after the birth of her second child, Todd, four years later, Ellen filed for divorce.

The decision to become a nurse, Ellen explained, was the result of a stock-taking done after the divorce. She was twenty-two, had two young children, a former husband with an unstable work history, and possessed no work skills beyond clerking and waitressing. This was a familiar story in Kingsville, and Ellen knew from friends how the story usually ended: in a trailer park, or in a four-room house next to an overgrown field, with hand-me-down clothes for the children, a welfare check, or a 7-Eleven job for the woman and no consolations beyond Garth Brooks and jelly doughnuts.

"I had a better opinion of myself than that," Ellen declared.

I asked her where she went to nursing school.

"Houston. The kids stayed in Kingsville with Mama while I was in training." After graduation Ellen moved the family to Houston.

"What about Todd and Caroline's dad?" I asked. "Is he still in Kingsville?"

Ellen frowned. "No, here. Houston. After Tom settled down, he followed us on up here."

As I conducted interviews for the project, I was growing truly astonished at the enormous role substance abuse and work instability played in marital dissolution. A number of the participants in our sample of working- to upper-middle-class families told us that they had left a first marriage at least in part because of a spouse's substance abuse problem or work instability. Ellen was one of these subjects, although apparently her first husband was settled down in a stable job.

"Not that that's helped him much," Ellen said during the interview. "Tom is still a difficult individual."

At this point, Andrew interrupted, to (sort of) defend Tom. He said Tom Dietrich, for all his faults, loved his children and had a good heart.

Ellen let out a whoop. "Andrew, did Caroline tell you what her daddy did last week? He told her he was going to take her and Todd to Hawaii at Christmastime. Tom is four months behind on his support payments, and he's promising his kids he's going to take them on a cruise to Hawaii!

"I said to Caroline, I said: 'Honey, if I were you, I wouldn't pack my bags just yet.' "

Ellen turned to me. "Tom Dietrich never has done one thing in his entire life he said he was going to do. He's a dreamer."

After Todd called Ellen into the kitchen, I asked Andrew about himself.

He said he was thirty-two, born in Virginia, but moved to Dallas when his father was transferred to IBM's Dallas office from Washington, D.C. "I was ten when we moved," he said.

Andrew's adult life seemed to be full of detours. He dropped out of the University of Texas midway through his junior year to go to Los Angeles and try his hand at film work—mostly, I gathered, acting. Four years later, upon returning to Texas, Andrew tried to write a book about his California adventures but abandoned the project midway for lack of money. Thereafter, he worked in a series of what he described as "people" jobs: counselor in a drug rehabilitation center, welfare case worker, and, briefly, probation officer. Currently, Andrew said, he was a family services coordinator at the hospital where he and Ellen worked. He counseled the families of the chronically ill. "Emotionally, it's a very demanding job," he said.

"Is this your first or second marriage?" I asked.

"First."

Andrew anticipated my next question. "We don't plan to have children. I don't want any. And Ellen doesn't want any more—do you, hon?"

"No," Ellen said firmly. "No more kids."

CHARACTERISTICS OF THE
MATRIARCHAL STEPFAMILY

At the time of my first visit, Ellen and Andrew had been married six months and, like most couples in the first cycle of stepfamily life, were struggling with many divisive issues. But their "problem" issues were not typical first-cycle issues. They did not involve children or parenting; rather, their problems involved their relationship with each other.

Before the marriage, Andrew had promised Ellen that he would finish the course work for his college degree at night at the University of Houston. This promise was part of another promise he made to Ellen. Once he got his degree, the Lawtons were going to move to Austin, a city Ellen loved. Andrew would become a lobbyist in the state capital, make a six-figure income, and then the Lawtons would buy a house—a big, lovely brick house on a hill.

However, it was now six months later, and Andrew had done absolutely nothing to redeem his promises. This was a very big issue for Ellen.

"Andrew has trouble finishing things," she said toward the end of the interview. "He gets all excited and enthusiastic about a thing for a week or two, then—" Ellen paused. "I don't know how to say this."

Suddenly Andrew threw up his hands as if he were expecting a blow. "Here it comes, Dr. Bray. Whenever Ellen starts a sentence 'I don't know how to say this,' I know I'm going to get slammed."

Ellen frowned. "Well, you have to show a little more ambitiousness, Andrew. Finish what you start. Sloth does not become a man."

I considered whether Ellen was beginning to wonder if she had married another dreamer.

Andrew's principal complaint about Ellen was that she worked too much. Her fifty-hour weeks were unreasonably long, he said. Ellen was hardly ever at home, and when she was, she was either with her children, sleeping, or on the phone with her mother. "We don't have a social life anymore."

Tom Dietrich, Ellen's former husband, was also a source of contention in the Lawton stepfamily. But I found it difficult to get a handle on why Tom was a divisive figure or, indeed, to figure out how Andrew and Ellen really felt about him. I noticed that whenever one Lawton criticized Tom, the other would leap to his defense. Tom seemed to function in the family like a big, clumsy, annoying, but basically lovable dog: a pet everyone complains about but whom no one can live without.

However, the Lawtons were in perfect accord on one very important issue: Andrew and Ellen agreed that the parenting responsibilities were solely Ellen's province. Such a division of labor is characteristic of our second stepfamily type, the Matriarchal family. Besides this signature trait, this form of stepfamily, which accounts for 25 to 30 percent of stepfamilies, has several other defining characteristics—among them, a relatively low level of cohesiveness, a vulnerability to change, and, most especially, a unique combination of personality types.

All kinds of men and women formed Neotraditional and Romantic stepfamilies. But only one kind of man and one kind of woman formed a Matriarchal stepfamily.

Andrew and especially Ellen are good examples of the two personality types.

Most of the authority and decision-making power in a Matriarchal stepfamily is centered in the woman. She is the intellectual and financial nerve center of the family, and also its heart—the person other family members come to for comfort, advice, and companionship. To put it more simply, in a Matriarchal stepfamily the woman leads and the man follows—not all of the time but enough of the time to make it clear who is the principal authority in the stepfamily and who is not.

The structure of the Matriarchal stepfamily suggested that it might be populated by egalitarians. This gender ideology, closely associated with modern feminism, holds that the sexes are so alike in abilities and talents that roles like leader and decision maker can be played interchangeably by a man or a woman. But it turned out that the Matriarchal stepfamily is an expression of an older type of egalitarianism, rooted not in a belief system but rather in the woman's personality.

Our Matriarchal women actually had rather conventional—which is to say rather traditional—views about men and women. Matriarchal women lead because they possess an innate ability to lead, to command. Put a Matriarchal nurse in a hospital and, as Ellen eventually did, she will become a ward supervisor; put her in an office and she will become an office manager; leave her at home and she will end up running half a dozen school and neighborhood committees. Put a Matriarchal woman in a family and she will lead it.

Energy and ambition are two other common characteristics of Matriarchal-stepfamily women; but a strong family orientation and often modest circumstances give the Matriarchal woman's ambitions a domestic cast. Typically, she would rather have a new house in a nicer neighborhood than shatter a corporation's glass ceiling. Unusually high competence is another common trait. But the Matriarchal woman's competence is not, like Sarah Goldsmith's, a matter of knowingness. It is practical and resourceful. It knows how to turn leftovers from a Sunday pot roast into four other dinners and how to turn last Halloween's Dracula costume into this year's pirate costume. Another expression of this competence is a very high level of parenting skill. Often Matriarchal women are content to exercise sole responsibility for parenting because parenting is something they do very well.

Virginia Kelley, President Clinton's mother, is a good example of what a Matriarchal woman can do with a child.

Matriarchal men tend to be low-key and easygoing; but temperament is not the only reason they are content to follow their wives. The rituals, joys, and comforts of stepfamily life are of secondary interest to a Matriarchal man. He does some of the things other stepfathers do; he attends birthday parties and graduations and tags along on trips to Disneyland—and he enjoys these activities as much as everyone else in the family. But the Matriarchal male always stands a little apart, a little distant from the principal centers of stepfamily life, because family and children are not what brought him into the stepfamily. He joined it for the companionship and affection of his wife. Usually (although, as we shall see in a moment, not always), as long as his wife continues to provide him with both of these things, he is content to let her run everything else.

A fourth characteristic of the Matriarchal stepfamily flows directly from the character of the Matriarchal man. In Neotraditional and, to an extent, Romantic stepfamilies, the tasks of family building are used to nurture the marriage. In the course of developing a common strategy on parenting, on former spouses, on money, and on a dozen other issues, the man and woman slowly begin to forge a shared vision, values, and outlook that are the building blocks of a good marriage.

In a Matriarchal stepfamily, the marriage is nurtured differently. It is constructed through couple's activities: through frequent nights out and adults-only vacations and expeditions. Neotraditional couples also engage in some couple's activities; indeed, all successful stepfamilies do. They are essential to keeping a marriage vital and vibrant. But in Neotraditional homes, couple's activities represent an "in addition to," a supplement to the main source of marital nurturance. In Matriarchal homes, the man's wish for companionship but not for family responsibilities make couple's activities the main (and often the only) source of marital nurturance.

Matriarchal stepfamilies are also unique in one other respect. Neotraditional and Romantic stepfamilies have predictable trajectories: The former almost always succeeds, the latter almost always does not. The course of the Matriarchal stepfamily, in contrast, is variable. While many of our Matriarchal families did well, a few did not, usually because someone reneged on the unspoken Matriarchal marriage contract. Either the man grew dissatisfied because he stopped getting the companionship he wanted, or the woman did, because she stopped getting the domestic control she desired.

The Matriarchal stepfamily's ability to nurture its children also can vary. Healthy development was the norm among our Matriarchal children, and a few of these youngsters did exceptionally well. But we also had a minority of Matriarchal children who did not do so well; despite their mothers' maternal competence, these boys and girls developed behavioral and emotional problems. And, in most cases they did for the same reason. The unusual structure of the Matriarchal family deprived the child of the support he or she needed to overcome the trauma of divorce.

CHILDREN AND THE STEPFAMILY:
HEALING THE WOUNDS OF DIVORCE

It is near the end of the Lawtons' first interview, and Ellen and I are sitting on a couch in the living room trying hard not to overhear Andrew, who is standing a few feet away in the hall, talking to a friend who called a moment ago.

Ellen, self-conscious about the interruption, is apologizing for the call, when six-year-old Todd wanders into the room. Todd, who has Ellen's blond hair and lazy, lopsided grin, holds a brochure in one hand and a model aircraft carrier in the other—except that the carrier is not exactly being held; Todd has it tucked under his arm like a commuter's newspaper.

"See the ship," Todd says. On the cover of the brochure he hands me is a picture of a sleek white luxury liner on an electric-blue sea. The ship sails under the banner HAWAII.

"Tom left that silly book when he was here Wednesday," Ellen says.

Todd ignores the disapproving tone in his mother's voice.

"For Christmas," Todd tells me, "we're all gonna go on a boat to an island." Then he turns slightly to his left so I can get a better look at the aircraft carrier under his arm. "I told my dad I want to go on a boat like this one."

Ellen sighs wearily. She has been through this before. "Todd, honey, we're not going anywhere. We don't have any money for a big vacation. Besides, I have to work and so does Andrew."

"No," Todd says, "we're gonna go. We're all gonna go. Me and Caroline and you and Daddy." Todd pauses and repeats the last word much more loudly. *"Daddy,"* he insists. *"DADDY!"* Then he begins to cry.

It has been clear since the 1970s that children in stepfamilies are at greater developmental risk than children in nuclear families. But only recently has it become clear why they are more vulnerable to emotional, psychological, and developmental problems. Early researchers blamed the vulnerability on the complicated structure of the stepfamily itself. They argued that children were confused and overstressed, made angry and resentful by the family's complex web of relationships and obligations. "No wonder boys and girls in stepfamilies have problems," these early investigators seemed to say. "Look at all the relationships stepchildren have to figure out, all the people they have to adjust to." Even now, the legacy of the early research lingers on in the feelings of inferiority that beset so many stepfamilies, in their members' sense of being second-class citizens, of belonging to a just-barely-"good-enough" family.

This legacy is especially tragic because it is wrong. It rests on a misreading, a mistake. We found that the experience of divorce is at the root of many of the behavioral problems that the early reports attributed to the complicated structure of the stepfamily. Take, for example, the often-commented-on rebelliousness and contentiousness of the stepfamily adolescent. Like Dr. Judith Wallerstein, who wrote about this second-wave behavior in her book *Second Chances,* we found that adolescent rebelliousness is often not a by-product of stepfamily life but, rather, a delayed reaction to a parental divorce. Four, five, six years after the breakup, the child experiences a second wave of emotional and behavioral problems. Dr. Wallerstein, borrowing a term first coined by Mavis Hetherington of the University of Virginia, called the delayed reaction "the sleeper effect"; Wallerstein noted that the time lag involved often puzzled adult members of the stepfamily. The child suddenly erupts after several years of seemingly healthy adjustment to stepfamily life.

I will have more to say about the sleeper effect later. Suffice to say now that we found it to be even more widespread than Dr. Wallerstein had observed in her study of seventy-six families. She described the sleeper effect as unique to girls. In our study sample of two hundred families, we found that the sleeper effect operates in boys as well.

One of the most troubling and sad conversations I had during the project's nine-year course was with an eight-year-old named Roger Leek. A few days before our talk, Roger, one of our target children, had gotten himself into a great deal of trouble. During a lunch break, he and another boy had exchanged words in the school yard. Words led to fists and fists led to a one-week suspension for Roger, who managed to knock the other boy down, bloody his nose, and blacken his eye before a teacher was able to intervene.

Roger's mother, Margaret, asked me to speak to him the afternoon I visited the Leeks for a videotaping session with Margaret and husband, Gary.

Usually, when I sat down with a target child, I just listened. I let the child explain what he did and why he did it, then I asked a question or two. My questions were designed to provoke thought about the behavior.

Roger began by explaining the reason for the fight. At morning recess, he said, he accidentally bumped into the other boy; the boy made a remark that Roger did not like, and Roger, who has a history of temper problems, decided to even the score at lunch.

"Why didn't you try to talk to the other boy first?" I said.

Roger shrugged. "Didn't think of it, sir."

"I'm curious," I said. "How did you think hitting him would solve your problem?"

Roger frowned the frown of the deeply wary. On top of all his other problems, he was now about to receive another lecture from another adult.

"I know hitting's wrong, sir," he said. "I know I shouldn't do it. But sometimes it just happens, like it did with my daddy." This last statement had slipped out accidentally, and Roger tried to amend it immediately. "It didn't happen much, just at the end, just before they got, you know, the divorce."

"It happened with your mom?" I asked.

Roger was not looking at me anymore. He was staring at the floor. "Uh-huh, with my mom."

A few minutes later I was packing up my gear in the Leeks' living room when Margaret came in. She asked about my conversation with Roger.

I told her what he had said. I also told her that I was surprised: At the Leeks' intake interview Margaret had said that financial problems had destroyed her first marriage. There had been no mention of domestic abuse.

Neither of us said anything for a moment. Then Margaret apologized. "I'm sorry," she said. "I was embarrassed, James. I was embarrassed to let anyone know that I let another human being treat me that way."

Conflict may be the most serious legacy of a parental divorce. But the most common legacy among younger children, especially, is self-blame. An amazing number of our six- and seven-year-old subjects were able to articulate why a parental divorce gives a child a low opinion of herself. "I think Daddy left because he was mad at me," one six-year-old girl told me, while a seven-year-old boy explained that his father took a new wife " 'cause he stopped liking me and my mom."

Our identification of the Matriarchal stepfamily coincided with an important new project finding about divorce. In the mid-1980s our data began to show that both the old conventional wisdom about divorce—it leaves no long-term scars on a child—and the new—it does leave long-term scars—were wrong. Instead of both of these extremes, we were finding that after two or three years of residence in a well-functioning stepfamily, most of our target children were healing and overcoming the effects of their parents' marital transitions.

When we looked at this healing effect in Matriarchal stepfamilies, we found a less consistent picture.

While many of the youngsters in these families recovered from divorce, some did not. And a key variable in determining whether—and to what extent—recovery took place was, ironically, the parental role of the Matriarchal man. Even the supercompetent Matriarchal woman benefits from some backup support. Typically, Matriarchal men provide that support in one of two ways. The way that worked best for the child—and for the family—was for the man to adopt the role that Andrew played in the Lawton stepfamily: monitor.

During one of my visits to Melton Street, I noticed that Caroline was missing. When I asked where she was, Andrew, not Ellen, answered. To my even greater surprise, Andrew had a pretty detailed knowledge of his stepdaughter's whereabouts. He said she was at her friend Lurlene's. Lurlene, Andrew explained with a half smile, was Caroline's second best friend. The two girls were having dinner at Lurlene's; afterward they were going to do their homework together.

The majority of our Matriarchal men played a similar monitoring role. The monitoring stepfather was usually not involved in the child's emotional life, but, like Andrew, he knew a lot about the child's daily life: where she was, whom she was with, and what she was doing. The monitor also checked homework and daily chores—and he often provided companionship. One thing I could count on when I arrived at the Lawtons' is that Todd and Andrew would be sitting together on the couch watching a baseball, basketball, or football game.

Often Neotraditional men play a monitoring role at the start of stepfamily life; but whereas a man like Jeffrey Goldsmith uses the role to create a more intimate stepparent-stepchild relationship, a man like Andrew Lawton has no ambitions beyond being a "buddy" to a stepchild. The Matriarchal man's parenting duties also remain fixed. They don't expand beyond serving as the Matriarchal woman's second set of eyes and ears.

Since detached parenting is thought to be unhealthy for a child, we expected to see a high incidence of new behavioral problems and an exacerbation of old divorce-related problems in the Matriarchal stepfamily. But something unexpected occurred: Not only did new problems fail to appear, but old, divorce-related disorders like low self-esteem began to disappear. Part of the credit—a significant part—belongs to the Matriarchal woman and her superb parenting skills. But, the man's monitoring was a real aid to his stepchildren. When we looked more closely at this unexpected finding, we found that there were several reasons for it.

One was that the monitor's intelligence-gathering function—his knowledge of what the children were doing and whom they were doing it with—allowed the woman to make more informed, and usually better, parenting decisions. More surprising, our data show that monitoring also had an emotional benefit. Children may complain about questions like "Where are you going?" "What time will you be home?" and "Have you done your homework?" but the questions make a boy or girl feel cared for, watched over, and valued. In time, children who feel valued tend to develop a good opinion of themselves.

The Matriarchal man's relative parental detachment also can serve his marriage.

Once, while I was at the Lawtons', Caroline arrived home in a terrible mood from a visit with her father. She slammed doors, stomped around, swore. Well, actually, she did not really swear. What she said was "I hate this 'frigedarian coat," but Ellen acted as if she had used the other F-word.

"Don't you dare use that word!" she shouted at Caroline. "Don't you dare even think that word in this house, young lady." Caroline shouted something back and a terrible row erupted.

Such acting-out behavior is common after a visit with a nonresidential parent, and in homes where a man is heavily invested in parenting, the result is often a family-wide disruption. The man, seeing himself as paterfamilias, criticizes the child for criticizing her mother. The child, reverberating from the visit with her biological father, tells the man to mind his own business; he is not her biological father. The man, now hurt and feeling rejected, tells the child she is rude—and, anyway, who does she think is paying for her food and for the roof over her head? Then the wife, upset that her child has been attacked, tells the man not to talk to her little girl that way.

Everyone loses in such fights, and the biggest loss is to the marriage that holds the stepfamily together.

When a biological parent–and–child argument erupts in a Matriarchal family, usually the man does what Andrew did. As soon as Ellen and Caroline began shouting at one another, he picked up his newspaper and announced he would be out on the porch reading if I wanted him. Andrew's exit from the fray may look like uninvolvement, but it was enlightened uninvolvement because he was removing himself from a situation that had the potential to spin out of control and sour his relationship with his stepdaughter and/or his wife.

In Matriarchal families where the scars of divorce lingered and caused developmental problems, stepfather withdrawal was also common, but, in these families, the man withdrew *permanently*. He refused to assume responsibility for even minor parenting tasks.

A principal reason why Matriarchal men withdraw is displeasure with a wife. The man is in the family for the woman, and if, for a variety of reasons, the woman becomes unable to provide sufficient affection and companionship, the Matriarchal man loses interest not only in her but also in *her* family.

However, the most common reason why Matriarchal men withdraw is an almost zero tolerance for difficult or annoying behavior in the child.

"I hate the way he talks to me. He talks to me as if I were a piece of garbage." The subject of these remarks is a project youngster, Jamie Harmon; the speaker, Jamie's stepfather, William Nixon. Having been present at one of Jamie's outbursts, I have to admit that William has a point. At times, Jamie's obnoxiousness approaches the transcendent. But Jamie is thirteen, and most parents, biological or step, are willing to extend an extra measure of tolerance to an adolescent because they know the youngster is just going through a stage. Part of being a thirteen-year-old is being obnoxious to your parents.

But William was not a typical parent. He listened politely while I explained all of the above, then told me that he did not marry Myrna (Jamie's mother) for the privilege of being insulted by her child. Either Jamie would "shape up, or—." William did not define the option on the other side of his "or," but he left me in no doubt about what it might be. When we looked at our data at the end of the study, we were not surprised to find that withdrawal created new (and exacerbated old) divorce-related problems in a child. Nor do you need to be a psychologist to understand why. Withdrawal tells a child whose esteem has already been damaged by a divorce: "You don't matter to me."

MANAGING CHANGE IN A STEPFAMILY

Ellen's house on Melton Street sits a hundred yards from an overpass. Beyond the overpass, the small businesses of city life—auto body shops, a machine tool factory, commercial warehouses—line both sides of Melton until it flows into the interstate, five miles away. Ellen's side of the bypass is largely residential. Small, boxlike houses with picture windows in front and TV antennae on the roofs (cable has not yet arrived in this part of Houston) line both sides of the street. The sherbet colors of the houses—pinks, oranges, and lime greens—are supposed to be festive; but under the relentless, unshaded Texas sun, they make the street look oddly forlorn, cheerless.

Two doors from Ellen's, I pass a steamroller with thick black diagonal lines painted on its back. It and two City of Houston trucks are repaving the street's badly pockmarked surface on this September afternoon. When I pull up in front of the Lawtons' house, Todd is standing on the lawn watching the work crews smooth the newly laid tar with rakelike tools. Todd is eight now but still in the habit of finding a compatible toy when a grown-up's persona or task excites his imagination; today he is holding a bright orange Tonka cement mixer in his hand.

As my assistant and I get out of my car, the front door of the house opens. Ellen emerges in a black tank top and a pair of jeans. Once she mentioned that in high school she had been a cheerleader; her figure is still sleek and athletic. A few of the men in the work crew stop and notice her. She waves when she sees me, then shouts, "Kids, c'mon. Lunch."

As Todd dashes up the stairs, Ellen lets out a whoop. I think she has a special affection for Todd. I think that in the boy she sees something of herself and believes that in him she may at last have found a male who will not disappoint her, who will live up to her expectations for him.

Inside, Ellen picks up a photograph from the dining-room table. She holds the photo up above her shoulder so I can see it. It is a picture of a house, a semidetached condominium. The house is modest-looking but still a notable improvement over her current home.

"I looked at it yesterday," Ellen says over her shoulder. She is still walking, moving toward the kitchen where Andrew is waiting for us. "I'm trying to decide if we can afford it."

"Rent or buy?" I ask.

Another whoop. "Rent!"

I don't ask about Austin, about the Lawtons' plan to move there, to buy a big house on a hill. It is now a year and a half since my first visit; Andrew is still only talking about school, and lately I notice that he talks about it less. I think the subject is too volatile, too fraught with accusations and failures to be talked about casually anymore.

Andrew and Ellen know why my assistant and I are at the house today. Last week I called Ellen and told her that I wanted to videotape an interaction among her, Andrew, and Todd (whom we have designated the family target child) this afternoon. Before I set up my camera, I remove a "topic" list from my briefcase and hand it to Ellen. I ask her and Andrew to select an issue that they would like to discuss with Todd. We use these topic lists, which contain ten possible areas of discussion, to keep family interactions focused. Ellen selects "discipline." She says Todd's manners are not all that they could be. Today's exercise will give her an opportunity to remind him about the importance of being polite.

"Well, Toddy does not say 'thank you' nearly as much as he should." It is now about five minutes into the interaction and Ellen has worked herself into a state of agitation over Todd's rudeness.

"So he forgets once in a while," Andrew tells her. "Big deal. He's a terrific kid." I thought the Lawtons' interaction might be one-sided, all Ellen. But Andrew has turned out to be an unexpectedly spirited contributor. Even more unexpected, he is quite critical of Ellen's strictness. "You're too hard on poor Todd," he says.

"I am not," Ellen replies. She is clearly annoyed at Andrew for criticizing her.

"Yes, you are," Andrew insists. "You criticize Todd too much."

As the argument escalates, Todd, who is sitting between Ellen and Andrew at the kitchen table, begins to cry. But the Lawtons are too preoccupied to notice.

"Andrew, you don't know diddly about kids," Ellen says.

"I know enough to know you're being overbearing with Todd."

This last remark is too much for Ellen. "Andrew," she warns, "you are puttin' your nose where it does not belong. I do not like your attitude at all."

Finally I decide to interrupt the interaction. But as I am about to call attention to Todd's distress, Ellen notices that he is crying. She leans over and puts her arms around her distraught son, then she looks across the table at Andrew. "Look, look, how you upset him," she says.

It is fifteen minutes later now and Andrew has not moved. He is still sitting at the kitchen table. He has barely spoken since Ellen took Todd into his room. He is looking out the window but not really looking at anything. I know Todd's crying has upset him, but I think Ellen's contentiousness during the interaction is troubling Andrew too. I sense that he learned something new about his wife and his marriage this afternoon and that he is upset by it.

Ellen also seems preoccupied when she returns to the kitchen. She glances over at Andrew but does not say anything. She looks very cross.

At the door, when Ellen says good-bye, I notice that she does not smile. Did she forget because she was preoccupied? I wonder. Or did something else make her forget?

In addition to the practical tasks of stepfamily life that must be negotiated and mastered, couples like the Lawtons and the Goldsmiths face another task.

Change is a constant in all families. Children grow up, marriages grow old. But in a stepfamily, the pace of change is greater and the ability to control it more limited. Partly, this is because more potential agents of change are on the scene. Every child has three to four parents and six to eight grandparents, and the reappearance or disappearance of any supporting player can alter a family's functioning, sometimes significantly. The other reason why the stepfamily is so prone to change is that its members often undergo changes of heart and mind as the family develops and matures.

How should change be managed? Should it be embraced as inevitable? Should it be resisted as a threat to family cohesion and functioning? Or should a middle course be charted? Developing a unified policy on change is also an essential task of stepfamily life.

Our data indicate that flexibility is the most effective policy to adopt toward change. Human beings are not static, not frozen, and neither is a family with several sets of parents, grandparents, uncles, and aunts. Over time changes of heart are bound to occur—among the principal members of the family and among its large supporting cast—and out of those changes will come new attitudes, feelings, and goals. Flexibility means learning how to integrate the new and the different into the fabric of family life without producing major disruptions.

The Matriarchal stepfamily handles certain types of change very well. For example, the Matriarchal man's low investment in the parenting role makes him much less vulnerable to jealousy if—as sometimes happens in adolescence—the stepchild grows closer to his or her biological father. But this form of stepfamily is much less adept at managing changes that threaten its signature trait: the one-sided division of domestic responsibilities.

Later I learned that after the taping, Andrew (briefly) tried to play a more active parenting role.

"He told me he thought I was way too strict with Todd," Ellen said at our next interview. "We had some real battles over it—wars practically."

I was a little stunned. I told Ellen I was sorry to have caused her and Andrew marital difficulties. It was the last thing I had intended.

Suddenly Ellen's voice went from upset to exasperated. She thanked me for my concern but said that wasn't why the session with Todd and Andrew had upset her. Parenting was her responsibility, *her* domain, and by orchestrating the interaction, I had disrupted the arrangement by inviting Andrew into it. Worse, now that he was in her domain, Ellen was having great difficulty shooing him out again.

"Andrew's very sweet," Ellen said, "but he does not know the first thing about raising kids. His idea of being a good father is buying a kid an ice-cream cone every time the kid asks for one."

You can't talk about why Matriarchal women resist change without also talking about another of their qualities, one that I think is implicit in everything else I've said about them: the need to control. A controlling personality is often an asset to a stepfamily because it helps make the trains run on time. It ensures that chores are done promptly and that rules on curfews, homework, and discipline are observed—that bills are paid on a regular schedule. But the Matriarchal woman's need to control can become a serious problem when a change threatens her domination of the family.

The kind of sharp reaction that Ellen visited upon Andrew's unsolicited parental advice is a common occurrence in Matriarchal stepfamilies. A Matriarchal woman's desire to control the parenting domain is a desire so deeply rooted, it sometimes can pull a stepfamily apart.

A large group of project participants were from the Midwest. These families moved to Houston from Detroit, Chicago, and Pittsburgh in the mid-1980s to take jobs in Houston's growing medical industry. Mike and Kristen Devon, both hospital administrators, were in this contingent of "snowbirds." Kristen and Mike moved from Ohio in 1987. A year later Kristen, who had a six-year-old named Ethan, gave birth to a second child, Moira Ann Devon.

Usually a new baby adds cohesiveness to a stepfamily. But a new child also alters the parenting dynamic within the family in a way that can threaten an individual invested in controlling this domain.

The reason? A new baby often brings a man deeper into his stepchild's life.

I have to admit that this response surprised me. At the start of the study, I expected to see new fathers begin to pull away from their stepchildren after the baby arrived. But an "ours" baby turned out to affect a man in two ways I had failed to anticipate.

In a general way, a baby increases a man's emotional investment in the stepfamily as a whole. In a more specific way, a new baby makes a man feel more like a real parent, more like a real father. And among other things, real fathers have a large voice in how their children are educated, the clothes they wear, the movies and television programs they are permitted to see, and how much money is spent on them. In Neotraditional and Romantic stepfamilies, this greater involvement in the parenting role was welcomed and praised, but such was usually not the case in Matriarchal families.

Kristen Devon reacted sharply to her husband's growing intrusions into the parenting domain. Moreover, once Mike stepped more deeply into this territory, the whole delicate structure of the Devons' Matriarchal stepfamily began to unravel, as it often does in such situations. Men in Matriarchal stepfamilies are usually as passive about financial decisions as they are about parenting decisions. Generally the man in such a family simply hands over his salary to the Matriarchal woman and lets her decide how to spend the money. After Moira's birth, Mike wanted a large voice, not only in parenting, but in financial decisions as well. Kristen, feeling her control and leadership of the family beginning to ebb away, resisted these encroachments. She and Mike fought for a year and then decided to split up.

When I contacted Kristen for this book, she and the children, Ethan and Moira, were back in Cleveland. Mike, who had married for a third time, was still in Houston, still at the hospital he had been working in when the Devons enrolled in the project.

A few years later another couple in our midwestern contingent also divorced. Shortly after the Devons arrived in Houston, Isabel Lefkowitz was transferred to Texas to open a new southwestern office for her employer, a Chicago software company. Isabel's husband, Steven, although unhappy about leaving his position as a high school guidance counselor, moved with her, as did Isabel's two children. The Lefkowitzes' divorce, which came three years later, had, as all divorces do, many causes. Steven was never able to put down roots in Houston. The large difference between his and Isabel's salaries (she made approximately three times more than he) was a source of tension too. But the Lefkowitzes' breakup had a third cause, and it illustrates how a man's resistance to change also can undermine a Matriarchal stepfamily.

Shortly after arriving in Texas, Isabel found her near-magical ability to balance a high-powered job and family responsibilities disappearing. Too much had to be done. She could not work ten- and twelve-hour days, parent a five- and an eight-year-old, and run a house, even with the help of a part-time housekeeper. Desperate and exhausted, Isabel turned to Steven. Could he help with the children? Steven was very empathic, very understanding about the request. He suggested to Isabel that she put the housekeeper on full time. He suggested hiring a college student to sit for the children. He even offered to put up posters in the neighborhood—but that was as far as he would go. The children—Isabel's children—were *her* responsibility, he said. He would help out around the edges of family life, but he had his own life and his own job. Isabel had always said she "wanted it all." Well, Steven reminded her, she now had it all: a good job, a family. It was up to her to figure out how to make it "all" work.

In most stepfamilies—in most *families*—Steven Lefkowitz's straightforward refusal to do more would lead to a straightforward conflict about the division of labor. But because the Matriarchal stepfamily brings together two unusual personality types, a division of labor conflict often ends up becoming something else: a conflict about spousal authoritarianism. Frequently, when the man refuses to do more, the competent, energetic, ambitious Matriarchal woman decides: "All right, I will do it all myself." Then the pressure of attempting to do everything transforms the woman from a family leader into a family dictator, because only a family dictator can do everything that needs to be done.

Isabel began undergoing the transformation from authoritative to authoritarian family leader about a year after the Lefkowitzes joined the project. Isabel began drawing up a daily schedule for family members, which deeply offended Steven. Even more offensive to him was that his breakfast and dinner hours were now fixed—and fixed rather inconveniently, at that. "I am not six years old," he told Isabel. "I do not need to have my eating hours dictated to me."

"I'm sorry you find my schedule so offensive," Isabel replied. "Not everyone in this house is free to float around the way you do. For once you could show a little understanding."

Resistance to additional responsibilities was not an uncommon occurrence in our stepfamilies. Many project men balked when an overburdened wife asked for more help. But usually at a certain point—out of guilt, empathy, or some combination of the two—the men relented and agreed to do more. Steven Lefkowitz never did, and in the end, his refusal to change cost him his marriage.

Two stories below me, Andrew and Todd are playing baseball on the lawn. Andrew self-hits a pop fly; he strikes the ball harder than he intended, I think. It shoots up past the porch where I am sitting, before finally arching in the blue summer sky. Todd is waiting when the ball hurtles back to earth. His catch is effortless, elegant almost. Delighted, Andrew claps his hands together.

During this visit, my first to the Lawtons' new home (the semidetatched condominium in the photo Ellen showed me last September), I have noticed that Andrew and Todd's relationship has changed. Tom Dietrich remains the primary male figure in Todd's life, and I suspect he always will. But Andrew and Todd, little more than casual acquaintances on my last visit, have now developed a real friendship. They are, as Andrew said during the just-completed interview, "true buddies."

This change was made possible by another change.

Ellen, who is inside now preparing a pot of coffee, underwent a change of heart.

Some Matriarchal women eventually do learn how to control their need to control, and interestingly, two studies—ours and one by Dr. Mavis Hetherington of the University of Virginia—have found an intriguing biographical similarity among Matriarchal woman who become change-embracers. These women rose to the challenge of divorce and single parenthood by becoming even more competent and accomplished than they already were. This interesting biographical detail is also an important psychological marker. It indicates the ability to adapt in the face of crisis.

Or, to put it another way, the marker suggests that change-embracers are supple and flexible; they are capable of doing whatever needs to be done to meet a crisis. We found that when a change-embracer found her domination of the family challenged, initially she did what all Matriarchal women do: She resisted. But change-embracers also did something that other Matriarchal women (women like Kristen Devon) did not do. They made an effort to reality-check their resistance. They sought advice from someone outside the family.

Sometimes the "someone" was a professional, a psychologist or family therapist. But most of our change-embracers consulted a friend or relative; even more commonly, they did what Ellen did—they spoke to a clergyman. After a conference with the pastor of her Baptist church in Houston, Ellen decided to relent and let Andrew in a little.

Change often begets change, and recently Ellen, who still exercises most of the control in the parenting domain, has been the recipient of a welcome change. Last May Andrew began working toward his degree. During the interview he told me he is currently taking two early-bird courses at the University of Houston.

I think that perhaps one day Ellen *will* get that big house in Austin. Matriarchal women have a way of making their dreams come true. But it is important to note that they are also patient dreamers. Matriarchal women know that stepfamily life is not going to give them everything they want immediately. They know it takes time for a marriage and family to cohere; and equally important, they also know that the process of cohering often involves bumps in the form of conflicts, disappointments, and setbacks.

Realism—knowing what *reasonably* to expect from stepfamily life, particularly early stepfamily life—was an important element in the success of Matriarchal and also of Neotraditional stepfamilies, who shared this trait. Conversely, a lack of realism was perhaps the principal reason why our Romantic stepfamilies were so prone to shocks and setbacks.

In the next chapter we look at why.

POINTS TO KEEP IN MIND

- The signature trait of the Matriarchal stepfamily is the leadership role of the woman. She is the decision-making power in the family. The Matriarchal man's primary concern is the companionship of his wife. His interest in parenting, while genuine, is limited. On domestic and family issues, he is content to follow her lead. The Matriarchal stepfamily nurtures the marriage through couple's activities rather than through child- and family-centered activities.

- Monitoring a stepchild's activities is an excellent way to begin getting involved in the parental role. This helps the biological parent in her role and signals the children that the stepparent is interested in their lives.

- Change is a constant in stepfamilies. It is there in the beginning and continues throughout the family's life cycle. Much of the change is uncontrollable, since it is influenced by factors outside the immediate family, such as the nonresidential parent. Flexibility and acceptance are the most effective policies to adopt toward change.

chapter three

The Romantic Stepfamily:
Dwight and Joanne McDougal

Dwight McDougal and Joanne Honeycutt met at a church dance. The dance was held at St. Peter's, the Episcopal church Dwight joined after he moved to Houston with Pamela—the same flamboyant, endlessly charming, endlessly ambitious Pamela who was to cause Dwight and Joanne so much trouble later. Dwight was a first-timer at St. Peter's. After the divorce he promised himself that he would start attending dances at the church regularly, but Pamela had humiliated him so badly, Dwight needed nearly six months to talk himself into actually going. Every time he thought about it, he thought: Who would want to dance with me, a man who has just been dispatched (dumped, really) by his much more successful wife? As Lester, Dwight's best friend, never tired of noting, that was the kind of thing that was supposed to happen to a woman, not to a man.

Joanne, unlike her future husband, was already a regular at St. Peter's. She began going to the dances at the church rectory three months after she left Tray Honeycutt. This early display of gumption, Joanne's friends agreed, was admirable, particularly in the light of the awful way the marriage to Tray had ended: his business in ruins, walking out on Joanne for a twenty-five-year-old secretary.

Not that Joanne's friends were particularly surprised at Tray's behavior. After the collapse of the Houston real estate market, Tray, a land speculator, had become completely unhinged. Esther Thornton, Joanne's best friend, told their other friends that the real miracle was that Tray had not done something stupid sooner.

Actually, in an indirect manner, Esther was instrumental in bringing Dwight and Joanne together. Joanne had grown tired of the St. Peter's dances. More to the point, she had been growing tired of the men she met there. They were nice enough gentlemen, and good dancers; men in their sixties almost always were, Joanne noticed; they were part of the last generation of men who really prized a graceful two-step. But what woman wanted to spend a Saturday night dancing with men old enough to her father? Besides, none of the men at St. Peter's had hair. This was a particular pet peeve of Joanne's. After all she had been through, she was modest about her life goals. But she did not think it was asking too much from life to want to dance occasionally with a man who had a full head of hair.

"The men are all so elderly and wrinkled," she said when Esther asked if she was planning to go to St. Peter's this month.

"Now, that's not true, Joanne," Esther replied. "Plenty of the men who go to St. Peter's are in their forties."

"Plenty?" Joanne said.

"All right, *some,*" Esther conceded. But she pointed out that anything was better than sitting home alone on a Saturday night watching *Dr. Quinn, Medicine Woman.* Even St. Peter's.

To this Joanne had no reply. "All right," she said, "pick me up at eight. I'll get a baby-sitter for the boys."

Joanne noticed Dwight first, and what she noticed first was his hair. Actually, Dwight's hair—blond and very fine—is thinning on the top;

but that night, in a sea of shiny bald heads made all the shinier by the rectory's overhead lights, his blond hair looked positively leonine.

"He's cute," Esther said, when Joanne pointed Dwight out to her. "Maybe he'll ask you to dance."

But Dwight, always shy in social gatherings, and shyer still at this, his first real "dance" in nearly fifteen years, did not ask anyone to dance. He and Lester stood by the punch bar at the back of the rectory talking and watching other people dance.

When the young priest MC announced a Ladies' Choice, Joanne decided to seize the initiative. She walked across the floor to the punch bar and asked Dwight if he would like to dance. Dwight stammered helplessly for a moment, then recovered and apologized for acting so flustered. It had been a long time since he had danced with a woman other than his wife—he corrected himself: his former wife. He told Joanne he would be delighted to accept her invitation.

The first song the McDougals ever danced to was "Memories" from *Cats*. Joanne remembers that Engelbert Humperdink sang it.

After the dance, Dwight asked Joanne if she and her friend Esther would like to join him and his friend Lester for a cup of coffee. This first semidate more or less set the pattern for the McDougals' other early dates. For the first few months of the courtship, Dwight and Joanne kept their dates short. They would meet at some public place— a diner or a restaurant—for a cup of coffee or lunch, then go their separate ways. Neither wanted the pressure of having to entertain the other for an entire evening; and after their first experiences with marriage, neither was in a hurry to get deeply involved again.

However, Dwight and Joanne's cautious policy was only partially successful. The average interim between divorce and remarriage among project participants was roughly three years. Romantics even before we designated them as such, Joanne and Dwight were already "completely and totally in love" by their fourth coffee date. They married eight months after they met—fourteen months after Dwight separated from Pamela and thirty-three months after Joanne left Tray Honeycutt.

Often, when you ask people why they fall in love, they seize on little things. When I asked Joanne, for example, what the first thing was that attracted her to Dwight, she said it was the way he bowed at the end of the Ladies' Choice. "When the song was over, he went like this." Joanne bowed her head slightly. "Then he said, 'Thank you very much for asking me to dance, ma'am.'

"I have always admired good manners in a man."

Dwight said he fell in love with Joanne's laugh before he fell in love with her. He does not remember the precise moment he noticed the laugh, but he does remember what delighted him about it; its sound, a ladylike titter. He described it as the laugh of someone who was a little embarrassed to be laughing as hard as she was.

However, I think some other qualities drew the McDougals to each other. I think Dwight, blond and boyishly slim, with the open, eager face of a car salesman, and Joanne, thicker and more weathered-looking, admired each other's gentleness and sensitivity. I also think that the McDougals saw in each other a person who could understand what the other had been through, could understand what it was like to be betrayed and belittled by someone you thought loved you.

And I think, finally, a shared dream of recovery drew the McDougals to each other. Dwight and Joanne both value the comfort and security and rituals of family life, and I believe each saw in the other a mate who would value those things too.

CHARACTERISTICS OF A ROMANTIC STEPFAMILY

The McDougals were married on a sunny Saturday in early June at St. Peter's by the young Episcopal priest who had served as MC the night they had met. Like the Lawtons, they came to the project via one of our recruitment posters. A few weeks after the wedding, a graduate student who worked at the project office had posted a study announcement on a bulletin board where Joanne worked. Joanne saw it the next morning, wrote down our number, and called my office when she got home. Two weeks later I paid a first visit to the McDougals, who lived in a modest brown-and-white raised ranch-style house in Pasadena, a middle-class Houston suburb.

As always, I began the interview by asking the McDougals background questions.

Joanne, who went first, said she was thirty-six, had grown up in Houston, and attended college here. "Do you want to know about my first marriage?" she asked.

I told her yes.

Joanne said that during the last three years of her ten-year marriage to Tray Honeycutt, Tray lost control of himself. "I tried to be understanding," she said. "I knew Tray's business was collapsing and he was under horrible pressure. I put up with a lot in those years, believe me: the women, the debts. I wanted to be supportive, but when he took up with that girl . . ." Joanne stops and begins to shake her head.

I asked her if her ex-husband still visited his sons.

Yes, Joanne said, but she was not happy about his visits. Her ex-husband was not a suitable positive role model, she said. Tray was deeply in debt and having relationship problems. "Plus, he always tries to undermine Dwight. You know, the boys are at that stage with language. But Dwight has a rule, terms like 'butt-breath' and 'dickhead' are not allowed. Tray knows that, but he lets the boys use any language they please. I just wish he would go away, disappear somewhere."

After Joanne finished her story, I asked Dwight to tell me about himself.

He said he was forty-two, a father of two, a six- and eight-year-old, worked for the Gap, and had an AA (Associate in Arts) in retailing from a community college in Atlanta, his hometown.

He came to Texas six years ago with his former wife, Pamela, who had been recruited by the marketing department of a large Dallas department store. According to Dwight, during the Dallas years he was the primary parent to his and Pamela's two children, Kendall and Dale. "I was the one who came home every night and took care of the kids," he said. "Pamela was hardly ever around; she was always at the store or off somewhere networking."

Another separation followed when Pamela moved to Houston to accept a management position at a large department store. Dwight, who had just been made an assistant manager at a Gap outlet, elected to stay in Dallas until the company could guarantee him a similar position in a Houston store. Dale and Kendall elected to stay with their father.

A year later an assistant manager position opened up in a Gap store in Houston, and Dwight and the children moved here. Two weeks later Pamela, now a vice president at the department store, asked Dwight to leave. He came home one night to find his bags already packed and Pamela waiting for him in the living room. "She said the marriage was over; she wanted me out. No warning, no discussion, no anything. Just 'get *out*.'

"I guess she thought I wasn't good enough for her anymore."

I asked Dwight how his children reacted to the separation. "You were the primary parent," I noted. "It must have been a tremendous loss to them."

"They were very sad," he said. "But what could I do? Pamela was their mother. She had an important position. A court would never give me custody."

Joanne, apparently feeling Dwight had not done justice to Pamela, interrupted at this point. "Pamela," she said, "was super-selfish, and super-, super-ambitious."

Dwight smiled at me. "You know what Joanne calls Pamela? She says Pam's a Yuppie on steroids."

"Well, she is," Joanne insisted. "She's a total 'me' person, and manipulative. You know what Pamela had the nerve to do last week? Her pool was clogged, so she called Dwight; could he please come over and unclog it? The nerve! We barely have a bathtub and Pamela wants Dwight to come over and unclog her pool."

Dwight shook his head. "I told her no way, José, didn't I, Joanne?"

Joanne put her hand on top of her husband's. "Dwight's totally different from Pamela. He's like me, he's a giver. He gives and gives. We're both givers and we were married to two takers."

During the interview, the McDougals displayed an unusual amount of physical affection. They kissed and touched often, and when they were not kissing and touching they were holding hands. Also unusual was the lack of issues—points of conflict—between them. The McDougals were in the middle of the conflict-prone first year of stepfamily life, yet Joanne and Dwight insisted that they had yet to encounter a single issue on which they disagreed. "We are so grateful at having each other, we don't ever want to fight," Joanne said.

Normally, it took us two to three years to figure out what kind of stepfamily a couple would form. But at the end of my first visit to the McDougals, I was already fairly confident that Joanne and Dwight would form a Romantic family, the third type of stepfamily. On the surface, Romantic and Neotraditional stepfamilies look similar. Indeed, Romantic and Neotraditional couples each begin stepfamily life wanting the same things: a cohesive family unit, an intimate stepfather-stepchild relationship, and at the heart of the family, a stable, satisfying marriage.

But whereas Neotraditionalists often achieve these goals, Romantic stepfamilies don't. The most notable characteristics of the Romantic family are difficult relations with stepchildren and former spouses, an inability to accurately identify areas of disagreement between family members, and a failure to nurture the marriage at the heart of the stepfamily.

These characteristics are all a reflection of the Romantic stepfamily's signature trait: unrealistic expectations. Couples like the McDougals enter stepfamily life expecting instant family cohesiveness, instantly high marital satisfaction, and instantly obedient and respectful children. In other words, Romantics enter stepfamily life expecting the impossible.

I think two things account for this. One is a strong allegiance to the nuclear family. More than our other participants, Romantics yearned for the closeness, the security, and, above all, for what they perceive to be the *authenticity* of the nuclear family. On some level, couples like the McDougals believe a family does not become a "real family, a true family" until it looks and acts and feels like the kind of family the Beaver and Wally Cleaver and Ricky and David Nelson used to come home to.

On occasion, I think there is a compensation factor at work. Romantics sometimes hope and expect a second marriage to compensate for an unhappy first marriage.

THE DANGERS OF GREAT EXPECTATIONS

The irony of the Romantic stepfamily—and I don't think it's hyperbolic to describe it as a tragic irony—is that the Romantics want their stepfamily to work very badly. Romantics are highly motivated and often value family life tremendously. But usually, these strengths are undermined by high or unrealistic expectations.

Romantics believe, indeed expect, that love and love alone will see them through, so they avoid the hard work of stepfamily building. In a Romantic family, there are no special nights out to nurture a marriage, no agonizing discussion about when to introduce the future stepfather to the child, no strategy session on how to deal with former spouses and nonresidential parents; all the central tasks of stepfamily life are left to solve themselves.

The research of Penn State psychologist Dr. Jay Belsky highlights a second way unrealistic expectations work against a Romantic couple.

According to Dr. Belsky, how we perceive an experience is determined not just by its nature—how easy or difficult the experience actually is—but also by the expectations we bring to it. Simply put, if a bad experience is the emotional equivalent of being hit over the head with a lead pipe, a bad experience that also violates our expectations of how bad it will be is the emotional equivalent of being hit over the head by a lead pipe with spikes on it. The reason for the compounding effect, Dr. Belsky says, is tied to the mobilizing role of expectations. If we expect a

situation to be difficult, sometimes consciously, sometimes unconsciously, we begin to mobilize psychological resources to deal with it.

How difficult the experience actually feels then becomes dependent
on how accurate our expectations for it are. If we overestimate the
experience's severity, often it will feel a little easier than it really is
because we have mobilized more psychological resources than we need.
Conversely, if we underestimate its severity, often the experience will
feel worse than it really is because, due to our rosy expectations, we
have undermobilized and don't have enough psychological resources to
cushion its effect.

Translated into stepfamily life, Dr. Belsky's work on expectations
explains one of the paradoxical characteristics of the Romantic stepfamily—the fact that the normal ups and downs of stepfamily life feel
more painful to couples like the McDougals than they do to more
realistic Neotraditionalists and Matriarchalists.

"You think 'Oh, this won't be too bad.' Then when you're in the
trenches, it turns out to be very difficult, more difficult than you imag-
ined."

This is my second visit to Joanne and Dwight. I am sitting in the
McDougals' living room, and Joanne is telling me how hard stepfamily
life has turned out to be. Funnily enough, she says, what she thought
would be the easiest part—dealing with the boys (Evan, our target
child, and Tray, Jr.)—has turned out to be the hardest part. The relationship between Dwight and Tray, Jr., has been particularly problematic. According to Joanne, last week there was an ugly incident between
them. Tray told Dwight that he hated him, then he cursed his stepfather and called him an "asshole."

Joanne flushes slightly when she utters the last word. She is uncomfortable using it, even for illustrative purposes.

I ask her what provoked the exchange.

"Dwight caught Tray in a lie," Joanne declares, then stops and corrects herself. "Actually, it was more serious than lying. Last week

Dwight caught Tray and a friend, a boy named Will, stealing." Tray and Will collect hubcaps from four-wheelers, from Jeep Cherokees, Jimmies, and Chevy Suburbans, Joanne says. Supposedly the hubcaps were being supplied by a benefactor, the manager of an auto body shop near the McDougals' home; the man was, according to Tray, Jr., allowing the boys to take hubcaps from the wrecked four-wheelers the shop salvaged. "Once or twice I thought those vehicles must be awful dangerous," Joanne says ruefully. "Tray and Will must have nearly a hundred fifty hubcaps. But I have to say, it never occurred to me that the boys were stealing them."

"I don't know why Mr. Blake suspected Tray," Joanne says. "But the other morning Mr. Blake came right over here when he noticed the hubcaps on his Land Rover were gone. Tray denied taking the hubcaps, but Mr. Blake didn't believe him, and neither did Dwight."

"That's when they had the confrontation?" I ask.

Joanne shakes her head. "No, not until that night. After Mr. Blake left, Dwight called Will's parents. They confronted Will and he 'fessed up. He said there was no manager; he and Tray have been stealing the hubcaps. We had a terrible row here that night. Dwight accused Tray of lying. Tray shouted 'I hate you, I hate you,' then he swore at Dwight."

Joanne's eyes are suddenly very moist. "It broke my heart seeing two people I love fight like that, Dr. Bray."

STEPDAUGHTERS, STEPSONS, AND STEPPARENTS

The stepparent-stepchild relationship, like the marriage, is a hub of stepfamily life; its spokes point outward in several different directions: toward the marriage, the child, and the general cohesiveness of the family. Accordingly, identifying the elements that shape the relationship was a major project goal. Earlier I described two of its elements: how soon the man integrates himself into the stepchild's life and his level of parental involvement.

However, there are also two other elements in the relationship. One is the stepfamily's attitude toward the child's biological father. Do the adults in the family criticize the nonresidential parent in front of the child? Do they respect or ignore the rules he sets for the child? The values he wants to instill?

The last and perhaps most surprising mediating factor in the step-parent-stepchild relationship is the child's gender.

At the start of the project, family scholars were divided about whether stepdaughters or stepsons got along better with a stepfather. We found that in the stepfather-stepchild relationship, gender interacts with arithmetic. In family-wide situations—that is, in situations where mother, stepfather, and child are present—girls relate better to a stepfather. But in one-on-one interactions, girls are often aloof, distant, and noncommunicative.

We also found something else, an x-factor that helps to explain the distance in many stepfather-stepdaughter relationships. The explanation begins with the different ways stepfathers and stepchildren—boys as well as girls—define affection. To men, affection is physical—it is hugs and kisses and other forms of touching—to children, it is verbal; it is compliments and friendly conversation.

A good deal of the first-cycle wariness we saw in our target boys and girls and confusion for stepfathers was rooted in these two different interpretations of affection. In many new stepfamilies, the child responded negatively to a stepfather because she felt uncomfortable with the kind of affection he was offering. But in families with stepdaughters, a new and more complex dynamic developed in the second cycle—years three through five. This time, it was the stepfather who became wary and began to back off and, in most cases, he did because he was afraid his stepdaughter, who was becoming more sexually mature, or her mother, might misconstrue his affectionate hugs as something else.

Sexuality *is* a problem in stepfamilies. One recent study suggested that the incidence of intrafamily sexual episodes is eight times higher in stepfamilies than in nuclear families—and later in the book we will look at how to deal with it. But our data also suggest that many now-distant stepfather-stepdaughter relationships could be made warmer if the man understood how his daughter defined affection and differentiated intimacy from sexuality.

In the case of stepsons, gender and arithmetic also interact. In three-way interactions, boys often treat a stepfather as a rival. But, provided his physical space is respected, a boy is often secretly delighted to have another male in the house—a happiness that usually spills out in one-on-one interactions with a stepfather.

During my first visit to the McDougals, Tray, Jr., displayed several examples of this stepson friendliness. A few days before the interview, David Robinson had been drafted by the San Antonio Spurs. Tray wanted to know what Dwight thought of the acquisition. Tray also mentioned a fishing expedition he had taken with a friend and the friend's father. Did Dwight fish? he asked. When Dwight said yes, Tray immediately wanted to know what type of rod and reel he used.

Males use this kind of "sports talk" to bond. The day of my first visit, eight-year-old Tray, Jr., was clearly available for bonding. That day Tray acted like an eager puppy around Dwight.

The troubled stepfather-stepchild relationship I encountered at my next visit was the result of two missteps common in Romantic stepfamilies, and both are related to the expectation for "instant familyness." The first is skipping over the monitoring stage of the stepfather-stepchild relationship. The desire to be "a real parent" right away reflects the Romantics' belief that you don't have to work or invest time in building a bond with a child; wanting it to be so will make it so. Interestingly, in the case of the parenting function, the greatest Romantic is often the woman. In the desire to establish an instant family, many Romantic wives actively encourage a spouse to begin playing a substantial parenting role right away.

At the McDougals' first interview, Dwight described himself as the family "tracker." He said he tracked Tray, Jr., and Evan's TV viewing and whom they spent time with, whether their homework was done, and then reported his observations to Joanne. I thought he seemed happy with this role, but at the McDougals' second interview, I learned that Joanne was not.

"I told Dwight, if the boys do something you don't like, tell them right then," she said, "instead of waiting and telling me. It eliminates a step."

I think this change had a lot to do with Dwight's second-interview complaints about his stepsons. He said the boys were often rude and disrespectful to him. "Sometimes I'm treated like the junkyard dog around here. You know, if it weren't for Joanne . . ." Dwight stopped and let the rest of the thought speak for itself.

Romantics also frequently mishandle the biological child–father relationship, usually because the relationship threatens the Romantic ideology of nuclear familyness. How can the family be a real family with an emotional interloper in its midst? Romantic stepfamilies often try to discourage contact with the nonresidential parent, and if he refuses just to go away (and a number of men do drop out of their childrens' lives), they do what the McDougals began doing: disparage Tray, Sr., in the presence of Tray, Jr.

In fairness to Joanne and Dwight, their motivations went beyond ideological concerns.

Tray, Sr., embodied a particularly florid variety of failings, including irresponsibility and womanizing. At the second interview, Joanne told me that because of her first husband's bad example, Tray, Jr., "disrespected" women.

"One other reason I encouraged Dwight to get involved with the boys right away," Joanne said, "is that I thought he would make a good role model for them."

During the project we found evidence that positive role modeling by a stepfather can indeed offset negative role modeling by a biological parent. This is one of the most important ways a stepfamily helps to heal the scars of divorce in a child. But we also found that example is the type of role modeling that works best. The man who treats his wife with consideration and respect is teaching a stepson a lesson in proper behavior toward the opposite sex. But in their eagerness to do away with an inconvenient biological parent, Romantics sometimes have trouble limiting themselves to example.

Between my first and second visits, Tray, Sr., became a frequent topic of dinnertime conversation at the McDougal home. Joanne talked about his young girlfriend, Dwight about his irresponsibility. And both McDougals talked about what a bad father Tray, Sr., had been to his sons. There are not many one-on-one correlations in human psychology, but one is that a child who hears a parent attacked thinks, in some way, he is also being attacked; another reliable correlation is that the hurt and anger such attacks cause eventually will be acted out in destructive behavior.

THE BIOLOGICAL PARENT—CHILD RELATIONSHIP IN ROMANTIC STEPFAMILIES

"I remember you coming and doing all these tests on me. Remember, how I used to show off for the camera?"

I tell Maria I remember her as being an especially shy little girl.

She giggles. Seventeen now, she has turned out to be quite an exquisite young woman: olive complexion, thick black hair that falls down over her shoulders and drapes her neck like a shawl, a perfect oval face, and dark, searching eyes.

"Those days that was a totally different situation from now," Maria says. "It's really weird the way things turned out in my family. I haven't seen my parents, now, in probably in . . ." Maria stops to think.

"A year, Maria," Anna Ramirez says. "It's been a year now." Anna, Maria's grandmother, is sitting on the opposite side of the living room next to the television set.

Maria, whom I reinterviewed in the winter of 1997 in preparation for this book, also belonged to a Romantic stepfamily, the Estradas. The family included: stepfather Hector, a prominent businessman and leader of the Hispanic community in Houston; mother Consuelo; Maria; and an "ours" baby, Frank. The Estradas were among the last group of subjects to enter the project; they joined the study in 1987 and were officially designated a Romantic stepfamily three years later.

Maria's story makes a good companion piece to Dwight and Tray, Jr.'s because it illustrates how the nuclear-family ideology sometimes can poison the biological parent–child relationship in a Romantic stepfamily as well.

At the 1997 interview, Maria claimed that her abrupt departure from the Estrada household a year earlier had been a matter of self-defense, self-preservation, really. All the years I was visiting the family, she said, interviewing Hector and Consuelo and filming her, the Estradas had been harboring "a terrible secret." According to Maria, she lived in constant fear of her mother; Consuelo would lash out at her randomly, unpredictably, for any reason or no reason at all. "Sometimes I'd just be walking by," Maria said, "and Consuelo would grab me by the hair, just like that." Maria made a grabbing gesture with her hand. "Then, *whack,* slap me. Bitch. Consuelo's a crazy woman."

Here, Maria paused to reconsider. "No, actually, Consuelo's crazy like a fox. She wanted to get rid of me, she wanted to have Hector and baby Frank to herself."

I noticed that occasionally Anna would look agitated as her granddaughter spoke, but she did not say anything—not until Maria excused herself; around five, she said she had to meet her boyfriend, Travis. When we were alone in the Ramirezes' small parlor, I asked Anna if she had any thoughts about her granddaughter's story.

She frowned and said Maria's tales about Consuelo's physical abuse were made up, fabrications. Consuelo, Anna was sure, had never raised a hand to Maria—if for no other reason than Hector (Hector the prominent businessman and community leader) would never allow such a thing, such a "low-class thing," to happen in his home. But Anna said Maria was right about everything else; her mother did want to get rid of her, did deliberately drive her out of the family.

She asked me how much I knew about Consuelo's early life.

I told her I knew that Consuelo had married Manuel Ramirez, Anna's son, at sixteen, gave birth to Maria at eighteen, and that a year later Manuel was killed in a motorcycle accident. I said I also knew that Consuelo met Hector, then an up-and-coming young businessman, two years after Manuel's death.

"Manuel and Consuelo were very wild kids," Anna said. "Street kids. He was a handsome boy—Maria looks just like him, with those eyes. But, oh, Manuel was so reckless. He and Hector, they are like night and day. Hector is so proper. That, in my opinion, is what the big problem is.

"Hector can't stand Consuelo's old life; he hates it, *hates* it. Maria told me he was always trying to make Consuelo over. He hired a speaking teacher, a coach, for her. And I knew he made her go back to school and get her GED [high school equivalency degree]."

"And Maria was always there to remind both of them who Consuelo used to be," I said.

Anna nodded. "I don't think Consuelo could help herself. She wanted to be Hector's wife, a businessman's wife; and I think every time she looked at Maria, it made her feel like she was just pretending. The real Consuelo—she was not so fine, you know." Anna pauses and gives me a knowing look. "I knew her mother; Consuelo could *never* be what she and Hector wanted her to be." Another pause. "So Consuelo got rid of the evidence. She nagged at Maria and picked on her and made fun of her until Maria left. Our Consuelo's quite the proper lady these days. Have you seen her car? She drives a big Mercedes, belongs to a fancy country club, and has a big house. Maria says it has six bedrooms."

"What about Maria?" I asked. "How has she adjusted—" I stumbled for a moment. I did not quite know how to describe Maria's current situation.

"You mean how does she like living here with me and Raoul [Maria's grandfather]?" Anna asked.

"That and the separation," I replied. "Hector and Consuelo really have not spoken to Maria in a year?"

Anna nodded. "A year. On the outside, Maria pretends not to care. You saw yourself, she has a very tough shell. But inside, her heart is broken. She feels like she was tossed out like garbage. She's very angry too, I think. It is why she is always in so much trouble. She was thrown out of school last semester, and I caught that Travis boy in her bedroom twice. I think they are doing things together.

"I told Maria, if the behavior does not stop, she will have to move out. My husband and me, we are too elderly, we cannot be policemen for a wild teenager."

"Where will Maria live if she leaves here?" I asked.

"I don't know," Anna replied. "Maybe with that boy. I don't know. You'll have to ask Maria."

THE THIN MIDDLE GROUND
IN ROMANTIC MARRIAGES

The soft thump of a refrigerator door closing; the clang of a glass jar being set down on a Formica countertop; the noisy rattle of a hand rummaging through a silverware tray.

The kitchen sounds stop and Joanne speaks. "That's the last of the peanut butter, sweetie." Evan's reply is inaudible. His little boy's voice is still too soft to carry well.

Whatever he says, it tickles his mother. Joanne laughs. There is no embarrassed titter in her laugh now. It is full throttled, rich with delight.

Footsteps. Evan must be exiting the kitchen; the refrigerator door opens and shuts again. This is followed by the sound of a faucet being turned on and off. Joanne must be rinsing off the knife she used to make Evan's sandwich. Finally, the moan of a counter drawer sliding open. She is returning the knife to the silverware tray.

Joanne's hands are still wet when she returns to the living room. She wipes them dry on her apron, then sits down and apologizes for the interruption. Boys, especially little boys, are very demanding, she says. But I am not convinced by her aggrieved tone. Joanne loves to be annoyed by little boys, loves to make peanut butter sandwiches in the middle of the afternoon, loves everything about domestic life, family life. And so too does Dwight with his never-ending schemes and projects to improve the McDougals' modest little ranch house in Pasadena.

The nuclear-family ideology has a deep bond on the Romantic imagination for a reason. Romantic men and women have a special affinity for family life. This is reflected not only in the Romantic's love of domesticity but also in his—and her—flair for the unifying rituals of family life. Romantics tend to be very attuned to the important role family vacations and family meals and family trips to the movies play in promoting a sense of "us-ness," a sense of family identity. Romantics also put more effort into creating these activities than other stepfamilies. Not many Neotraditionalists and even fewer Matriarchalists are willing to spend an hour trying to enforce a dinner rule on a resistant eight-year-old. But many Romantics are. At the McDougals', for example, there are no exceptions. Every night the entire family eats dinner together.

At other elements of stepfamily life, however, Romantics are less good. They rarely do things together as a couple; nor do they sit down and try to work out a common strategy toward the tasks of stepfamily life. Since even our Matriarchal couples occasionally strategize together, we wondered what accounted for this peculiarity. Why do Romantics rarely talk to each other about important issues such as parenting or former spouses? The answer turns out to be the assumptions fostered by the nuclear-family ideology.

Psychological studies show that people with deeply held beliefs often assume that other people think like them. Romantics do this—they assume (usually correctly) that their partners share their view of family life. But Romantics frequently take the assumption a step further by also assuming that their partners have a detailed understanding of how the Romantics would like the shared ideology to be expressed in the family's day-to-day life. In other words, Romantics assume their partners will know automatically—through mental telepathy or the magical power of love—what the Romantics want to do about parenting and a former spouse or nonresidential parents, about managing change, about all—or almost all—the central tasks of stepfamily life.

One by-product of these assumptions is that in Romantic marriages, the middle ground runs thin because Romantics do not have the kind of discussions that help forge a shared vision, a shared worldview. A second by-product of the process is a high incidence of misunderstanding; Romantic husbands and wives constantly step on each other's toes. I am sure a communication survey would find that the most frequently repeated phrase in a Romantic home to be "But I thought you knew."

A third by-product of the assumption habit is conflict. Romantic couples tend to have more conflict than more communicative Neotraditional and Matriarchal couples. The McDougals are beginning to acquire this characteristic. According to the results of our latest conflict assessment, Joanne and Dwight are now fighting a great deal. I do not know it yet but they are about to have another fight now in front of me.

It originates in a story.

Last week, Joanne says, Dwight's children, Kendall and Dale, were invited to a birthday party. Since the children were going to be at the McDougals' the afternoon of the party, Pamela, Dwight's former wife, asked Joanne if she would mind taking the youngsters.

"I should have known better," Joanne says. "With Pamela there's always an angle."

"Boy, tell me about it," says Dwight, who has just joined us in the living room.

Joanne ignores the interruption. "It turns out that Pamela doesn't know what time the party starts or where the child having it lives. I mean, Pamela knew the name of the boy's street, but not his house number. I said to her, 'Pamela, how am I supposed to take the kids to a party when I don't know where it is or what time it starts?'

"You know what she said? 'Call information, Joanne. Get the child's telephone number and call the parents.' "

Joanne shakes her head. "I told Dwight last night: Never again. Never! This is absolutely the last time I will get involved with this woman. She's horrible—terrible. It's a miracle Dale and Kendall don't have more problems than they do."

Dwight suddenly looks annoyed. "What do you mean, Joanne?" he says. "They're good kids."

Joanne tells Dwight she does not want to be critical, but Kendall and Dale are not well-adjusted children. "It's not your fault, Dwight," she reassures him. "You did everything you could."

Dwight now looks very annoyed. "Not well adjusted? If anybody is not well adjusted," he declares, "it is Tray, Jr. Remember the hubcaps, Joanne? Tray is dysfunctional. He's going to end up just like his father."

Dwight looks over at me. "I told Joanne. Tray, Jr., shouldn't spend so much time with his dad. It's bad for the boy. In my opinion, it's *very* bad."

During the first year of stepfamily life, conflicts like the McDougals' were common. In Neotraditional and Matriarchal homes, however, disagreements about former spouses and nonresidential parents became rare later in the stepfamily cycle, but not in Romantic homes. In Romantic homes, they often became a permanent feature of the marriage; and as the years passed, many times the disagreements grew uglier and more bitter.

This lingering effect was partly due to poor communication. But to understand why Romantics are unable to communicate effectively on issues like former spouses and children, it is first necessary to understand why it is so important to be able to talk openly and frankly about these issues.

THE INVISIBLE MEMBERS
OF THE STEPFAMILY

Dealing with significant others in the form of former spouses and nonresidential parents is the fourth task of stepfamily life.

What kind of relationship should a stepfamily have with these figures?

In the case of the nonresidential parent, some family scholars argue that the lack of a relationship does not affect the child. According to psychologist Glenn Clingempeel, author of several studies on the influence of the nonresidential parent, contact with a biological father has no effect one way or the other on children's development.

However, scholars like Mavis Hetherington and Judith Wallerstein suggest that regular visits, when there is low parental conflict, are important to children's self-esteem and also to ease their adjustment into postdivorce life, including their adjustment to stepfamily life.

Our findings support the Hetherington-Wallerstein view, but with three significant qualifications. The first involves time. In the early years of stepfamily life, we found a developmental benefit for regular contact with a nonresidential parent, but over time this benefit waned. Boys and girls in four- and five-year-old families—that is, youngsters in families where a stepparent-stepchild relationship has had time to develop—did not appear to be affected one way or the other by regular paternal visits.

The child's sex also acted as a qualifier. On the whole, both boys and girls benefit from regular parental visits, but we found the benefits to be mixed for boys; regular visits make boys less vulnerable to destructive and family-disruptive acting out. But, curiously, in boys, we found a correlation between regular contact with a nonresidential parent and a drop in self-esteem. There are several possible explanations for this surprising relationship. It may be that our data measured a chicken-and-egg phenomenon: Low self-esteem may be a *cause* and not an effect of ongoing paternal involvement. The boy is troubled, the father feels guilty about that, so he visits regularly.

Alternately, maternal and stepfather criticism may damage the self-esteem of a boy who identifies closely with a biological father. "They don't like him so they must not like me," a boy like Tray, Jr., thinks when he hears his biological father criticized by the adults in the stepfamily. A third possible explanation is that regular contact with a biological father gives a child fewer opportunities to engage in esteem-building peer activities like sports.

The final qualifier in the nonresidential parent–child relationship is the presence of conflict. Chronic animosity among a biological father, his former wife, and her current husband produces hurt and confusion; the youngster feels caught in the middle, pulled in opposite directions. And, often, this pain and confusion manifest themselves in poor school performance and disruptive (and often destructive) acting-out behavior like stealing hubcaps.

In a 1994 paper for the professional publication *Family Journal,* I noted that despite the self-esteem risks and the waning benefit posed by regular contact, such contact was, on the whole, desirable and to be encouraged—since everything we know about a child's development suggests that the steady love of two biological parents is better, much better, than the steady love of one parent.

In that paper I also noted that regular contact is most likely to produce developmental benefits when the following three measures are taken:

1. The child is allowed to move freely between the stepfamily and the nonresidential parent.

Nonresidential parents like this policy because it gives them ready access to their youngsters; children like it because it allows them to move between a mother's and a father's home unencumbered by accusatory glances and questions.

2. Parents should avoid fighting in front of the child.

One way to minimize conflict between angry parents is by eliminating face-to-face encounters. Explosive and (to a child) frightening parental feelings are easier to control when stepfamily-nonresidential parent communication is conducted via the telephone or the even more impersonal letter. A second way of avoiding conflict is a nonaggression pact. The family agrees not to criticize the nonresidential parent in front of the child in return for a promise from the nonresidential parent that he will not criticize the family in front of the child.

3. Parents should observe each other's values and rules.

Project experience indicates that this step is particularly difficult to implement. Two people who could not see eye to eye on a marriage, unsurprisingly, are not prone to see eye to eye on issues of upbringing. But asking a child about an absent parent's policy on movies or curfews shows the child that, despite their differences, his mother and father still respect each other.

The project also made an important discovery about the nonresidential parent. Too much regular conflict with him can have a negative impact on the marriage at the heart of the stepfamily.

Exhibit A is the experience of Howard and Elizabeth Hailey.

Elizabeth spent over a year pursuing her former husband, Jonathan Pierce, through the Texas court system before a family court judge finally awarded her $9,000 in delinquent child support. The day she told me about the award, Elizabeth described it as a great moral victory. Finally, she said, her former husband would be forced to do the right thing, because she, Elizabeth, had done the right thing.

A year later, however, Elizabeth was not so sure that she had done the right thing.

Surprisingly, delinquent support settlements often have a negative impact on a stepfamily marriage. The reason: Men who begin to support their children regularly again usually want to see those children regularly again. And, often, when regular visits resume, the dynamic within the stepfamily alters in troublesome ways.

For example, about three months after Jonathan began visiting regularly again, Elizabeth's husband, Howard, suddenly became uncharacteristically petty. Howard complained about everything, and what he complained about most was Elizabeth. He didn't like her hair, her clothes, her cooking. She was putting on weight, spending too much time on the phone with her mother. The day she told me about Howard's sniping, Elizabeth also mentioned that Howard, who used to spend a lot of time with her son, Timmy, was now spending very little time with him.

"I may be crazy," she said, "but I think the two things are related."

I told Elizabeth I did not think she was crazy at all. In a complex organism like a stepfamily, a change in one area often produces two or three unanticipated changes in another. "Very likely," I said, "Howard is hurt and jealous about Jonathan and Timmy, and he is taking it out on you."

Howard agreed with this analysis a few days later, when Elizabeth mentioned my observation to him. He thought about it for a moment and then said, "Yes, I think James is right. In a strange way, I feel like someone has stolen my best friend. And I don't like it, I don't it at all."

Elizabeth and Howard talked about Howard's hurt and, probably equally important, Elizabeth talked to Timmy about Howard's hurt feelings. Once Timmy began spending time with his stepfather again, Howard's sniping stopped.

Exhibit B, the McDougals' argument I witnessed, shows how a non-residential parent—and a former spouse—can produce marital disruption.

Joanne's attack on Dwight's children was really an attack on Dwight. She felt Pamela was able to walk into the McDougals' lives any time she wanted because Dwight had given her permission—not directly, of course, but he signaled it through a certain attitude, a certain curious combination of obsequiousness and fear. Similarly, Dwight's attack on Tray, Jr., was really aimed at Joanne. Dwight was furious at her for being so tolerant of Tray, Sr.'s, delinquent support payments.

This displacement of anger was not unusual. During the first cycle we saw a lot of it in Neotraditional and Matriarchal stepfamilies too. But in these families, the anger usually sorted itself out in time, because the husband and wife were able to talk openly and freely about their feelings about everything, including each other's former spouses and children. However, a kind of emotional self-censorship inhibited this sorting-out process in Romantic families.

A nuclear family does not include former spouses. So Romantics are reluctant to talk about these figures. How can you admit you feel threatened by your husband's former wife when your husband is not supposed to have a former wife? Such is the power of the nuclear-family ideology. The danger in this kind of self-censorship, which is often unconscious, is that the feelings the former wife arouses get displaced into other things. The Romantic wife starts complaining about the amount of child support her husband is paying. And, once that problem is resolved, about how unruly his children are. And these complaints go on and on, fraying the fabric of the marriage because, unable to articulate the true source of her unhappiness, the Romantic wife and her husband are never able to address it.

POINTS TO KEEP IN MIND

- Most husbands and wives hope their new stepfamily will one day acquire the characteristics of a nuclear family. The signature trait of Romantics is that they expect this transformation to occur instantly. A second signature trait of Romantics is that they are also much more likely to hang on to their unrealistic expectations when reality intrudes.

- A biological parent should never be criticized in front of the child. This practice, common in Romantic homes, is a leading reason why the stepparent-stepchild relationship is often troubled in such homes.

- Stepfathers and stepchildren often define affection differently. In the first cycle, this difference can produce avoidant behavior from both boys and girls. In the second cycle, it becomes a particular problem with girls.

- The Romantic couple's attachment to the nuclear-family myth often gets in the way of clear, direct marital communication. The myth makes it hard for husbands and wives to identify what is *really* bothering them or to articulate concerns cogently.

part two

The Three Cycles
of Stepfamily Life

At the time of the project's launch in the mid-
1980s, there was not a large body of data on the new
American stepfamily—the family formed from divorce
rather than from death. In addition, the data were static,
consisting of snapshots, studies that looked at the stepfamily at a particular point in time.

I wanted to develop a more panoramic and dynamic
view of the new American stepfamily, one that would
show how this family grows and changes in its first decade. I thought that such a picture would not only answer
a lot of outstanding questions about the modern stepfamily, it would be immensely helpful to couples—and to
family psychologists, counselors, and therapists.

The picture of the stepfamily that emerged from the

project is the most complete and detailed assembled. And while its findings are based on the stepfather stepfamily—by far the most common type—the behavior patterns and dynamics identified in the study are applicable to all stepfamilies, including the stepmother families and families that form when the children are in adolescence.

In the chapters that follow, we explore the project's main finding— that the first decade of stepfamily life divides into three distinct cycles— and the implications this discovery holds for America's 20 million stepfamilies. What are the three cycles?

Cycle 1 encompasses the first two years. Even future happy stepfamilies often are unhappy in this period, which is characterized by high stress, disillusion, conflict, and internal division. In the first cycle, men often feel isolated, women torn, children confused and fearful, and most everyone feels disappointed. In the first period, stepfamilies come together, then move apart. A major challenge of early stepfamily life is to reunite the divided family and provide it with a more realistic ideology and belief system.

Cycle 2 runs from the end of the second year to the fifth year. This is the Happy Time of stepfamily life. Family members are now more realistic about what a stepfamily is, internal divisions are quiescent (at least for the time being), and an organizational structure is developed. Also, quite often the second cycle coincides with latency, ages six to ten, the most tranquil period of childhood. Even unhappy stepfamilies find ways to be happy in this period.

In cycle 3, things change again, this time usually for the worse. Between the fifth and ninth year, relationships, rules, accepted ways of doing things—the organizational structure of the stepfamily—come under stress for a second time. A major factor in the return of chaos is the child's passage into early adolescence.

In this section of the book we explore the three cycles via the experiences of the three project families you met in Part One as well as several other families. In chapter six we explore the challenges of being a stepmother, part time and full time.

As you watch our project families navigate through the first decade of stepfamily life, I think you will learn not only a great deal about the three cycles themselves but also about your own stepfamily and how to ease its journey from a collection of individuals bound by ties of acquaintanceship to a real family bound by ties of love, devotion, and respect.

chapter four

Hope and Expectation:
The Turbulent First Two Years

Often a single moment embodies the helter-skelter quality of early stepfamily life. For Sarah Goldsmith, that moment arrived carrying a grudge on a gray, wettish February Saturday four weeks after the Goldsmiths (newly wed, and not feeling as happy as newlyweds are supposed to feel) moved into their new home, a large, low-slung, wood, stone, and glass structure with a lovely patio in back, a sun-dappled street in front, and in the middle distance, a view of Rice University's mock-Gothic spires rising into the Texas sky.

Ten years later, when I reinterviewed Sarah for this book, every detail of that awful day and every one of the unhappy events that led up to it were still vivid in her mind. Sarah said she was already in a "blue mood" when she woke up that Saturday; the Goldsmiths' new house was nagging at her. Actually, Sarah said, the house had nagged at her from the moment that she and Jeffrey had closed on it. Jeffrey adored the house, thought it handsome, discreet, architecturally significant, and a whole lot of other good things. Sarah was more restrained. The house was indeed very handsome and in a wonderful neighborhood. From the front window you could see not only the spires but the broad green lawns of the Rice University campus. But the house was also very big, much too big in Sarah's opinion. It had fourteen rooms, fifteen if you counted the screened-off part of the porch behind the patio. It was dark too. The big oak trees in the front yard blocked out the sun; in the late afternoon, the front rooms filled with long, foreboding shadows, and the acres of still-packed moving boxes in the front rooms did little to alleviate the gloomy atmosphere. Sarah missed her old apartment. She missed its bright whitewashed brick walls, shiny pine floors, and cheery prints. The apartment was too small for three people, she knew, but it was bright, airy, and welcoming; it felt like home, like her home and Naomi's home. This new house felt like an aircraft carrier: *Jeffrey's* aircraft carrier.

That, said Sarah, is what really bothered her about the house. It had been Jeffrey's choice. He wanted a big, impressive house in a "nice" neighborhood, a neighborhood full of professionals, a neighborhood where no one would ever guess that Jeffrey Goldsmith was a kitchen supply wholesaler.

Sarah said she went along with Jeffrey because she liked the academic atmosphere of the neighborhood too and because the house excited him. He was like a little boy when he talked about it. But on some level Sarah felt she had been taken advantage of. Jeffrey was very clever about getting his own way. On the surface, he was Mr. Solicitousness, always so eager to please, but the Goldsmiths always seemed to end up doing what pleased Jeffrey.

The events of the previous evening were also contributing to Sarah's blue mood. Yesterday, leaving for work, Jeffrey had asked Sarah to pick up his son, Aaron, at the airport. Ten-year-old Aaron was flying down from New Hampshire to spend the midwinter school break in Houston. "Your office is only ten minutes from Hobby Airport," Jeffrey said as he was putting on his coat in the kitchen after breakfast. "Why don't you pop over at noon and pick up Aaron?"

Sarah hesitated for a moment. She had a client at one-fifteen. But the round trip from Hobby to the house to her office should only take forty-five minutes, an hour in traffic.

"Okay," Sarah said. If there was time, the two of them might even have a quick lunch together.

Jeffrey said he would like that.

Sarah was at Hobby at noon—but Aaron was not. The woman at the American Airlines ticket counter checked the computer screen, then shook her head: There was no Aaron Goldsmith booked on the noon flight from Nashua, New Hampshire, she said.

Jeffrey cursed when Sarah told him.

"Are you calling from a pay phone?" he asked.

"Uh-huh."

Jeffrey asked for the number, then ordered Sarah to stay put. As soon as he spoke to Barbara, he would call her back. Sarah wanted to tell him: "Please hurry." It was twelve-thirty; she was already on the verge of missing her appointment. Instead, Sarah said, "Okay." Jeffrey had enough to deal with already. Aaron could be God knows where, with God knows who. What kind of wife would think of herself in a situation like that?

At one o'clock Sarah called her secretary and told her to cancel the one-fifteen appointment. At one-thirty, when Jeffrey still had not called, Sarah put a quarter in the pay phone. She had two other clients this afternoon. She dialed the first four digits of Jeffrey's office number, then stopped. What if something terrible had happened to Aaron? What if poor little Aaron had been kidnapped? What was the matter with her? How could she think of herself at a moment like this? How selfish could she be? She hung up and, a moment later, heard a *clink*. Her quarter. Sarah picked it up, put it back in the pay phone, and dialed her office number. She told her secretary to cancel all appointments for the rest of the afternoon.

At two forty-five Sarah was still standing in front of the pay phone, wondering whether Jeffrey was going to blame her for Aaron's kidnapping—after all, she had been sort of entrusted with Aaron's care, hadn't she?—when a voice on the PA system announced that a Mrs. Sarah Goldsmith had an emergency call in the airport director's office. By the time Sarah arrived at the director's office, the kidnapping had metamorphosed from a Sarah Fantasy, one of those little nightmares she occasionally conjured up for herself when she was feeling very anxious, into something real. She was now convinced that Aaron had been kidnapped; Jeffrey was calling to tell her and to say that the kidnapping was her fault. But why didn't Jeffrey call on the pay phone? Maybe it was the kidnappers? Maybe the kidnappers were calling with a ransom demand?

A man in the director's office told Sarah her husband was on line four. The man punched a blinking red button at the bottom of the phone, then handed Sarah the receiver.

Jeffrey apologized for the page. He said he had misplaced the pay phone number.

But he had good news: Aaron was safe. He was still in New Hampshire, in fact.

"Barbara didn't have enough money to buy him an airline ticket," Jeffrey said. "She was going to call us this morning and tell us, but she overslept."

Sarah knew better than to ask what happened to the $500 the Goldsmiths had wired to New Hampshire for Aaron's airfare.

"Is there anything you want me to do?" she asked.

There was a six o'clock flight from Nashua to Houston via New York. Barbara could get Aaron to the airport on time if Sarah bought him a ticket.

"Put the ticket on your American Express," Jeffrey said. "Then go over to the bank. Barbara needs gas money to get to the airport. Wire her a thousand dollars."

Barbara could drive all the way to Houston and back with a thousand dollars. But Sarah knew that it would also be pointless to mention that.

She sighed and said: "All right, Jeffrey."

The next morning, the gray February morning Sarah could still remember so clearly ten years later, began with a dull, rumbling, unhappy feeling in the pit of her stomach and the murmur of voices outside the bedroom door. Jeffrey and Aaron were talking in the hall. Jeffrey was telling Aaron that Sarah would take him out for breakfast this morning—him and Naomi.

"Dad has to go into the office for a few hours," Jeffrey said.

An hour later Sarah was in the upstairs bathroom wondering how Barbara and her boyfriend were going to spend the Goldsmiths' gas money, when she heard a horrible shriek; someone was shouting: "Save me! Help me!" It was Naomi! Sarah threw her housecoat on and ran out into the hall. Her very frightened-looking daughter was running up the stairs a few steps ahead of her very angry-looking stepson.

"She bit me!" Aaron yelled after Sarah had separated the two children.

"I did not!" Naomi yelled back. She pointed an accusing finger at Aaron. "He hates girls."

"No I don't!" Aaron screamed. "I hate *you.*"

Sarah was inclined—more than inclined—to believe Naomi's version of events. Aaron was a high-strung child; he had gotten only a few hours sleep last night—and Barbara was his mother.

Sarah suggested a truce. Naomi and Aaron would shake hands and make up. Then the three of them would go out for a big breakfast.

"She started it," Aaron said, ignoring the peace offer. "She bit me." Aaron stuck out his tongue. "Bitch, bitch, bitch," he yelled at Naomi. "I'm going to call my mother. I'm going to tell on you." Sarah had grabbed Aaron by the arm and was marching him down the hall to the guest room. At the door, Aaron wrestled his arm free and said, "I'm going to tell my mother you're mean to me."

Ten minutes later the phone rang in the kitchen. Sarah put down her coffee and picked it up. Barbara. "I'm going to sue your ass off," she hissed from snow-covered New Hampshire. "You're a child abuser."

Sarah slammed down the phone. A moment later it rang again—

Jeffrey this time. His voice was very small and very tight. He said he had just spoken to Aaron; the boy was very upset.

Sarah started to describe the chase up the stairs, but Jeffrey cut her off.

"Aaron says Naomi bit him. He says he was in the playroom watching television and Naomi walked in and bit him on the arm for no reason at all."

The accusation was preposterous. Aaron was just saying that because he was mad at Naomi!

"Naomi would never bite anyone," Sarah said.

Jeffrey asked if Sarah had examined Aaron's arm.

In all the commotion, Sarah had not thought to. "No," she said, "I didn't."

"Would you please now?" Jeffrey asked. His voice was getting smaller and tighter by the second. "Aaron claims he's bleeding."

Aaron was not bleeding, but Sarah found two ugly purple-black toothmarks just above his wrist. Sarah swabbed Bactine on the bite, then put a Band-Aid over it.

"Feel better now?" she said, and smiled.

Aaron ignored Sarah's smile. "The bitch bit me," he said.

"It was his fault," Naomi screamed when Sarah confronted her in the playroom. "Aaron hates girls. Aaron hates everyone."

Sarah told Naomi to go to her room. Then she called the family pediatrician and made an appointment to take Aaron in for a tetanus shot. After that Sarah went into the bathroom, locked the door, sat down on the toilet, and began to cry.

I would like to be able to report that Sarah's experience is unusual, that very few people go through what she went through, that the conjunction of events that reduced her to tears on that gloomy February Saturday is rare. But actually her experience is fairly typical for the first cycle of stepfamily life. Parents and children alike find this period difficult—in some cases, very difficult. Over the nine years the project ran, there were a total of nineteen divorces in our stepfamily group and most occurred within the first two years of the family's formation.

We began the study expecting to find an unusual amount of turmoil in the first two years, especially the first. The available data, although limited, suggested that the process of fitting together—of learning how to live as a family—created a great deal of tension and stress. In addition, my personal experience as a psychologist—counseling stepfamilies as well as studying them—supported this view.

Nonetheless, everyone involved with the project was surprised at just how troubled the first two years turned out to be.

Some of our findings about this period came from the Life Events Survey, a questionnaire that study participants (including the nuclear families in our control group) were required to complete at the end of each cycle. The LES is a compilation of seventy-six common life events, changes, and stresses. Every event personally encountered in the past year has to be checked off and rated on a six-point scale ranging from extremely negative (−3) to extremely positive (+3). Typical LES questions include:

- Have you recently had a major change in living conditions?
- An extended separation from your child?
- A major change in social activities (increase or decrease)?
- A change in residence?
- Incurred a major new debt ($10,000 or more)?
- Had sexual difficulties?
- Trouble with an employer?
- A major change in financial status (better or worse)?
- A major change in closeness of family members (increased or decreased closeness)?

A special pediatric version of the LES was administered to the target children in each family. Items on the pediatric LES included:

- Moving to a new home
- Changing to a new school
- New brother or sister (step or biological)
- Increased absence of parent from home

- Trouble with classmates
- Extended visit away from home (a month or more)
- Losing a best friend

The first-cycle LES scores of our stepfamilies were remarkable in two ways. They were the highest of the three cycles, and there was an enormous stress gap between them and our nuclear families.

For example, the average stress score for women in new stepfamilies was three times higher than that for women in nuclear families: 13.4 vs. 4.3. Among males the difference was more than two times greater; the average stress score for men in nuclear families was 3.5 vs. 8.3 for men in new stepfamilies.

The same pattern held for girls in new stepfamilies; they scored nearly twice as high on stress as girls in nuclear families: 5.5 vs. 3.7. The one bright spot in this otherwise gloomy picture were new stepsons. Probably because males welcome the presence of other males in the family, the stress scores of boys in stepfamilies actually were the same as boys in nuclear families, 5.0 vs. 5.1.

Not surprisingly, these high stress levels often impacted on behavior within the stepfamily.

Among new stepchildren, we saw a considerable increase in acting-out behaviors and some increase in regression. Several girls and boys (temporarily) slipped back a developmental stage under the pressures and demands of stepfamily life. Naomi's reversion to biting—something she had not done since she was three—was one example of the regressive behavior we encountered; a more common one was clinging.

Adult participants also seemed to suffer from a form of stress-induced regression. One area where this turned up with striking regularity was in parenting skills, particularly mothering. Stress often interfered with a woman's ability to attune to her children—to track their thoughts, feelings, and needs carefully. Preoccupied, the woman would miss the youngsters' distress signals.

Relationship skills also were casualties of stress-induced regression. Project men and women seemed to lose the ability to talk to one another. Spouses often tightened up. Thoughts and feelings that once flowed easily and unguardedly were now left unspoken or half spoken. The inability of the usually nimble Sarah to finesse Jeffery's more unreasonable demands (in other words, to tell him no in a nice way) is a very common first-cycle phenomenon.

I think many new stepfamily couples lose their conflict-resolution skills for the same reason that they lose their communication skills: first-cycle overload. In many situations it is just easier for a frustrated, stressed-out, or overwhelmed husband or wife to say "Do this!" or "You're *wrong*" than to ask "How can we work this out?" The frequent use of such blunt shorthand during the first cycle was responsible for another disheartening study finding: The incidence of marital conflict soared in new stepfamilies.

In the talks I give to stepfamily groups from time to time, I always insert a little preface before I describe our first-cycle findings. I warn my audience that, out of context, the numbers they are about to hear will sound scary. But the numbers do have a context. The context is one of growth, change, and development.

A stepfamily is a living organism, and our figures on stress and conflict are, in a very real sense, a barometer of the organism's birth pangs. The feelings and behaviors that the numbers reflect are a normal part of the process of adhering, of coming together, of learning—of a new family being born.

A FATHER'S TROUBLED MEMORY

I am surprised at how little Jeffrey Goldsmith has changed when I visit him a week after my talk with Sarah. The laugh lines around Jeffrey's mouth have deepened. But otherwise he looks like the Jeffrey of five years ago: imposing, thoughtful, intelligent, solid. I do notice one change, though. That tight, slightly censorial quality Sarah used to complain about is gone, or is at least less evident. Jeffrey is pleased when I tell him he seems more relaxed now; he smiles and tells me that the last few years have been happy ones.

I have arranged to interview the Goldsmiths separately for the book because I thought Jeffrey and Sarah would speak more freely if the other spouse was not present. However, I was a little apprehensive about Jeffrey's willingness to sit for a reinterview. Sarah told me that he was very busy these days. Recently Jeffrey and his brother opened a new office-warehouse complex in Dallas; until the complex got off the ground, Jeffrey was spending a couple of days each week there. Sarah also said that temple affairs were taking up a lot of his time.

But apparently Jeffrey, the intellectual, was intrigued when Sarah told him that I was reinterviewing project couples for a book I was writing on stepfamilies.

A few days later, when I call his office, a secretary says Mr. Goldsmith has been expecting to hear from me, then immediately puts me through to Jeffrey, who arranges to meet me at his office the following Tuesday afternoon.

"The boys are doing very well," Jeffrey says when I ask about his sons. Aaron, the younger Goldsmith son, is now a senior in college and on the dean's list.

"Aaron has begun to talk about medical school," his father reports.

The older Goldsmith son, Mark, works in New York City. He is on the copywriting staff of a prominent advertising firm.

Jeffrey and I exchange small talk for a few minutes, then I explain the reason for my visit. I tell him about the book and say I would like to talk to him about the Goldsmiths' stepfamily experience.

"Where should I begin?" he asks.

"The beginning, the first months," I say.

Jeffrey's first few recollections are abstract and detached. He could almost be talking about another couple, a couple he is rather fond of but does not really know very well. But as soon as I ask about Aaron's visit—the incident Sarah still remembered so clearly a decade later—I notice a change.

Jeffrey stiffens slightly, then answers my question with a question of his own. "Have I ever told you about the conversation I had with Aaron and Mark after I left Barbara?" he says.

I tell him no.

Jeffrey nods and leans back in his chair. "I think it was the second or third weekend I had the boys. On the way home from an Astros game, the three of us stopped at a little Tex-Mex place near my apartment for dinner. After the waitress took our orders, Mark and Aaron began acting oddly. They got very fidgety and started shooting glances back and forth. Finally Aaron said: 'Go ahead, Mark, tell him.'

"I put down my menu and said: 'Tell me what?'

"Mark stared at me for a second or two, then he began to make a little speech. I think he and Aaron had prepared it beforehand. Mark said that he and Aaron wanted me to come home. They missed me. He also said that the boys were not getting along with their mother."

I notice that Jeffrey is not looking at me anymore. He is staring out the window.

"That night, after the boys went to bed," he says, "I was sitting on the couch trying to lose myself in a book when I felt something wet on my cheek. I felt the spot. It was wet. I was crying. Mark's speech, it was . . . I felt awful, I mean, my boys . . ." Jeffrey stops. He seems to be completely transfixed by a warehouse across the street.

Neither of us speaks for a moment, then I ask a question. "But you couldn't bring yourself to go back to Barbara?"

Jeffrey shook his head almost wearily. "I believed if I went back to Barbara something terrible would happen to me. I'd get sick, I'd die. It was a kind of magical thinking, I know. But I had had so much of Barbara's craziness by that point, I was getting a little crazy myself. I believed the only way I could survive was to stay away from her. But I felt guilty, horribly guilty about Aaron and Mark; when we separated, they chose to stay with Barbara. But I still felt I was abandoning them. I was saving myself and leaving them to fate. It was not a happy thought.

"You're probably wondering what all this had to do with Aaron's first visit," Jeffrey says. Then he answers his own question. "When I married Sarah, I had a little fantasy. I was going to give Sarah and Naomi a new home and life and then, when the three of us were settled in, had become a family, I was going to bring Aaron and Mark down from New Hampshire. Sarah couldn't understand why I wanted such a big house. *That's* why. In the back of my mind I always planned that one day Aaron and Mark would come and live with us. But I didn't mention the plan to Sarah because I knew that she had a lot of issues with the boys, especially Aaron."

Jeffrey pauses, then asks: "Did you ever meet Barbara?"

"Sarah showed me a picture of her once," I say.

Jeffrey nods. "Aaron and Barbara look alike, and Aaron has a lot of her mannerisms. I think, in Sarah's mind, Aaron became a kind of surrogate. I mean, Barbara's a difficult person but Sarah made her into Evil Incarnate. Barbara was taking all of our money, Barbara was try-ing to steal me back, Barbara was never going to let us have a normal family life. Barbara was going to drop a thermonuclear device on Hous-ton. But Sarah couldn't do anything about Barbara. She lived in New Hampshire and, anyway, she was a little scared of her, I think. I don't want to say Aaron became a target for all Sarah's frustrations and anger about Barbara, but sometimes I think she did get him confused with his mother.

"Sarah started out being very critical of Aaron: He was rude; he was hyperactive; he had bad manners. Some of the things she said really upset me, but I tolerated the criticism because I knew where it was coming from and, considering the alternatives, I figured it was a rela-tively harmless way for her to work through her feelings about Barbara. But that morning Sarah went over the line. She landed on Aaron directly. That's why I got so upset. I don't know if she told you, but she didn't even ask Aaron for his side of the story."

"Sarah did tell me that she felt very guilty about what happened," I say.

A rueful smile. "Good. She should."

THE MOST COMMON EXPECTATIONS
OF NEW STEPFAMILIES

Most popular writing on the stepfamily blames the turmoil and conflict of the first two years on the same four or five factors. New stepfamilies fight a lot because the stepfather's authority is unclear, because no family rules have evolved yet, because former spouses still loom large in mind and heart, and because a lot of practical but emotionally charged issues like money have to be resolved quickly. And, indeed, many first-cycle stress levels can be explained in terms of these factors. However, we found that they are actually manifestations of a larger phenomenon.

As we listened to our subjects agonize over surly stepchildren and intrusive former mates, we realized something surprising. At the start of cycle 1, *everyone,* even the most realistic Matriarchalists and clear-eyed Neotraditionalists, harbor many unrealistic expectations about stepfamily life.

We were helped in our understanding of this process by Emily and John Visher, two pioneering stepfamily clinicians who identified many unrealistic expectations for stepfamilies. This led us to reconsider the role of the usual suspects in cycle 1 conflicts. While differences about money and children and stepchildren do make a contribution to the turmoil, the real culprit is Dr. Belsky's lead pipe phenomenon. The normal problems of settling in and learning to live together felt worse to our participants because they had not expected them—in their heads many had, but not in their hearts. In their hearts, even our cynics were revealed to be cockeyed optimists.

I don't want to sound scolding about expectations. The impulse to hope (and expectations are a form of hope) is a fundamental part of the human condition. And few things are more likely to inspire hope than a new beginning, a fresh start.

In new stepfamilies, hope takes many different forms, but we found two themes dominated: people hope for healing and for redemption.

The new stepfamily is going to heal old wounds, and it is going to provide the man or woman with a new opportunity to prove that he or she really is a good spouse, a good parent, a good person.

According to our data, here are the most common expectations people bring to stepfamily life.

The Nuclear-Family Myth

In the 1980s, when the study was launched, the problems of stepfamily life were already being widely written about, so I assumed that people would be fairly realistic about what to expect. I was wrong.

Even our very realistic couples often expected their new stepfamily to function like a nuclear family—and to do so from the beginning. Indeed, this expectation was so common, we gave it a name, the nuclear-family myth.

At first, I thought the myth was so popular because it expressed a longing for a certain kind of family—the white-picket-fence, 1950s-style family—but, as the project progressed, I realized our participants clung to it because the nuclear-family myth speaks to certain fundamental human longings and desires. It is about the need to belong, to be nourished and nurtured by close human relationships; it is about the yearning to give and to receive love, about the wish for a secure haven in a heartless world, and about the need to feel whole and authentic.

The Rescue Fantasy

Jeffrey Goldsmith, like many men, was particularly attached to a variant of the nuclear-family myth I call the rescue fantasy. I first encountered the expectation one day early in the project during a discussion about—of all things—Galveston. I do not now remember how Jeffrey and I got onto the subject, but I do remember that as I was describing my parents' vacation home there, he interrupted. He wanted to tell me about a weekend he, Sarah, Naomi, Aaron, and Mark had spent in Galveston before the Goldsmiths were married.

Jeffrey told me the name of the hotel where the five of them had stayed and the restaurants where they had eaten. Then, rather surprisingly, reserved Jeffrey began to describe a memory—an image, really—of the trip. One morning, in a hurry to get to the beach, Sarah, the boys, and Naomi had left the hotel ahead of him. A few minutes later, walking out of the hotel, Jeffrey saw the four of them on the other side of the street. Sarah was bending down to wipe Popsicle dribble from Mark's chin, while Naomi was crouched on the sidewalk, her arms wrapped around her mother's legs.

I think this little street scene made such a powerful impression on Jeffrey because it spoke to his dream of family unification. A great deal has been written about the tendency of men to abandon their children emotionally and financially after divorce. But many men, Jeffrey among them, are devastated by the end of marriage. They hate the isolation, loneliness, and alienation of being single. They feel whole only in a family, in a fathering role.

Often such men associate parenting—fathering—with masculinity. Frequently what such men want, without quite realizing it, is what Jeffrey wanted and eventually got: family reunification. On some unconscious level, the man enters the stepfamily expecting to unite his biological children and stepchildren into a "real family," a family that will restore him to the paterfamilias role and renew his authenticity.

The Just-Us Expectation

Sarah, who thought she had prepared so assiduously for stepfamily life, was seduced by another version of the nuclear-family expectation. A quarter of a century of divorce and remarriage is supposed to have made Americans comfortable with the idea of multiple serial mating. But the impulse toward mate exclusivity also runs very deep in the human character, and often the impulse gives rise to another unconscious expectation, what might be called "just us." One mate unconsciously expects the other to devote himself exclusively to her and her child. Or to put it another way, at the start of stepfamily life, the woman expects the man's inconvenient past, in the form of ex-wives and biological children, just to disappear.

According to a new discipline called evolutionary psychology, the "just-us" expectation is more common among women because of their enormous biological investment in children. Unlike males, females have a finite reproductive span; they can produce only so many eggs per month and so many children during their reproductive years. Consequently, say evolutionary psychologists, over time, women have become genetically "wired" to be fiercely protective of their children. And one of the ways female protectiveness expresses itself is by demanding *exclusive* material and emotional support from a man.

Today, of course, mate exclusivity is less important to female reproductive success than it was 5,000 years ago. But genes do not change as fast as material circumstances and social trends, so women continue to act on this ancient impulse. In modern stepfamilies, one way the impulse manifests itself is through complaints that are designed to drive a wedge between a man and his past.

Exhibit A of this phenomenon is Sarah and her frequent complaints that Jeffrey was spending too much money on his former wife, and that his children, unlike her child, were rude and undisciplined.

"Instant-Love" Expectation

Careful, wary, sweet Joanne McDougal displayed this variant of the nuclear-family expectation when she described the five-month drum roll that preceded Dwight's introduction to Tray, Jr., and Evan.

"I talked about Dwight a lot before I brought him home to meet the boys," she told me at the intake interview. "I would tell Tray, Jr., and Evan what a fine man he was and how he liked the same things that they did: camping and fishing."

Joanne must have seen that I was puzzled by her drum roll, because she stopped at this point to explain that the stories were part of a plan she and Dwight had devised. The stories were going to make Evan and Tray, Jr., so fond of Dwight that when she finally brought him home, the boys would never want him to leave.

"I was sure Tray, Jr., and Evan would fall in love with Dwight right away, the same way I did," Joanne explained.

The "Better-Than" Expectation

I encountered a fourth variant of the nuclear-family expectation in a project mother called Karen Johnson. One day, during a visit, Karen said she had something she wanted to show me. Before I had a chance to ask what, Karen disappeared into the kitchen. When she reappeared, there was a manila envelope in her hand. Inside were a dozen photos of the Johnsons' new home in a Houston suburb.

Karen took the pictures out of the envelope and laid them on the coffee table. "I'm so proud of the house. I've been showing these pictures to everyone, James." She picked up a photo and handed it to me. It was a picture of the living room in the Johnsons' new home. "Much nicer than this living room, isn't it?" Karen said, waving her hand dismissively around the small, dark room we were sitting in.

It took Karen and me nearly fifteen minutes to work our way upstairs and downstairs and into the backyard of the new house. Every time we visited a new room photographically, Karen enthused. Wasn't this room bigger or better or prettier than its counterpart in the house we were sitting in, the house of her first marriage?

Midway through the tour, I realized that Karen was not really giving me a preview of her new house. She was giving me a preview of her new *life*. Karen was showing me how much bigger and better and happier that life was going to be in comparison to her bad old life.

Since stepfamilies are usually a by-product of divorce, people—most adults anyway—enter them with the expectation that the new family will be better and happier than the old family, which divorce destroyed. But people who have had a particularly traumatic first marriage often have a particularly intense version of what might be called the better-than expectation. Most often the source of the trauma is a very difficult first spouse, like Karen's first husband, Clement. Clement, an emotionally remote man, ignored his wife and their son, Ethridge.

The danger of the better-than expectation is the often impossible standards it sets for the new spouse. David Johnson, Karen's new husband, was a warm, funny man. But the targets of better-than have to be much more than warm and funny, much more than just companionable. They have to be—are expected to be—paradigms of good fathering and good husbanding. And because these are almost impossible standards for anyone to meet, the man and, perhaps the stepfamily as well, is doomed to fail.

Egalitarianism

A final variant of the nuclear-family expectation is egalitarianism. The man—and this expectation is most common among new stepfathers—expects to enter the new stepfamily on an equal emotional footing with the other members. He expects his opinions, feelings, desires, and needs to be valued as much as theirs. He expects the other family members to open their hearts to him as readily as they do to each other; he expects to feel just as at home in the family as they do.

Often a confusion is at the root of this expectation. The man mistakes the legal equality conferred by a marriage document with emotional equality. But they are not at all the same; the first is conferred by the state, the second by the human heart. Normally, one to two years are required to penetrate existing family relationships, to be totally accepted by family members, especially older members. The greatest danger of the egalitarian expectation is not that it makes a man give up. Men do not like to enter stepfamilies as second-class citizens, but most are willing to put in the work and time to acquire first-class citizenship. However, there is another aspect of stepfamily life that egalitarians can never reconcile themselves to, and this is that some relationships and people in the family may *always* be unavailable to them, no matter what they do.

Expectations of the Matriarchal Stepfamily

While the Matriarchal family is less vulnerable to the nuclear-family expectations than Neotraditionalists and Romantics, Matriarchalists are not free of expectations. However, the distinctive Matriarchal personality tends to produce distinctive expectations.

I caught echoes of one common Matriarchal expectation in the complaints of Dana Vincennes. Dana was not a project participant; I saw her in my capacity as a psychologist.

Dana was deeply upset by the unreliability of her husband, Michael. "I can't count on him," she told me during her first visit. "Michael will promise to do something, then forget. Like last Thursday. I had a doctor's appointment in the evening, so I asked Michael to pick up Tommy [Dana's four-year-old] at the day care center. He said 'Sure, I'll do it on my way home from work.' But as I'm walking out of my office at five, the phone rings. It's the day care worker. 'Isn't anyone coming by to pick up Tommy?' she says.

"When I reminded Michael about the pickup that night, he hit his head and said, 'Oh, geez.' Can you believe it? A thirty-two-year-old man and best he can do is hit his head and say 'Oh, geez.' "

As Dana talked, I began to suspect that more than Michael's unreliability was making her unhappy.

Most Matriarchal men do not expect to be burdened by family responsibilities or obligations, but they are willing to help out around the edges—to pick up a child at day care when a wife has a doctor's appointment, for example. They are also usually mature and adult; for many men, one attraction of the Matriarchal structure is the time and emotional energy it leaves free for them to spend with their biological children.

But the Matriarchal structure sometimes attracts another kind of man, a Peter Pan type who, like Michael, is emotionally immature. The Matriarchal woman's competence, particularly her maternal competence, is very attractive to this man. He wants to be taken care of, and since the Matriarchal woman is a superb caretaker, he imagines that she will be able to take care of him. Men like Michael usually bring two related expectations to stepfamily life. They expect not to have to play *any* role in family life at all, and, more centrally, they expect the husband-wife relationship to be a version of the parent-child relationship, with themselves playing the role of a needy, semihelpless child.

Matriarchal men who have not been married before are vulnerable to another kind of expectation. They expect stepfamily disruptions, but they do not expect the disruptions to impinge on their lives. In other words, they never expect to have to deal with interrupting children or to have to negotiate about family holidays and vacation schedules, or to find themselves having to make small talk with a spouse's former husband.

Expectations Among Stepchildren

In terms of expectations, the youngest members of the stepfamily often are the most clear-sighted. Expectations of instant love or instant familyness are rare among children, although many youngsters do expect more normalcy in a stepfamily—at least, normalcy in an outward sense. Once again they will have two parents at home. And now, on holidays, mother and child won't have to travel to someone else's family for dinner. At the intake interview, Naomi told me that the best thing about stepfamily life was not having to fly to Chicago to celebrate Passover with her grandparents. From now on, the two of them could celebrate at home in Houston with Jeffrey. Another new stepchild told me, with some pride, that this Christmas, instead of eating at a relative's house, relatives were coming to his house for dinner.

Many children also expect more money to be available in a stepfamily. This is another expectation that is often realized—and quickly. Usually stepfamilies do have more money available for clothes and vacations and dinners out than single-parent families.

Children also expect something else, and while the expectation has nothing to do with stepfamily life directly, it affects the quality of that life tremendously. In their heart of hearts, almost every boy and girl dreams and hopes and expects that one day, Mommy and Daddy will learn to love each other again, that their family of origin will be reconstituted, that order and sanity will reign in the universe again.

Adults often think that a stepfamily puts an end to this fantasy. It doesn't.

"You'll see," eight-year-old Boyce Hopkins assured me one day. "Mom and Dad are going to get married all over again."

I asked Boyce, one of our target children, what would happen to his stepfather, Lyle Applecroft. I knew that Boyce and Lyle were pretty close.

"Nothing," Boyce said. "Lyle's going to stay here and live with us."

"With you and your mom and dad?" I asked.

Boyce seemed surprised by my surprise. "Why not?" he said. "Dad and Lyle are already in business together. I've heard them talking on the phone a couple of times about money."

I later learned—not entirely to my surprise—that the money conversations Boyce overheard were about child support payments, which Boyce's father never paid on time. However, Boyce's fantasy of family reunification, plus the stepfather, was pretty common among children who liked their stepparents. Among those who did not, the reunification fantasy called for the bad stepparent to be sent packing after the parental remarriage.

Sometimes, the emotional tug of the reunification fantasy, if not the fantasy itself, will linger into adult life. A patient told me that the day of her wedding, she burst into tears when she looked out into the church and saw her remarried mother and father sitting on opposite sides of the aisle.

Parents often feel guilty when I tell them about these fantasies. Thus, it is important to keep in mind that a stepfamily can also be the beginning of a new, and better, dream for a child. I know this for a fact, because I saw new and better dreams arise in dozens of project families.

HOW TO DEAL WITH UNREALISTIC EXPECTATIONS

Is it possible for a couple to identify and deal with unrealistic expectations before their marriage?

I frequently counsel men and women on the cusp of stepfamily life, and I always tell them three things about expectations:

1. Couples should sit down before the marriage and explore each other's expectations; next, they should do a reality check to see how on target those expectations are. The check should include talking to people they know who live in stepfamilies and reading about stepfamily life. Most local libraries contain hundreds of popular magazine articles and books.

2. Keep talking. Sharing disillusionments and disappointments not only takes some of the sting out of them, it creates a sense of "we-ness." The couple begins to develop a sense of going through the stepfamily experience together. And husbands and wives who feel that they are sharing a joint adventure are much more likely to blame the impersonal processes of family formation, and not each other, for problems.

3. Don't expect to identify every unrealistic expectation beforehand. The project husbands and wives who engaged in expectation conversations premaritally all told us the same thing. Some expectations are so subtle that identifying them beforehand is impossible. You have to actually live in a stepfamily—have to experience some first-cycle disappointments—before you realize all the things you expect it to give you.

Unrealistic expectations and the disappointments they produce are a normal part of first-cycle life. Moreover, as we shall see in the next section of the book, most expectations self-correct. In a stepfamily, time and experience do not diminish the capacity to dream, but they do teach family members how to dream more realistically.

POINTS TO KEEP IN MIND

- Conflict and disagreement are a normal part of early stepfamily life. *Everyone* feels stressed.
- Unrealistic expectations often add to the stress. But such expectations are also normal; everyone enters stepfamily life with a dream in his or her heart.

- The most seductive expectation of stepfamily life is the nuclear-family myth. Everyone—everyone but Matriarchals, that is—wants to transform the stepfamily into a nuclear family.
- Husband and wives shouldn't blame disappointments on each other. They have to recognize that a certain degree of disillusionment is also a normal part of stepfamily formation.

chapter five

Bridging the

Insider-Outsider Gap

There is a bright yellow Whiffle bat in the corner of the office, next to the window. Jeffrey Goldsmith stands up, walks over to the bat, and picks it up.

"Do you play ball?" he asks me.

"No. In high school I played football."

Jeffrey takes a swing. I am surprised at the speed of his cut.

"I played all the time when I was a kid." Jeffrey puts the bat back in the corner and returns to the desk. "Sometimes I play for the company team now. We have one here. Second base, mostly."

I had been apprehensive about how forthcoming Jeffrey was going to be in the reinterview, but it has been nearly an hour and he hasn't stopped talking. We are discussing his stepdaughter, Naomi, and the talk seems to be stirring troubling memories.

Jeffrey says that the first year he and Naomi spent together was very difficult. "I would have imaginary conversations with Naomi; I would tell her what a good person I was and what a lucky little girl she was to have me as a stepfather. I was very persuasive. Naomi would always beg me to give her another chance, but I would tell her 'No, Naomi, you had your chance to be my daughter. You were too mean to me. It's too late to make amends now.'" Jeffrey stops and smiles ruefully. "It reminded me of the kind of thing I used to do when a girl rejected me. That was the level I was operating on the first year. Dreaming up revenge scenarios against a child. I'm embarrassed to talk about it now."

"Being an adult doesn't stop you from being human," I say.

Jeffrey nods, then says something that surprises me. He says he reached a point where he almost gave up on Naomi. "I had decided to withdraw completely," he declares. "The final straw was a school play I went to with Sarah. Afterward the three of us were standing in the hall when another girl walked up to us—I think it was one of Naomi's classmates. Naomi got this funny little expression on her face when the girl pointed at me and said, 'Is that your father?' I could have lived with Naomi's first answer. She introduced me as her 'mother's husband,' but she couldn't stop there. She had to add a kicker. She told the girl, 'He'll never be my father.'"

Jeffrey leans back in his chair. "When we got home, I told Sarah, 'No more, that's it. I started out hoping Naomi would like me, then all I wanted was for her to be civil to me. Now I don't want anything. She's all yours. I'll say hello to her in the morning and good night in the evening, but from now on that is going to be the extent of our interactions. I have had it. Thank you.'"

Between the third and sixth month, typically, two things happen in stepfamilies. The first thing is that by now, the usually overwhelmed couple begins to believe that unending stress is the defining characteristic of stepfamily life. It isn't, but there are so many unexpected emergencies and crises in this period, it is understandable why husbands and wives feel this way. The other thing that happens—and that adds to everyone's general stress level—is that the man and woman begin to realize that the stepfamily is really two different families: The Outsider Family consists of the stepfather—and, if he has them, his children when they visit on weekends—while the Insider Family consists of the woman and her biological child or children. Insiders are insiders because most stepfamilies are built around the mother-child bond, which usually shapes the culture of the new stepfamily. Outsiders are outsiders because they know very little about this culture and how it operates. Since marriage crystallizes and sharpens the differences between Outsiders and Insiders in a way that dating and even living together do not, the (usually temporary) division of a new stepfamily into two families is a normal part of the family formation process, just as holding expectations is. But the division is problematic, because it means that Outsider and Insider Family members will experience and perceive the new stepfamily in different ways and will have different feelings about it.

To understand how this gap develops and why it is intimately connected to a couple's expectations, it helps to understand how Outsiders and Insiders perceive stepfamily life in the first two years.

THE OUTSIDER EXPERIENCE

The primary Outsider experience is isolation: Often new stepfathers perceive the mother-child bond as an impenetrable biological force field. Sometimes the impenetrability seems deliberate. Consciously or unconsciously, the Insiders have decided not to let the Outsider in to join them. But more often than not, the bond is impenetrable because it is built on a history and on experiences, values, and ways of relating that the man does not yet share or understand. Thus, even when the Insiders make an effort to let the Outsider in, the man still feels left out because he does not know how to relate to the mother and child the way they relate to each other. Said one project stepfather: "My wife was very open to me at the beginning and so was my stepchild, much more than I expected. But it didn't help. There were eight years of history in every word Carol [his wife] and Ben [his stepson] said to each other. And I didn't share that history. Some things just take time and the dailyness of a life lived together."

The sense of inhabiting someone else's culture frequently intensifies the new stepfather's sense of isolation. "No one even heard of *Monday Night Football* in this house until I arrived," said one irritated man who married a woman with a teenage daughter. This stepfather made another complaint about the dominant culture in his new family, a complaint I heard from several men who married women with daughters. The man said that the portions of food his wife served were too small. "I'd get a little teeny piece of meat and one slice of bread—one! Ashley [his wife] has forgotten how men eat."

Weddings, bar mitzvahs, baptisms, and other family functions often add to the new stepfather's sense of isolation. Most new stepfamilies celebrate events in just the Insider's family, so each person the new stepfather meets at family celebrations presents him with yet another opportunity to contemplate his Outsider status, his growing feeling that he is living on Mars. Said one project stepfather: "I spent a year going to parties where I literally did not know a soul."

Along with isolation, many Outsiders also are haunted by a sense of powerlessness. Even when a man has a special expertise in a subject, his opinion does not seem to count for much with the Insiders. A colleague of mine at Baylor wanted to enroll his new stepdaughter in a summer math camp at a local private school. "Suzanne's math skills are a year behind where a fifth grader's ought to be," the colleague told me one day at lunch. "I think she really needs some tutoring."

But my colleague's wife thought the math camp was a bad idea. "Elizabeth said it would not be fair to Suzanne," the colleague told me. "She said Suzanne was only ten, and as a ten-year-old she should be allowed to have her summers. I wanted to protest but . . ." My colleague shrugged and began to pick at his salad.

Sometimes a stepchild evokes surprising and disturbing feelings in a new stepfather, feelings the man not only did not expect to feel but that on some level embarrass and dishearten him because they do not bear any resemblance to the love one family member is supposed to feel for another.

"In my wildest imagination I never thought I would find myself jealous of a nine-year-old," one project man said. "But I am. I'm envious of my nine-year-old stepson. I see how completely unstinting my wife is with Bobby [his stepchild], and, frankly, it makes me jealous. I practically have to make an appointment to talk to Ann [his wife]. Bobby gets her total rapt attention any time he wants."

Another frequent surprising stepfather emotion is resentment. The new stepchild ignores a bid to start a conversation or introduces the man to a friend as "not my real father." Suddenly the man feels resentful—then, almost immediately, guilty. "I'm an adult and I am the child's stepfather," the man tells himself. "I should be more understanding and accepting." But the child's behavior still rankles.

The little humiliations new stepchildren can inflict frequently intensify another Outsider experience: divided loyalties. The men in our study, like stepfathers generally, devoted most of their time and resources to the stepfamily, which meant that the stepchild often received more emotional and material support than the man's biological child. Many men felt guilty about this.

In a candid moment, Tom Effinger, one of our project stepfathers, told me that 80 percent of his time and 60 percent of his money went to his stepson, Wilson, about whom he felt ambivalent. "Elliot [Tom's biological son], whom I love, gets the leftovers," Tom said. "Tell me how that happened."

Tom and I talked about Wilson and Elliot for a while. Then I asked him how he was adjusting to stepfamily life otherwise.

"It's been interesting," Tom said, following the remark with a half smile I was not sure how to interpret.

I asked him how he thought his wife, Mandy, was doing.

The question seemed to surprise Tom. "Mandy? Terrific," he said.

"But why shouldn't Mandy be terrific? Mandy has barely had to make any adjustments. Lucky Mandy."

Many new stepfathers feel this way. They believe a woman has to make far fewer emotional adjustments—and in one sense they are right. Often the woman is transferring a known civilization and a known relationship from one kind of family structure to another. But the woman is the reason the family exists—why the man and child are in the family—and the emotional responsibilities this fact creates can produce far greater turmoil than anything a new stepfather experiences.

THE BURDEN OF INSIDERNESS

I am sitting in Lotte Ardman's kitchen on a sunny Thursday morning, examining a small, freshly polished ball on the kitchen table. Actually, the ball, which is the color of brilliant July sun and is mounted on a chocolate-brown plastic rectangle, is not a ball at all; it is a globe. Thin, interlocking metal strips curve around its circumference to form a perfectly round sphere. The metal plates on top of the strips are supposed to represent the seven continents. Inside, in the middle, the globe is hollow. Below Australia, I can see the bottom of the salt shaker on the other side of the table.

"I got it at the World's Fair," Lotte says when she sees me looking at the globe.

I pick it up. The inscription on the plastic base says NEW YORK WORLD'S FAIR 1964.

"Your parents must have taken you in a stroller," I say.

Lotte laughs. "I wish. I was eleven."

I am interviewing Lotte, a former project participant, for the book, and I have caught her just in time. Tomorrow is her moving day. She is returning to New York, back to Long Island Sound, back to Smithtown where she grew up. The marriage that brought Lotte to Houston fifteen years ago is over now. It ended last year in divorce. With no compelling reason to stay in Houston, Lotte has decided to return to family and friends.

"Home is where the heart is," she says now.

"And your heart has never been here?"

Lotte shakes her head, then takes a sip of her coffee. When she puts down the cup, she says that she has just been out to San Francisco. "I went to see Paul."

Paul Puskoft is Lotte's younger child. I remember him as a thin, anxious, distant ten-year-old. I also remember that Paul and Lotte have had a troubled relationship.

I ask how the visit went.

Lotte does not exactly answer my question. "Sam [Lotte's twenty-two-year-old daughter] says Paul is gay. That's why he doesn't have a girlfriend, why he lives where he does."

"Have you ever talked to Paul about it?" I ask.

"About being gay?" Lotte shakes her head. "Paul never talks to me, James. You know that."

"I thought that might have changed."

Lotte takes another sip of coffee. "I missed a connection with Paul. He never got what he wanted from me. He stopped wanting anything from me after that."

Lotte does not define "that." She doesn't have to. "That" is part of our special language. We have talked about "that" a half-dozen times or more over the years. In terms of the things that can happen in a stepfamily, in any family, "that" was really not terribly dramatic. It was a small incident—painful, upsetting, but still small. One evening at dinner Edwin Ardman, the man Lotte moved to Houston for, asked Paul to mow the lawn after dinner. When Paul said he had homework to do, Edwin lost his temper.

"I asked you," Edwin said. "Now I'm telling you, Paul, I want you to mow the lawn as soon as you finish eating."

Lotte believes her life, Paul's life, the Ardman stepfamily life—everything—changed when Paul turned to her and said, "Mom?"

"I should have stood up for him," Lotte declared the last time we talked about the incident in 1991. "I should have taken Paul's side against Edwin. I should have acted like a mother."

"You tried to negotiate," I reminded her for the fifth or sixth time. "You did what anyone would have done."

Lotte had stopped listening to me. "Paul didn't eat with us again for a year, James. You know that. And he got out of here as soon as he could. Remember how devastated I was when he moved back to New York to live with his father? He was only twelve and I was losing him already."

I am not a great believer in life-transforming moments. I believe people and relationships change gradually over time, pushed by the slow accretion of small events. And, indeed, our data had shown difficulties in Paul and Lotte's relationship before "that" happened. But what I believed and what our data showed did not matter to Lotte. She believed that the incident had presented her with a life-defining choice and that because she had chosen wrongly, she had lost a son.

"I'm afraid you're going to break that, James," Lotte says crossly, and takes the globe out of my hand, wraps it in a old copy of the *Houston Chronicle,* then puts it in a moving box.

If men are surprised at how isolated they feel in a new stepfamily, women are surprised at how frequently they feel like Lotte: caught in the middle; torn between a husband—who desires and pushes for change and the child who, having undergone one major life transition—his parents' divorce—does not want to make any more changes—at least for a while.

"I think that's why I disliked Jeffrey at first," Naomi said on the lovely April afternoon I reinterviewed her on the Goldsmiths' patio. "I was just adjusting to the divorce, and now suddenly here's this guy who wants to turn my life upside down *again.* I didn't want any more changes. Besides, I liked the life Mom and I had created for ourselves.

We had gotten super-close. She used to tell me about the guys she dated, about the things that happened at work . . ."

I was a little surprised. "You were only six when your mother remarried, weren't you?"

"Seven, just seven." Naomi was beginning to look a lot like Sarah. She had the same dark, alert eyes and olive complexion.

Naomi anticipated my next question. "I know, I was a little young to be told about boyfriend problems . . . but Mom was lonely then, and I was the only person she could confide in; her family and friends were all in Boston. And I didn't mind. I liked being her confidant. It made me feel like a big girl. I also liked all the other things we used to do together: lying on the bed, eating Chinese and watching television, going to movies on Saturday nights. I think all the togetherness helped me get over the divorce. After a while I was almost glad Dad was gone. I could have Mom all to myself.

"Was I a selfish little girl?" Naomi asked in a self-dramatizing twentysomething voice.

"I remember you as a pretty normal little girl," I said.

Naomi giggled and took a sip of ice tea. "I was afraid Jeffrey was going to destroy all of that. And he did. He made us move here." She waved toward the house. "I hated this place at first. It looked so big and dark and lonely. I felt like I was moving into a mortuary. I hated everything about our new life; no more confidences, no more Chinese on the bed. Just Jeffrey with that dour, dour face." Naomi imitated her stepfather's expression. "I resented Jeffrey, but I was really angry at Mom. First, she left Dad; now she was destroying this wonderful life we had built together."

Naomi paused and took another sip of her tea. "I don't know if anyone ever told you, but the summer she got married, I wanted to leave. I told her I wanted to spend the school vacation in Boston with my grandmother. Mom burst into tears when I asked if I could go. I guess it was some kind of final straw; she was afraid she had already alienated Jeffrey."

"Because of Aaron?" I asked.

"Uh-huh. Now she was afraid she was going to lose me too. Poor Mom. She must have felt pulled every which way."

As Naomi spoke, I found myself thinking about the recurring dream another project mother had told me about. It was a dream about fire and fear and choice. The woman began having the dream about four months after her marriage, and it continued intermittently until she and her stepfamily arrived in the more tranquil second period of the stepfamily cycle.

The dream always started the same way. The woman would awaken in the darkness to shouting voices, but before she could identify the voices, a thick, acrid smell began to fill her nostrils. Smoke! A moment later a lick of bright red-orange flame shot through the open bedroom door. The house was on fire, the woman realized. As she bolted out of bed, there were more shouts. This time the voices were identifiable. Her husband and child were calling her. Each was trapped and needed her help. But one voice was coming from the kitchen downstairs, the other from the bedroom at the other end of the hall. The woman knew she would be able to reach only one caller in time.

THE HIGH COST OF DENYING
THE INSIDER-OUTSIDER GAP

One of the biggest surprises to emerge from project data was the subtle way expectations continued to add to our participants' stresses during the first cycle.

Earlier I described one example. Expecting only good things, many of our participants were psychologically defenseless when bad things happened. Their lack of preparation made the bad things feel very bad indeed. But as the study progressed, it became clear that expectations also could intensify the normal stresses of new stepfamily life in a second way, through denial. To our surprise, even Neotraditional and Matriarchal couples often hung on to a few cherished illusions despite the contrary evidence of reality. The isolated husband would continue to insist that he was not isolated, the caught-in-the-middle wife that she was not caught in the middle. This insistence often intensified normal cycle 1 stresses because the husband or wife invested so much emotional energy into maintaining a fiction that he or she then had very little energy left over to cope with the normal ups and downs of early stepfamily life. Therefore, those ups and downs, which were stressful anyway, began to feel very stressful.

An example is some of the data we collected from the Life Events Survey. Respondents were asked to rate several essentially neutral events, such as moving or changing a job. There is nothing inherently negative or stressful about either; both events can be interpreted positively or negatively, depending on the person's perspective. Indeed, moving to a new house usually is a positive experience for a new stepfamily because the move helps to defuse the potentially volatile issue of territoriality. Children, in particular, are less likely to complain about invasions of space because no one in the family has had the time to lay claim to space.

However, people who clung to their unrealistic expectations often rated moving as a minus-two or minus-three event—very painful. They complained about clumsy movers, intrusive real estate agents, and losing old friends. And some people did, indeed, have wearying moves. But more often than not, what made the move a minus-two or -three experience was psychological exhaustion. So much energy was spent denying the palpably self-evident that the move felt like a root canal— minus the anesthetic.

Why do couples stress themselves needlessly by holding on to beliefs they know to be untrue?

They need to dream.

A new stepfamily is more than just a physical entity, a collection of individuals assembled under a common roof. It is a kind of dream—a wonderful, astonishing dream. It is a dream about making a fresh start, of doing it right this time, of correcting old wrongs, of healing a child's hurt, of reestablishing one's identity and sense of self. It is a dream about love and security and pride and respectability. People cling stubbornly to such dreams because these dreams involve so many things that give meaning, purpose, and direction to life.

Equally important, many people in the study were reluctant to acknowledge the troubling—sometimes even embarrassing—emotions stepfamily life can arouse. Jealousy and resentment are not exclusive stepfather emotions; nor are anger and fear. Women in stepfamilies have them too.

At the end of the study, we found that one of two things happened to deniers. Stubborn deniers, usually Romantics, often ended up divorcing. These individuals spent so much energy denying the obvious that the normal difficulties of early stepfamily life began to feel intolerably stressful. Other deniers—usually Neotraditionalists and Matriarchalists—eventually surrendered to reality and began to edit their hopes and dreams more carefully. The man began to admit to feelings of isolation, the woman to feeling caught in the middle sometimes. At a certain point, the men and women in this group realized making the family work was more important than pursuing a fantasy.

Some deniers proved to be very vigorous editors; almost all of their wildly unrealistic expectations were lying on the cutting room floor by the end of cycle 1. Other deniers—usually Romantics—were more reluctant editors. They let go of enough expectations to survive cycle 1, but they still held on to a few. The stepfamily might not feel exactly like a nuclear family now, a Romantic husband or wife would think, but someday it would. During cycle 2, all our families reported less stress and more happiness. But in families where unrealistic expectations persisted, the dip in stress and increase in happiness were relatively modest.

We noticed another phenomenon among Romantic families who clung to a few of their illusions. Often they got stuck. Three, four, five years later, they were still functioning like a new stepfamily in some areas. And while denial was not solely responsible for freezing them in place, it played a major role because it absorbed energy other husbands and wives used to bridge Insider-Outsider differences and to solve the major tasks of stepfamily life: parenting, managing change, dealing with the child's nonresidential parent, and coping with the ghosts of marriages and families past.

LETTING GO

Here's a story Sarah told me at her reinterview:

One night, a few weeks after Aaron returned to New Hampshire, Sarah and Naomi were in Naomi's room lying on her bed when Jeffrey, in an uncharacteristically perky mood, bounced into the bedroom. He smiled elaborately at Sarah and announced that a new barbecue restaurant had near Rice Village. Would she and Naomi like to try it tonight? The three of them could be there in ten minutes.

Sarah said: "Thank you, but I'm in the mood for Chinese tonight."

Jeffrey looked at Naomi and smiled again. "How about you, young lady?" he said in his most appealing voice. "Would you like to join me for some barbecue? We could eat in peace. No lectures from your mother on our bad manners."

Sarah put down the take-out menu. "Naomi was in the mood for Spicy Amazing Chicken," she said. "We were just about to order out. Right, hon?"

Naomi nodded, but her eyes did not leave Tom Cruise, who was also smiling elaborately, but not at her. Tom was telling Larry King how much fun he had making his new movie, *Top Gun*.

"I guess we'll take a rain check," Sarah said. "Another night, maybe."

"Jeffrey seemed fine when he left," Sarah told me at the reinterview. "He asked me to order him some Peking Duck, then went downstairs and read the paper."

But later that night Sarah learned that Jeffrey was not fine. He had a little temper tantrum after Naomi went to bed. He claimed that Sarah and Naomi had ignored him in the bedroom. "He was really upset with Naomi," Sarah said. " 'She didn't look at me once while I was standing there,' he shouted at me. 'It was like I wasn't even there for her, like I don't exist in NaomiWorld.'

"I told him lots of people don't exist in NaomiWorld, including me half the time. Naomi is eight. Eight-year-olds are supposed to be self-absorbed. I also told him not to take Naomi's behavior so personally. I didn't. It was just a stage she was going through."

Sarah began to toy with her wedding ring. She twisted it round and round on her finger for a moment, then looked at me again. "At that point Jeffrey said something so obvious I felt stupid for not landing on it first. He said: 'You have a context for Naomi's behavior, Sarah; you know what she's thinking and feeling. You're her mother. I don't. I don't know what's going on in that little head. All I know is that when someone behaves the way she behaved to me tonight, I feel rejected and humiliated.' "

The timing of this conversation was significant. Sarah and Jeffrey both said that after Aaron's visit their ideas about the Goldsmith family began to change.

The change occurred independently; Jeffrey and Sarah did not consult one another. It was a case of two people traveling on parallel tracks and arriving at the same place at the same time. Jeffrey pulled into the station the morning he put Aaron on the plane to Nashua. Driving home, he said at the reinterview, he realized it might be two or three years before he got his boys back. There was a possibility, a real possibility, that he might never get them back. Sarah and Barbara might, for their own different reasons, block his dream of family reunification.

Sarah pulled into the station the morning after the conversation about Naomi. At the reinterview she told me she woke up very depressed. "First I accuse Aaron unfairly, now Naomi humiliates Jeffrey. I was sure everything was going to come undone. Jeffrey was going to tell himself 'Who needs this?' and walk out."

In retrospect, however, Sarah said, she realized that Jeffrey was not what was depressing her. "In my heart of hearts, I think I knew he would never give up on us. If anything, Jeffrey sort of likes problems, analyzing them."

I told Sarah I had the same impression.

She stopped twisting her ring and put her hands on her lap. "I was depressed because I was working some things through. I was trying to come to terms with two things I definitely did not want to come to terms with: My fantasy of Jeffrey and Naomi falling madly in love with each other was just that, a fantasy. It was not going to happen, at least, not any time soon. I also realized that Barbara and Mark and Aaron were going to be in my life for a long, long time to come."

Sarah smiled ruefully. "Let me tell you, the thought of having Barbara in your life for a long time would depress anyone."

Sarah and Jeffrey's difficulties dealing with Naomi, Aaron, and each other illustrate the "how" of a point I made earlier. Energy depletion is one reason parenting and partnering skills deteriorate in cycle 1. Husbands and wives devote so much emotional energy to defending their expectations, their dreams, that functioning in other areas of family life begins to decline.

Once a couple begins to let go of their unrealistic expectations, as Jeffrey did on the way home from the airport and Sarah did after the talk about Naomi, the regressive downslide usually halts, then reverses itself. Stresses grow more tolerable because more emotional and psychic energy becomes available to deal with them. And feeling less harried and stressed, the man and woman begin to recover old parenting and relationship skills. In a sense, what happens to couples at this point is not too different from what happens to a boat after it has been hit by a big wave. It bobs unsteadily back and forth in the water for a few moments, then gradually regains its equilibrium.

The unusually frank conversation Jeffrey and Sarah had after the incident in Naomi's bedroom is typical of the kind of talks couples have as equilibrium is regained. Jeffrey's willingness to express his feelings about Naomi openly, and Sarah's willingness to listen, indicated that they were now abandoning their illusions and were ready to take the first step toward resolving the differences that divided the Goldsmith family into Insiders and Outsiders.

BRIDGING THE INSIDER-OUTSIDER GAP

The principal bridge across this gap is made up of mutually agreed upon compromises. The couple and the family negotiate back and forth about Insider-Outsider until they come up with solutions that give everyone in the new stepfamily a little of what he or she wants.

The man says, "I feel isolated only seeing your side of the family"; the woman says, "I like my family and you should too." They go back and forth on the issue for three or four or five months, and out of this give-and-take emerges a policy on seeing relatives that pleases both parties.

Our Neotraditionalists were particularly good at bridge building. Two factors in particular accounted for their success in creating "Ours" families. The first was frankness; Neotraditional husbands, wives, and children were not hesitant to speak up about aspects of stepfamily life that displeased them. This may seem surprising at first; expressing complaints in a fragile new stepfamily would seem to be divisive and destabilizing. But the honest ventilation of an aggrieved and sometimes angry perspective turned out to have an important purpose: The frank and honest disclosure of feelings and perceptions served as durable raw material for bridging differences. In order for a compromise to work, it has to incorporate the perspectives of both parties, and it is very hard to do that if one or both parties cannot state his or her perspective clearly and forthrightly.

The observation brings me to the other reason why Neotraditional families were so successful at bridge building. Their frankness was facilitated by six traits:

1. The ability to recognize and express feelings clearly
2. Mapping

3. Conflict resolution
4. The ability to state a complaint in a way that evokes empathy
5. Develop rituals
6. Acceptance

The Ability to Recognize and Express Feelings Clearly

At the start of stepfamily life, couples often engage in a kind of expectations-induced self-censorship. Feelings and perspectives are left unstated because they are embarrassing or troubling, or might lead to a fight. But even after unrealistic expectations begin to be edited out, Insider-Outsider divisions often linger because many couples do not know how to articulate their concerns and perspectives to each other; in other words, they do not know how to complain about the stepfamily in a way that makes it clear why they are unhappy. Without knowing that someone is unhappy, other family members cannot suggest bridge-building compromises and solutions.

A good example of this inarticulateness is the problem many of our participants had in identifying a feeling. "I'm unhappy," a new stepfather might think—but usually he would stop there, instead of thinking his unhappiness through to the point where he could link it to a specific emotion, such as anger, fear, or jealousy.

Other participants knew what they felt but had difficulty explaining why they felt it.

"This is hopeless," a project stepfather said to me one day. "My wife's never going to change. Nothing is ever going to change in this family."

I told the man I sympathized with him. But I also told him that change requires information; his wife needed to know why the stepfamily felt hopeless to him before she could do anything to remedy his complaint. The only thing "This is hopeless" and "I feel angry" (the man's other favorite pronouncement) tell a spouse is that she has had the misfortune to marry a big pain.

Self-aware (and expectation-free) individuals are able to do what

Jeffrey did: Put a label on a feeling (humiliated), then connect the feeling to a specific incident or behavior (because Naomi didn't look at me once). Stated this way, concerns become minibridges; the information they provide can help a mate implement change. Knowing why Jeffrey was upset, Sarah could build one bridge across the perception gap. She could tell Naomi to look at Jeffrey when he talked to her.

Mapping

The purpose of mapping is to identify differences in feelings, perceptions, and values that need to be bridged to transform the Insider-Outsider Families into Our Family. The hallmark of a good mapper is insatiable curiosity. He wants to know how every other member of the family feels about every aspect of stepfamily life. How does life in the family make these members feel: Happy? Sad? Confused? Angry? Lonely? Afraid? What situations and practices in the family trouble them? What behaviors of what family members would they like to see changed? What would make an Outsider feel like an Insider and an Insider stop feeling torn?

When I use mapping in my clinical work—which I do quite frequently with new stepfamilies—I tell the husband and wife that I want them to become reporters. I want each spouse to interview the other about the stepfamily experience. No subject is off-limits; the interviewer can ask the interviewee about anything. The only ground rules are no loaded questions and no generalizations. The interviewer is there to gather information and understanding—not to provoke, not to settle scores. It is also important for the interviewee to observe the no generalization rule in his answers. The only information a statement like "You never listen to me" conveys is global condemnation. Like Jeffrey, the interviewee has to put a specific name on what he is feeling, and he has to tie the feeling to a specific event. He also has to be highly specific about recommendations. A response like "I wish Naomi would be nicer to me" is not as helpful as "I wish Naomi would look at me when I talk to her."

Youngsters also need to be included in the interviewing process; but since seven-, eight-, nine-, and ten-year-olds have even more trouble sorting out feelings than adults do, some assistance from the interviewer will be required. One technique I recommend to parents and stepparents alike is *reflection*.

Children frequently respond to adult queries about stepfamily life with global statements, such as "I hate this stepfamily." Although awful to hear, these blanket condemnations say more about children's cognitive immaturity than they do about their real feelings. Something about the family is obviously troubling the child, but, unable to identify what it is, he or she falls back on an all-purpose word like "hate." Reflection is designed to help children accurately identify a feeling and then accurately identify the reason for it. To illustrate how the technique works, imagine a parent-child dialogue that begins with the statement "I hate this stepfamily."

Instead of asking Why? the parent should respond with a statement that reflects the emotion in the child's statement, for example, the parent may say, "You sound angry." While this may seem like an indirect reply, responses that reflect emotion rather than content force children to examine feelings in a way that they otherwise would not do. "Am I really angry?" a youngster thinks. "No," she decides, she is not angry. She has another feeling. What is it?

Say the child decides that what she really feels is sad. Her reply might be "I feel kind of sad, Mom."

A second parental reflection of emotion such as "Why do you think you feel sad?" will initiate a second wave of self-examination. Now the child begins to think hard about why she is sad.

Children who embark on these kind of parent-initiated self-examinations often end up in unexpected places. A youngster may discover her sadness is about losing her old friends when she changed schools or about her absent biological father or about the new family next door, which reminds her of her family of origin. Reflection not only helps children (who are given an opportunity to ventilate a painful emotion) and the adult interviewers (who can now address the children's real concerns), it also helps the stepfamily by reducing the incidence of disruptive acting out. Temper tantrums become less frequent when children have had an opportunity to talk out their frustration.

The goal of mapping is to identify family hot spots—places where differences in feelings, values, and perceptions promote division and factionalism. And while sometimes working out differences takes months of back-and-forth talk, other times the mapping process itself leads to bridge-building solutions. An example is the way mapping helped the Kendricks, another project family, identify and deal with a very potent family hot spot: stepfather Nelson's decision to attend a PTA meeting at stepson Wesley's school with wife Ann.

"I thought you came with me because you wanted to get involved with Wesley," Ann said when Nelson interviewed her.

"No," Nelson said when Ann interviewed him. "I went because I thought you wanted me to go. I was trying to please you. But I felt awkward. I wasn't sure it was appropriate for me to be there. I've only been a stepdad for four months."

"Nelson was butting in," Wesley complained when Ann interviewed him. "PTA is for real parents. Nelson's not my real dad."

Out of this Rashomon-like brew of conflicting perspectives, the Kendricks were able to devise a strategy for managing the stepfamily task in a way that promoted family harmony. Nelson and Ann decided to table Nelson's appearance at PTA meetings until he and Wesley had developed a closer relationship.

Mapping interviews also serve another useful function. Often they encourage family members to explore the motivation for behaviors that promote Insider-Outsider differences. An example is what Jeffrey learned about himself when Sarah interviewed him about his former wife, Barbara.

"That first year I felt like we were being taken advantage of by Barbara," Sarah told me at the reinterview. "Every time Mark or Aaron was scheduled to come down, Barbara would call and say she needed an extra thousand or two. One night I finally worked up the courage to ask Jeffrey why he always gave in to her. He said, 'I'm just buying my way out of trouble.'

"I told him I didn't believe that. Something else was going on. And I was right, something was."

Money is about many things in stepfamilies. Sometimes it is about reality, about the real hardship of supporting or partly supporting two households from a single paycheck. But sometimes money is also about resentment and punishment—a support payment is withheld to get even with a wife—or about guilt.

Sarah's questions gave Jeffrey an opportunity to reflect about why he, normally prudent and economical, would say yes every time his ex-wife asked for extra money. "I think it's because I feel guilty about leaving the boys," he said.

"I think it's also because you feel guilty about leaving Barbara," Sarah said.

Jeffrey thought about this for a moment, then gave Sarah one of his tight little smiles. "Yes, I suppose you're right," he said. "I do."

This mapping session helped to produce two bridge-building agreements. The Goldsmiths concluded that giving in to Barbara's demands for money was not going to change the way Jeffrey felt about Mark and Aaron and that surrendering to her tactics would only encourage her.

I should add that, unlike the Kendricks, who learned mapping in family therapy, the Goldsmiths discovered mapping on their own. Jeffrey and Sarah, unlike people who are taught the technique in counseling, never sat down and formally interviewed each other. But after the conversation about Naomi, they began to share their feelings and perceptions with one another. I was not fully aware of the sharing until the follow-up interviews. But I was not surprised by it.

Conflict Resolution

Neotraditional couples, our best communicators, had an innate grasp of conflict resolution, which is critical to building bridges across the Insider-Outsider gap.

Recent studies have shown that negative communication—how a couple disagrees—is as important to marital happiness as positive communication. The reason: Disagreements and fights give a husband and wife an opportunity to share thoughts and feelings that, unshared, can lead to future misunderstandings, to ventilate grievances and frustrations that unventilated can lead to destructive acting-out behavior.

Many popular stepparenting books warn their readers that conflict is particularly bad for children. But we found the opposite to be true. Constructive fighting actually benefits children. It shows them how people can resolve their differences with each other in a healthy manner.

However, the reconciling power of an argument wanes when there is no mutuality, when one partner wants to end a fight but the other partner won't let her—when the argument becomes about inflicting punishment instead of resolving differences. This is destructive fighting, and because it exacerbates Insider-Outsider differences, destructive fighting almost always *permanently* subtracts from the sum of marital happiness.

Each sex has characteristic ways of signaling a desire to withdraw. Typical male emotional or physical withdrawal behaviors include whining, defensiveness, and agitated attempts to withdraw. Typical female signals include sadness and fear. Studies show that when these signs are ignored, an argument often spins out of control; the retreating partner turns on her attacker; she lashes out at him—or he at her—and the argument turns into a train wreck.

We rated videotapes of couples discussing areas of disagreement to see how cognizant project subjects were of a mate's withdrawal signals and how they responded. More consistently than other couples, Neotraditionalists heeded "halt" signals. Partners often returned to troubling issues later, but when a Neotraditionalist husband or wife signaled "I want to stop for now," the wish usually was respected.

The capacity to recognize and respect a partner's boundary line served Neotraditional couples well. It allowed them to fight about their differences in a frank and forthright way but also in a way that led to solutions that promoted a sense of mutuality in the marriage and in the family.

At the reinterview, Sarah said that she and Jeffrey usually were able to share their stepfamily experiences without arousing rancor. But one night they did have a huge fight. It began when Sarah put a name on her feeling about the Goldsmiths' wonderful new house.

"I took a deep breath and told Jeffrey that the house felt oppressive to me," Sarah said. She named some other unpleasant feelings that night. One was anger, and she tied it to a specific behavior of Jeffrey's. "I told him that he could be unbelievably controlling. I said 'Jeffrey, you decide where we live, how much money Barbara gets, you decide everything. I just get orders. I get told to take Aaron out for breakfast, how Naomi should behave when she speaks to you, and to change my work schedule around if you decide you need me.' I looked him right in the eye and said: 'Jeffrey, I want more reciprocity in the marriage.' "

Sarah began to laugh.

"You know what he said to me, James? 'You sound like Barbara.' Oh boy, did we have a fight that night; there was blood on the floor by the time we finished. But it was good. We worked out a lot of things."

"You're still here," I said.

Sarah looked puzzled for a moment. "Oh, you mean the house?"

I nodded.

"That's because I ended up loving the house too. Jeffrey told me I could decorate it any way I wanted, and when I finished I was so thrilled with what I did, I never wanted to leave. 'Girl meets house.' James, it's the oldest love story going."

According to Sarah, this conversation produced another behavioral change. "Jeffrey was—he is still—controlling," she said. "The only way

Jeffrey could *not* be controlling is to have a brain transplant. But he leaves me alone about work now. That's what used to get me really crazy. Work is important to me, to my identity. And my clients rely on me. I can't cancel on people because my husband wants me to run errands for him. I told Jeffrey that that night. He understood and accepted this."

The Ability to State a Complaint in a Way That Evokes Empathy

Neotraditional men and women enjoyed one other important advantage in fashioning bridge-building solutions. They knew how to state potentially upsetting concerns and perceptions in a way that evoked a partner's real, true understanding rather than anger and conflict. This capacity is especially important in resolving differences over what is often the most potentially volatile of the stepfamily tasks, parenting.

An example is the way the Goldsmiths resolved what became informally known in the project's offices as the goalie problem. The goalie is the woman, and goalie behavior often becomes a problem in cycle 1 because it interferes with the man's attempt to establish an independent relationship with his new stepchild. Even unobtrusive friendliness—the best strategy for a new stepfather—will not work if a goalie is stationed in front of the child's heart all the time—that is, if the mother constantly interposes herself between the stepfather and the child by answering questions he directs at the child, discourages stepfather-stepchild activities, perpetuates parent-child activities that subtly exclude the outsider—such as eating Chinese food in front of the TV—and ignores the stepfather's suggestions and observations about the child.

It is important to stress that goalie behavior is usually unconscious. The goalie is acting out of an old habit of heart and mind; the woman and child usually have a long history and, in a stepfamily, especially in the early years, history has a habit of repeating itself.

Matriarchal men rarely object to goalie behavior, but Romantic and

Neotraditional men do. Jeffrey told Sarah the biggest problem in his relationship with Naomi wasn't Naomi, it was Sarah. "Sometimes I feel like I'm trying to get in between a pair of Siamese twins," he said one night. But he told me Sarah still couldn't see what she was doing. "She just didn't get it."

Often the hardest thing for a woman to see is the biological force field she and the child create. Project mothers told me time and again that they made it a point to invite a husband into biological parent–child activities. But even when family members were gathered together in front of the television set or at the kitchen table, many project stepfathers said they still felt cut off and isolated. Complained one man: "It's like Eileen [his wife] and Davy [his seven-year-old stepson] have this invisible shield around them. Even when I'm with them, they somehow manage to be with themselves."

The best way to help a woman "see" is to do what Jeffrey did. He evoked a situation where the woman felt the same sense of exclusion and isolation.

"One day," Jeffrey said at the reinterview, "I reminded Sarah of a remark she made to me once after a ball game. We had just dropped Aaron and Mark off, and we were driving home when out of the blue Sarah said: 'No more ball games with the Goldsmith men.' She said she felt like a fifth wheel."

Jeffrey said the remark surprised him. He thought he and the boys had been pretty attentive. But when he mentioned that to Sarah, she smiled and said: "You were all very sweet. But the three of you have a special way of relating to one another, and I feel like I interfere with it; I feel like what the three of you really want is for me to disappear so you can start being yourselves again."

Shortly after this conversation, Jeffrey said, Sarah's goalie behavior began to end; Naomi was allowed to answer his questions by herself, the Chinese-and-TV nights were phased out, and Sarah's hovering decreased. Now she occasionally left the room so Naomi and Jeffrey could be alone together.

And Jeffrey proved very adept at taking care of these opportunities.

Sometimes unobtrusive friendliness alone will draw a child into a stepfather's orbit. But mistrust, indifference, fear of betrayal—a number of factors can make youngsters wary of even a friendly stepfather.

"We—Jeffrey and I—got off to a terrible start," Naomi told me the lovely spring day I interviewed her on the Goldsmiths' patio. "That first six months we had a lot of unpleasant encounters. I suppose most of them were my fault. Like I said, I was very happy with just me and Mom."

Naomi stopped and rearranged herself in her chair. "But Jeffrey wasn't exactly Mr. Rogers either. You know how he gets whenever he thinks his dignity has been insulted."

I told her I didn't, but I could imagine.

Naomi said she began to notice a change in Jeffrey at the end of the first year. "He sort of started to court me. I liked it."

Over the course of the project, we identified three strategies that were particularly effective in winning a child's friendship. These include going on group outings, developing an interest in what the child is interested in, and creating opportunities for one-on-one time. Naomi told me that Jeffrey had used all three.

Going on Group Outings

In the first six months especially, stepchildren often feel awkward in one-on-one activities, even when the activity involves something they normally enjoy, such as watching a baseball game or going to a movie. Instead of thinking: "Oh, good, I want to see this game," the new stepchild is prone to thinking: "Oh, God, three hours alone with my stepfather. What are we going to talk about?" Having another parent and a child along defuses this anxiety. Now, instead of one person, there are three other people to talk to. Also, another parent-child pair can help to ease the self-consciousness that is common in early stepfather-stepchild outings.

Developing an Interest in the Child's Interests

This is an unobtrusive declaration of affection. The stepfather is saying: "I care enough about you to care about what you care about." Additionally, a mutual interest can provide a way to relate to the child. Men especially feel more comfortable when they can relate around an activity or an interest.

In fourth grade, Naomi developed a consuming interest in gymnastics, which Jeffrey seized on to create a bond. He monitored Naomi's lessons and classes, attended meets when she began to compete in the fifth grade, and, in typical Jeffrey fashion, turned himself into an enthusiast. At her reinterview, Naomi told me that Jeffrey was always surprising her with little pieces of arcana about the sport.

Creating Opportunities for One-on-One Time

This strategy has to wait a few months, maybe even a year, but when a mutual comfort level develops, the stepfather and stepchild should begin to do things together, whether it's watching television, going to the movies, or participating in their special interest together. Naomi said her gym meets were such a special Naomi-and-Jeffrey thing that she half resented it when Sarah tagged along. "I was so used to having Jeffrey to myself, I used to get jealous if I had to share him with anyone."

Develop Rituals

Neotraditional couples are successful in bridging the Insider-Outsider gap because they understand the importance of rituals.

A ritual is a form of symbolic communication, and what it confers on a family is a sense of distinctiveness and unity. The most obvious type of ritual is the celebration, a category that includes not only holidays such as Christmas but also rites of passage such as weddings, birthdays, bar mitzvahs, and first communions.

Family members are together almost every day even if they do not—as they do not in some stepfamilies—spend much time interacting. Celebrations provide an opportunity to extend the circle, to gather the larger stepfamily together—the uncles and aunts and grandparents who play a supporting role in the family and in many cases provide it with a support system. In terms of cohesiveness, celebratory gatherings play two important roles. First, the assembled uncles, aunts, and grandparents constitute a living history. They serve to remind a family that despite its newness, it does have a distinctive past. Celebrations also promote cohesiveness in a more subtle way. Among other things, a birthday party or a Christmas dinner guest list is an act of self-definition, a way for a family to define itself to the outside world and to itself, a way to say: "Here is who we are," and "Here are the people—the grandparents and aunts and cousins and perhaps, even the nonresidential children—who belong to our stepfamily."

Family traditions are a second form of cohesion-promoting ritual. A tradition is a form of self-representation. It is a symbolic way for the family to say not "Here is who we are" but "Here is what is unique about us, what makes us different from other families, what makes us special." A tradition can be made out of anything. It can be a vacation spot—a beach house, say—or a star on top of the Christmas tree. It can be the same dumb jokes told over and over again, or who sits where in the car, and who rides with whom.

Project couples were aware of the way family traditions can contribute to family cohesiveness. But as they set out to create a new set of family traditions, many couples fell into one of two traps. The first was artificiality. An event or behavior simply would be declared "a tradition." But the new "tradition" rarely lasted very long because no one, including its inventor, had a emotional attachment to it. What makes a tradition a tradition, what gives it emotional resonance and makes it a unifying symbol, is its history.

The second trap was using first-marriage traditions. While these do have histories, they are not histories everyone in the stepfamily can rally around. Eating Chinese food and watching television together may be a well-established custom to some stepfamily members, but it sends an exclusionary message to other members.

Family-of-origin traditions—things the husband and wife used to do with their parents—provide the best solution to the tradition dilemma. F-O-O-Ts have a history and they also have an emotional resonance. True, at the beginning, only one family member will feel the resonance, but her special emotional connection to the tradition ensures that she will uphold it long enough for other family members to develop a connection to it too.

It is important to blend F-O-O-Ts from both families to make a stepfamily work. Allowing the stepparent to contribute to these is an excellent way to bridge the Insider-Outsider gap.

Patterned interactions, the third type of family ritual, are not as common as they used to be. Who has time to eat together or do chores together—the most common forms of patterned interactions—when Mother gets home at six, Father at seven, and the child's favorite television program starts at eight? However, it would be a mistake to conclude that no one has time for these interactions.

Children often enter a new stepfamily feeling like spiritual orphans. They wonder where they belong now that the family that valued and nurtured them is gone, destroyed by divorce. The sameness, the routine, the reassuring predictability of a patterned interaction can help to quell these doubts and help heal the wounds of divorce. Not immediately, of course. But over time, an activity like a family dinner hour helps to promote a sense of identity and rootedness. Where does the child belong? He belongs right there, at the table, with the people he eats with every night, with the people who nag him about unfinished vegetables, who ask him to pass the salt, who love and value him as much as his old family ever did.

Acceptance

Acceptance is an important point for couples to bear in mind because not every problem that occurs in a stepfamily can be solved. Relationships and people and obligations can change, but there are limits to how much they can or will change.

Jeffrey, for example, would not be Jeffrey without his impulse to control people and situations. It is as much a part of who he is as his Houston drawl. Over time Sarah learned how to curb the impulse—she put her work off-limits to him—and when she could not, how to work around it. But her crack about the "brain transplant" was a tacit acknowledgment that she knew what Jeffrey's limits were. He would always be controlling, and, if she wanted the relationship, she would have to learn to live with that.

One day, while project staff members were discussing the Goldsmiths, the graduate student who scored their questionnaires said, "I don't know how Sarah puts up with him. He's a control freak."

"Jeffrey can be controlling," I acknowledged.

"*Can* be?" the student said indignantly. "I could never live with a man like Jeffrey, *never*."

Life, however, is often more complicated than graduate students realize. In most marriages, there comes a time where one spouse or the other has to make a decision about what is more important, being right or making the relationship work. I say "decision," but people rarely make this kind of choice consciously, particularly people who decide "it's more important to be right." This kind of inflexibility develops subtly, over time. Attachment to a particular idea becomes so strong in every situation, the person can see only two options: "my own way or no way."

THE OURS FAMILY

In my talks to stepfamily groups, I always say that cohesiveness is the most important cycle 1 goal. And in families who let go of their unrealistic expectations and map out the family hot spots, develop rituals, and employ the other techniques I've outlined, often a sense of cohesiveness, of an "Ours Family," begins to replace the Insider-Outsider gap between the eighteenth and twentieth month. This does not mean that everyone in the family will have found a way to love everyone else by the twentieth month—or indeed, that they ever will. Cohesiveness varies tremendously even in successful stepfamilies; however, to succeed, a family does need to have some sense of itself as a family.

POINTS TO KEEP IN MIND

- The Insider-Outsider gap is normal. People from different cultures and with different histories will inevitably see the new stepfamily different ways.
- Accept reality. The first two years of stepfamily life are full of difficult and often unexpected stresses. Clinging to unrealistic expectations makes those stresses worse and interferes with a couple's ability to close the Insider-Outsider gap and turn two families into one.
- Mutually satisfying compromises form the best bridge over the Insider-Outsider gap. The best way to unify the new stepfamily is to create solutions that show everyone, particularly the Outsider, that his voice matters. Often this strategy also deepens the Outsider's investment in the family's success.
- Successful bridge building involves six skills. The skills are identifying and articulating feelings clearly, mapping out family hot spots, fighting constructively, employing empathy to state one's case, creating family rituals, and acceptance.

chapter six

A Stranger in My Own House: The
Part-Time and Full-Time Stepmother

Dale and Leslie Cole moved after the project ended. The Coles used to live in upper-middle-class Memorial, a small, leafy section of Houston where country clubs and expensive cars abound the way pizzerias and McDonald's do in other less affluent areas. But two years ago big, lumbering Dale and angular, intense Leslie decided a rambling ranch house with a circular driveway, leaded windows, and a half-acre of front lawn was too much for two middle-aged empty nesters "who were itching to put a little fun back into their lives."

This is how Dale explains the Coles' move to me as we stand in the living room of the Memorial replacement, a cheery blue and white town house with a panoramic view. From the bay window behind Dale I can see a park, gray on this wet June afternoon, and, in the distance, the shimmering spires of downtown Houston.

Dale tells me he is forty-three now and still a stock broker at Dean

Witter. He is beginning to acquire the thick look of the ex-athlete slipping into comfortable middle age. The broad shoulders and big chest are all that remain of the once-powerful college linebacker's body. Dale's face is as I remember it, though, open and friendly and baby pink.

Leslie Cole is sitting on a white-on-white sectional couch when I arrive in the living room. She is almost as tall as her husband, five eight to Dale's six feet. She's pale, blonde, and poised. Everything in big, lumbering Dale seems to spill outward; everything in the perfectly made-up, impeccably dressed, tightly wound Leslie, inward. She has the crisp, authoritative, self-contained look of a TV anchorwoman or a certain kind of club woman.

Leslie frowns when she looks at Dale's shoeless feet. "Dale, you met Dr. Bray in your socks? You should be ashamed of yourself." Dale smiles a bad-boy grin.

Leslie shakes her head and scolds him. "Gorilla man."

The high-ceilinged living room of the Coles' new home is startlingly bright—everything in the room seems blond or white or some combination of the two. Mementoes and photos of the Coles' two daughters cover every surface. On top of a marble table behind the sofa are a half-dozen photographs of Leslie and daughter Christina in various poses and places. There is a picture of mother and daughter at the beach, taken when Christina was ten; at Disney World with Dale when Christina was fourteen, and at Christina's high school graduation. Christina's father, Wallace Lassiter, is in that picture. In another life, Leslie and Wallace and Dale and his first wife, Annabelle, were part of the same "set" at a country club in Memorial. During an early interview, Leslie told me that the Coles and Lassiters used to see each other all the time at club dances and dinners. "We used to be fairly friendly, the four of us," she said.

Photos of Amanda Cole, Dale's daughter, occupy a bookshelf across from the marble table. Next to a John Grisham thriller, there is picture of Dale and Amanda with Ronald McDonald taken when Amanda was five; a few books later, one of Amanda and Christina with Leslie, taken when Christina was twelve or thirteen; and finally, at the end of the shelf, Amanda alone in high school cap and gown.

"She's at Carleton College now," Dale says when he sees me looking at the graduation picture. "It's in Minnesota. It's a first-rate college. According to *U.S. News & World Report,* thirty-third in the country."

"I remember Amanda as a very good student," I say.

"Amanda was in all the gifted classes in high school," Dale declares.

"Christina also is doing quite well," Leslie interjects. "She's at UT Austin now. She's doing wonderfully well."

"I remember her as being a very good student too," I say.

Leslie qualifies my compliment slightly. "Christina always had to work a little harder. But she was willing, she always made an extra effort. Christina is a disciplined child, more disciplined than Amanda, I think." Leslie turns and looks at her husband, who has seated himself next to her on the sofa. "Don't you, Dale?"

THE PROJECT AND THE
PART-TIME STEPMOTHER

In the project we devoted a great deal of time, effort, and manpower to the study of the stepparent role. But our goal was to study the full-time stepparent. And since our study group of one hundred stepfamilies consisted entirely of stepfather families, that meant the stepparent role we studied in a scientific sense was the stepfather's. But 50 percent of project men had one or more children from a previous marriage. In interviews, project women often talked about the experience of being a part-time stepmother two or three weekends a month. Thus, informally, we also learned a great deal about stepmothering.

Many of the things project women told us about the role paralleled the things their husbands were telling us about the stepfathering. Women complained about poor role definition. What exactly did a part-time stepmother do? They complained about feeling isolated by the father-child biological force field, about rude and ungrateful stepchildren, about former spouses who were "poisoning" a child against them, and about the weekend visitors who brought havoc into their own well-disciplined homes.

Biology and socialization combine to make parenting a high priority for women. Thus often stepmother complaints contained an element of self-reproach that was missing from stepfather complaints. If there were problems in a stepmother-stepchild relationship, women were likely to blame themselves first. (Husbands and husbands' former spouses were criticized generously too.) Men, on the other hand, tended to blame everyone but themselves.

For a while, we did not hear any typical stepmother complaints from Leslie. At the Coles' intake interview, she described her relationship with stepdaughter Amanda as "very good"; Leslie also said that she expected the relationship to remain very good. She had some legitimate reason for optimism. Most stepmothers and stepchildren start out as strangers. Leslie and Amanda started out if not as friends, then as acquaintances. The two met for the first time when Amanda was three. Amanda does not remember the meeting, of course, but Leslie does. She remembers that the year before her marriage ended, the year before Wallace Lassiter walked out on her, saying he was bored, Leslie got a call from Annabelle Cole. Annabelle was planning a big party for Amanda's third birthday. Would Leslie and Christina like to come?

Leslie says her view of her stepdaughter's character as "sensitive and high-strung and sometimes difficult" did not develop until much later, until she and Dale had been married "for years and years." But I think most of the things Leslie came to think about Amanda were linked to something that happened at that birthday party.

In posh Memorial, birthday parties are pageants of affluence. Caterers, clowns, brightly colored lawn tents, and Japanese lanterns are as integral to party throwing as laughing children and cookies, cakes, and ice cream. The clown Annabelle hired for Amanda's party, a school bus driver named Harriet Woods, was a large, burly woman with pug dog jowls and a Cat-in-the-Hat tower of woolly, unkempt hair. Depending on your age and knowledge of Harriet, Harriet in a clown outfit is either funny in the way that *Seinfeld* is—absurd, surrealistically funny—or she is a garish, brightly colored, frightening monster.

Three-year-old Amanda thought she was a monster. "I think the clown makeup scared her," Leslie said when she told me about the party. "I think Amanda couldn't figure out who this person was supposed to be, and Amanda is such a high-strung child. Poor thing, she just flew off the handle. She cried so hard, Annabelle had to take her upstairs."

Leslie and Amanda renewed their acquaintance three years later. Dale, then divorced and living alone, thought a woman's companionship would brighten weekend visits for Amanda. But what woman? Dale immediately eliminated all the women he was dating. That kind of woman might confuse and threaten his daughter, and even if she did not, the girl might get the wrong idea. "Her mother was telling her that I left the family for another woman," Dale told me during an early interview. "I didn't, but I didn't want to feed into anything Amanda was being told at home about me."

Leslie provided Dale with a way out. She had the perfect résumé for a "safe" female companion. Amanda knew her already, Leslie had a daughter the same age, and, of course, she was divorced. The four of them ought to start getting together, Dale said one night when he ran into Leslie at a restaurant at the Galleria. "I think the girls would like it; it would give them companionship. We could go to the movies and stuff."

Leslie liked the idea. She was as worried about Christina having male companionship as Dale was about Amanda having female companionship. And Dale was a nice man, Leslie thought: easygoing, charming, and slyly funny. Christina and Amanda also got along well. Leslie called Dale a few days after the restaurant encounter and arranged the first of what turned out to be dozens of outings.

One thing that often distinguishes part-time from full-time stepmothers is that their expectations about the stepmother-stepchild relationship are pretty realistic, so Leslie's expectations vis-à-vis Amanda were pretty clear-sighted. Short, plucky, plodding, practical Christina was her daughter; willowy, blond, "sensitive," ethereal Amanda was Dale's—Dale's and Annabelle's; Leslie's ambitions with Amanda stopped at friendship. Maybe she, Leslie, could be a wise, helpful friend to Amanda, and during the outings that's how Amanda seemed to regard her.

Leslie had good reason to feel confident that marriage would not change the relationship. Amanda, along with Christina, had encouraged the romance with Dale—more than encouraged it, in fact. Amanda played matchmaker to Leslie and Dale the way Hayley Mills used to play matchmaker to shy mothers and fathers in Disney movies of a certain period. One day about five months after the Cole-Lassiter get-togethers began, Dale read a notice in a local paper. An old steam engine with four Pullman cars and a caboose in tow was passing through Houston two weeks hence en route to its final resting place in a New Orleans technology museum. The notice said the train would be open to the public on a first-come, first-served basis. Passengers could board in Houston and ride free to any destination en route to New Orleans.

Dale's original plan was to go only as far as Beaumont, ninety miles east of Houston. From there the Coles and Lassiters would take a bus home in the late afternoon. But the train was so much fun, Dale and Leslie decided to let the girls ride all the way to Lake Charles over the Louisiana border.

"It was already dark when we got off," Dale said when he told me about the train ride. "So I thought, 'Why don't we get a couple of hotel rooms and go back in the morning?' "

But in the hotel lobby, the girls announced that they wanted a room of their own. "I told Amanda, 'I'm not going to pay for three rooms,' " Dale said. " 'That's a waste of good money.' Amanda said I didn't have to. Leslie and I could share a room. At that point Christina chimed in. She said, 'We don't mind. But we're going to make you guys leave the door open. We don't want any misbehaving.' "

"It was like the girls were telling us they wanted us to be more than friends," Leslie said.

But a year later Amanda began to act as if she were having second thoughts about that. One night newlyweds Dale and Leslie were walking out of a movie hand in hand when Amanda suddenly thrust herself in between them, seized Dale's hand, and led him away as if he were an errant child.

"Dale seem embarrassed by Amanda's behavior, so I made a little joke of it," Leslie said when she told me about this incident. "I said, 'I think someone I know is jealous for her daddy.' James, you should have seen the expression on that child's face when she turned around and looked at me. It was pure venom."

THE PART-TIME
STEPMOTHER—STEPCHILD RELATIONSHIP

Within a few months of the incident in the theater lobby, Amanda's venom began to take a concrete form; it materialized as two problems that are often big issues for part-time stepchildren. The first was whose rules would govern Amanda's behavior during visits: the Coles' rules or the more lenient rules Amanda lived under at home with her mother, Annabelle?

The first place this became an issue was the dinner table. Leslie believed a child should not be allowed to leave the dinner table unless and until her plate was clean. But Amanda almost never finished her meals. She would eat half of everything on the plate, then ask to be excused. At home, permission was always granted; at the Coles' it was not. Exercising her stepmother's authority, Leslie would say, "No, Amanda, you have to finish your meal first." Amanda would comply but she would fall into such a terrible sulk that a pall would fall over the dinner table.

Leslie also had rules about TV viewing. One governed *Married with Children,* which was declared off-limits to everyone in the Cole household. This also upset Amanda, who was allowed to watch anything she wanted at home; she could not understand why a rule that applied in her mother's house should not also apply in her father's house.

How should a part-time stepmother deal with the rules issue? Most stepfamily authorities believe that regular visitors should be governed by the stepfamily's rules; infrequent visitors, for example, children who see a parent only for a month or two each year, by vacation-time rules.

I agree that if children are allowed to eat dinner in front of the television set at home, they should be allowed to do the same in the stepfamily's home. But I think this rule should apply to frequent as well as infrequent visitors. The reason goes back to a lesson I learned early in the project and have been reminded of many times since in my clinical practice: A very rigid part-time stepmother and a part-time biological father can begin to seem like villains to a part-time step-daughter or stepson.

Children are not just any visitors. They bring a complex blend of desire and wariness to a family that is not their own but that contains a parent who is theirs. The children want to be loved and accepted, but their fragile, divorce-shaped psyches are acutely attuned to any and all possible slights and injustices, an attunement that affects the way children hear things. Thus where another child might hear only inconvenience in a request like "Can you help out with the dishes?" the wary visitor may hear dislike. "They want me to do the dishes because they don't like me." She may even hear rejection. Doing the dishes is a way of "getting rid" of her.

I believe the best way to resolve rule conflicts between the stepfamily and frequent visitors is through negotiation, negotiation that gives frequent visitors some of the things they want but not all of them. Explanations also help. Children, particularly adolescent children, are more likely to obey willingly when the rationale behind the rules is explained to them.

For example, a good compromise for a rule conflict about eating—in front of the television as at home or at the dinner table as stepfamily rules require—would be an every-other-meal policy. During one meal the child would follow the stepfamily's rules about eating, during the next, home rules. The children in the stepfamily would have to be included in such a compromise; at every other meal they would have to be allowed to eat in front of the television set too. I know some parents and stepparents worry about the domino effect when a rule is relaxed—let children eat in front of the television set and they will never want to eat at the dinner table again. But I do not think the domino effect theory explains family behavior any better than it once explained geopolitics. In the nine years of the project's existence, I did not come across any empirical evidence to support the view that a temporary suspension of the rules produces permanent "ruin" or "spoiling" in a child.

Disputes about TV viewing can be resolved by way of negotiation and compromise, unless—and this is a very important "unless"—the dispute is really about cultural values rather than viewing habits. Value differences were a major problem for project families. Several of the native Texans in our study were married to snowbirds from the North, who often had different ideas about how children should dress, behave, and what television programs they should be allowed to watch. We also had a number of "mixed marriages" among native Houstonians. The city has a large cosmopolitan population of academics, medical researchers, and financial executives; it also has a large population of conservative Christians. Occasionally people from the two groups intermarried. The Coles were in such a mixed marriage.

Dale and Leslie came from similar backgrounds; they were both brought up in rural, deeply religious households. But twenty years of big-city life had changed Dale's ideas about a lot of things, including what was appropriate viewing for a child. Leslie, however, was more resistant to the effects of big-city life. She retained the traditional conservative Christian values of her youth, and according to those values, *Married with Children* was crude, vulgar, and sexually explicit.

I thought that the Coles solved their disagreement about *Married* rather skillfully. At the next interview, Dale told me that after a fairly heated discussion, he agreed to support Leslie's ban on the television show. He also said that when he presented the decision to Amanda, he was careful to present it as a reflection of stepfamily rules.

I thought this method rather skillful for two reasons. First, Dale and Leslie confined the decision-making process to themselves—value conflicts are too complex to involve a child in. Secondly, presenting the ban as a by-product of stepfamily rules took the blame off Amanda's mother. It made Amanda think, "that's how my dad and my stepmother do things in their family," not "my dad and my stepmother think my mother is a bad person." A youngster who believes the latter is also likely to think, "my dad and my stepmother think I'm a bad person," as children often equate parental criticism with criticism of themselves.

The Coles also did something else that was smart; they compensated Amanda for her loss. Children adjust more readily to defeats in the values court if they receive a quid pro quo. In Amanda's case, the quid pro quo was the right to stay up a half hour later than had been previously decided.

The Possessive Child

Some part-time stepmothers were happy when a visiting stepchild tried to monopolize all of "Dad's" time. It meant that they would be able to relax on the weekend instead of having to play baby-sitter to a husband's child. But other part-time stepmothers, Leslie among them, felt hurt and annoyed at being ignored. Leslie did not mind her stepdaughter wanting to have her dad to herself; it was the degree of Amanda's possessiveness that bothered her. Very early on Amanda made it clear that her sole purpose in coming to the Coles' was to be with her dad. While she usually would spend a little time with her part-time stepsister, Christina, when Amanda was with Dale she did not want anyone else to be with him. While Leslie sort of minded being excluded from movie and restaurant dates, she could live with those exclusions. "I'd like to tag along more," Leslie told me one day. "But I can understand that Amanda would like to be alone with her daddy."

However, what Leslie did mind very much was being excluded in her own home. "Sometimes Amanda acts like she owns him," Leslie said. "Like she's got a copyright on him or something. When she's here she's always pulling Dale into the living room or the backyard for little father-daughter talks."

Leslie stiffened in her chair. "Frankly, I wonder what the child is telling Dale. Why can't Amanda say what she has to say in front of me? I find that a puzzlement."

Possessiveness usually upsets a stepmother for one of two reasons.

The first is linked to maternal insecurity. Stepmothers who do not have children of their own and are insecure about their own parenting skills sometimes misinterpret possessiveness as a form of rejection. The youngster clings to the father not because she loves and misses him but because she does not like or want to spend time with the stepmother. Often a second misinterpretation follows the first. The woman thinks, "Why should my stepchild want to spend time with me? I'm not a very good mother, anyway."

In these cases, it is essential to clarify the reason for the child's possessiveness. A very sensitive mate can help explain it. But men are sometimes slow to pick up on signals of maternal insecurity, and often, when they do, their response is perfunctory. The woman gets a pep talk, a pat on the back, and the issue is forgotten.

Stepfamily support groups are a better antidote to parental insecurity. Group members not only provide insight into stepchild behavior, they also can help with a problem that often goes hand in glove with maternal insecurity: the expectation for instant love. Women who do not have children of their own often assume that parent-child love, whether step or biological, just happens. Stepmothers with some experience of stepfamily life know it does not. Their advice and counsel can help a new stepmother create more realistic goals for herself.

Also helpful is taking note of the stepchild's special interests and using those interests the way Jeffrey Goldsmith did—as a way to bond with the child. Many of the relationship techniques that work for stepfathers also work for stepmothers.

Possessiveness troubles women like Leslie Cole, women with children of their own (and who are secure in their parenting skills), for a very different reason. They find the stepchild's possessiveness threatening. In some cases the youngster is seen as a direct threat to the woman and to the marriage. Desirous of stealing Daddy back, the youngster tries to cut out the stepmother. Much more commonly, though, it is the man's former wife who is seen as the threat. The child is viewed as a kind of Trojan horse, who is sent into the stepfamily to woo the man back to his *real* family, which she does during all those hours she spends alone with her dad. Most of Leslie's complaints about Amanda's behavior sprang from this fear, although in Leslie's case, the fear was mixed with guilt.

About eight months after the Coles' marriage, Leslie's worst nightmare about Annabelle came true. She ran into her former friend in a suburban mall. It was more of a confrontation than anything else. Leslie thinks Annabelle saw her in the crowd and followed her into an Abercrombie and Fitch outlet. As Leslie was rummaging through a pile of jeans on a display table, she sensed someone watching her. When she looked up, a red-eyed Annabelle was standing on the other side of the table, trembling, the ghost of marriages past hovering unsteadily over a stack of Levi's 501 jeans.

"I didn't know whether Annabelle was going to kill me or faint on to the table," Leslie said when she described the encounter to me. "I have never seen an individual aquiver like that."

"Did you say anything to her?" I asked.

Leslie shook her head. "I tried to, but Annabelle cut me off. She hissed, 'Leslie Lassiter, you could have married any man in the world, but you had to marry my man.' At that moment, a salesgirl appeared and asked Annabelle, 'Can I help you?' I'm sure the girl thought Annabelle was going to take out a gun and shoot me. I am sure everyone in the store thought it. Annabelle is a very loud hisser, James."

Leslie paused. "I have no doubt Amanda hears terrible things about me at home. I'm sure Annabelle fills her little head with vicious lies.

And I'm sure Amanda repeats every single thing she hears about me to her daddy."

Most complaints about possessiveness are really expressions of fear about being undercut. In these cases, reassurance usually will resolve the issue. In the Coles' case, the wife should be reassured that (1) he and the child do not talk about her when they are alone, and (2) that the husband will correct any misapprehensions the child might have about her stepmother. It is also a good idea to repeat these reassurances periodically to let the woman know her concerns are a concern to her husband.

One thing a man should not do to reassure a wife is deny when he does talk to his child about her. Most men view denial as a form of protection. Often father-child conversations about a stepmother are corrective in nature. The child has a negative perception about the stepmother that the man wants to correct. But when the wife asks, "Were you two talking about me?" afraid of upsetting her, the man says no. The danger to this seemingly benign withholding of information is that if the woman discovers—as stepmothers often do—that her husband and stepchild are in fact talking about her, she is going to perceive her husband's denials not as an attempt to protect her but as lying.

I was pretty sure Leslie would let her stepdaughter have as much of Dale as she wanted if she knew she was not being undermined in father-daughter conversations. I was right. In a later interview Dale told me that Amanda's visits were going much better.

However, Leslie and Amanda never really became close in the way Dale and Leslie's daughter, Christina, eventually did. When I interviewed the Coles for this book, both agreed that Dale and Christina developed a better relationship. "We were just too different as people," Leslie said. "It's hard to connect on a deep level with someone who isn't the same as you."

I think Leslie's analysis contains some truth. She and her stepdaughter were and are very different. Leslie, like Christina, is concrete, emphatic, down-to-earth; Amanda is airy and ethereal. But I also believe that something more than just personality differences kept Leslie and her stepdaughter apart.

Amanda was prettier than Christina, and things came easier to her—not just in school, but socially too. Amanda was part of the "in" crowd at every school she attended, and as she grew older, she was very popular with boys. Christina had plenty of friends and plenty of dates, when she was old enough to date, but socially she operated on a different level. These differences never affected the girls' relationship with each other; over the years they became very close. But Amanda's "golden girlness" did affect Leslie. On some level I think she felt jealous of her stepdaughter's success. While Leslie did a relatively good job of controlling her jealousy and occasional resentment, I think Amanda sensed how her stepmother felt.

I did not encounter many other cases of jealousy among project families, but I see the problem fairly frequently in clinical practice. Not surprisingly, it tends to occur in families like the Coles, where the spouses' children are the same age or close to it and where there is a notable achievement gap between one child and the other.

The first thing I tell stepparents who become jealous is: "Don't be embarrassed by it." As I noted earlier, stepfamily life sometimes produces undesirable feelings. As long as the jealousy is kept under control—as long as it does not produce cutting or sarcastic remarks—it will do no one harm.

Moreover, there is an antidote to it. Every child has unique strengths and talents. Parents who focus on the things that make their child special often find the jealousy oozing away. Further, often the stepparent then is able to enjoy the stepchild's achievements as well.

Another technique that helps alleviate jealousy and also aids the stepsibling relationship is suggesting trade-off tutorials. The stepsibling whose special strength is athletics can provide tutoring in sports to the stepsibling whose special strength is academics, and in return the scholar can tutor the athlete in academics.

DEFINING THE PART-TIME
STEPMOTHER'S ROLE

Several project couples met in unusual ways, but I think the most unusual first meeting in our group was that of Earl and Nadine Archer, who met at an amateur Elvis Night at a Houston club. Earl, who has sad, hound-dog eyes and a slight paunch, was the fourth contestant of the evening, and when he walked onto the stage Nadine remembers smiling to herself. Never had she seen a King who looked so unroyally woebegone. Even in his white jumpsuit and glistening black pompadour, Earl looked like a lost little boy. But there was something sweet about him too—forlorn maybe, but sweet. Underneath the sad eyes, Earl had a shy, vulnerable smile that made you want to take him in your arms and hug him.

Earl's first impression of Nadine was visceral. After the show he was talking to a friend in the club bar when the friend turned suddenly and looked across the room. Earl noticed that the two men at the next table also were looking in that direction. Curious, Earl put his drink down and turned around. A tall blonde was standing in the doorway. She had a tough/pretty Ellen Barkin face and a figure so spectacular that Earl was glad he had thought to put his drink down first. Ten minutes later Earl was sitting at a table with the woman and her friend.

Earl liked Nadine's voice immediately; it was sandpapery with a slight South Texas twang underneath. He also liked her direct, plain-spoken manner, her throaty laugh, and of course, her spectacular figure. Earl told me later that he was already a little in love with Nadine when he left the club that night.

I met Nadine three years later when she visited the project office to enroll the Archers in our study. Three weeks later she introduced me to Earl in the living room of the Archers' modest two-story house in the Channelview section of Houston. I left that first meeting—an intake interview—confident that the strong-willed, competent Nadine would form a Matriarchal stepfamily with Earl (and her son, David). Sad-eyed Earl struck me as someone who would be happy to be taken care of.

Matriarchal women are not only good mothers but frequently good stepmothers too. The principal reason is that they are good at doing single-handed what should really be a joint task—defining the stepmother's role. While this role often evolves with time and circumstance and the feelings that do or do not take hold between stepmother and child, the woman needs some general guidelines to start with. So at the beginning of stepfamily life, there should be a candid exchange of views on this role. The man is the biological parent: What part does he see the woman playing in his children's lives on weekend visits or on vacations with the stepfamily? How much authority is he willing to cede her? Is the woman comfortable with the role the husband wants her to play and the authority he is willing to grant her? In project families where the stepmother's behavior became an issue later, it was almost always because the couple did not have this discussion until too late—until the woman did something that made the man feel that she had overstepped her authority or was ignoring his children.

In fairness, it was usually the man who avoided the definition conversation. Most often he avoided it because, like most men, he had a childlike belief in the existence of the "mommy gene." Many men believe that all women possess a special gene that automatically tells them what to do in every situation involving a child. Given the fabulous properties of the mommy gene, many men see no need for a parenting conversation. The mommy gene will tell the woman everything she needs to know to be a stepmother.

"But I thought you knew" was what a project man usually said when a project woman under- or overplayed the stepmother's role. But there is no way for a woman to know how to be a good stepmother unless the biological parent offers his view on how the role should be played.

I think the reason Matriarchal women usually were successful in defining the stepmother role by themselves is that they have an unusual child sense—an ability to sense what a child is thinking and feeling on a wide range of issues, including how much authority a child will accept from a part-time stepmother. However, Matriarchal women, like other project women, occasionally did make stepmothering missteps—and about a year after the Archers joined the project, Nadine made a fairly sizable one.

CHILD DUMPING

The term "child dumping" means being given *sole* responsibility for the visiting child, and it was the most common complaint of our part-time stepmothers. However, dumping is also a very sensitive issue with the potential to trigger a lot of other sensitive issues, so it has to be handled with great care—as Nadine learned through hard experience.

In the early years of the Archer stepfamily, Earl's children, eight-year-old Wendy and eleven-year-old Custer, usually saw their father two weekends each month. I say "saw" rather than "visited" because "saw" more accurately describes Earl's paternal behavior (and that of a sizeable minority of other project men) during visits. On Saturday mornings he would bring his children into the playroom and interrogate them for a half hour about their week. ("Hey, kids, how did your week go?") After the interrogation, Wendy and Custer would be deposited in front of the Saturday morning cartoons. Nadine, in the kitchen, would be paid a visit and get a promise: "I'll call you later, hon." Then the front door would open and Earl would vanish. At five, after a day of softball or bowling, he would reappear, engage Wendy and Custer in another round of questioning ("Hey, kids, how did your day go?"), then disappear upstairs to prepare for his Saturday night date with Nadine.

On Sunday, after another round of softball and bowling, Earl would drop the kids off, return home, take a beer out of the refrigerator, put ESPN on the kitchen TV, throw his feet up on the table, smile the smile of the self-righteous, and say to Nadine: "Wasn't it great having the kids this weekend, honey?"

Most part-time stepmothers had two reactions to behavior like Earl's, but the two reactions were connected by one overarching emotion: annoyance—often profound annoyance. In some cases, this arose from a feeling of being taken advantage of. Women who felt this way did not mind helping out during weekend visits. They were happy to prepare meals for stepchildren and do things with them, but they had their own children to look after. Besides, for the 90 percent of working mothers in our study, Saturday was a down day; many of our mothers resented having to spend the day playing full-time baby-sitter, particularly since the person they were baby-sitting for usually was off somewhere playing with his friends.

The women in this group opposed dumping for a second reason. They believed it was harmful to the stepchild. And they were right. "Dumping" a child who only visits twice a month tells him or her "you are not important to me" and reinforces his or her sense of loss about the divorce.

Another group of women did not mind baby-sitting, but they did mind not being asked if they minded. "Whatever Larry wants, Larry gets. That's life, according to Larry," erupted part-time stepmother Mindy Rooney one afternoon in the middle of a conversation about something else.

"You sound angry, Mindy," I said, a little startled. I had no idea what she was angry about, except that it obviously had something to do with husband Larry.

Mindy shook her head and said I was wrong. She was not angry, she was hurt, very hurt. Then she poured me another glass of ice tea and explained why.

The previous Saturday, Larry had marched four-year-old Will Rooney into the kitchen, pointed at Mindy, who was stacking dishes in the dishwasher, and said: "Mindy's a nice stepmother, Will. She's going to take you to see *The Lion King* this afternoon."

"I thought you said you were going to take me, Daddy," a puzzled Will said; then he burst into tears.

Larry bent down and hugged his son. "I know, Will, but I can't. I want to but I can't."

"Why can't you?" Mindy asked. "You promised him you would."

"Something's come up," Larry said.

"What? What's come up?" Mindy demanded.

Larry shook his head and said, "Not now, Mindy. Not in front of Will. I'll tell you later."

The information too delicate for Will to hear concerned a spare ticket to a Houston Oilers game. A friend had called Larry that morning to say he had one. The ticket belonged to a friend of the friend's, who had come down with the flu; Larry could have the ticket for free.

Mindy said taking Will to *The Lion King* did not upset her. On the contrary, she enjoyed spending time with her stepson. "He was a little dear." It was Will's father who upset her. Mindy said she resented the way Larry had just thrust Will and the movie on her without warning or consultation, without even troubling to ask if she had any plans. "In Larry's mind, selfish behavior never has any consequences," Mindy said. "But in the real world, it does. It hurts people. It hurts Will and it hurts me."

While we did not collect data, my anecdotal impression is that most men responded to complaints of child dumping by ceasing to see their biological children. It didn't happen immediately, nor would one or two complaints drive them to abandonment. But when complaints were chronic, over time the man would begin to see his children less and less, until finally—usually within a year or two—he would stop seeing them completely.

This is not an argument for accepting the practice. But I do think that in many cases, dumping complaints lead to child abandonment because the man misunderstands what his wife is complaining about. He thinks he is being told that his children are annoying, when in fact what his wife is trying to tell him is that *his* behavior is annoying. Thus in homes where dumping is or becomes an issue, clarity is vital. The woman has to make it absolutely clear what she is objecting to, and the man needs to listen carefully to what his wife is saying.

A woman who feels too overburdened to play full-time baby-sitter on weekends should make it clear to her husband that while she cannot handle his children and hers, she thinks it is important for him to live up to his parenting obligation; she also should tell him that she supports him in that role. Clarity is also important for a woman like Mindy Rooney, who enjoys spending a lot of time with her stepchild. This stepmother should make it plain to her partner that while she is happy to play full-time baby-sitter, she expects to be asked beforehand for her help and to be thanked and valued for it.

What a stepmother should *not* do is try to actively intercede between her stepchildren and their father. This was Nadine's misstep, and it is a very easy one to make because when children feel neglected, often they will do what Custer and Wendy Archer did—complain to their stepmother.

One Saturday afternoon, while Nadine was in the backyard sunbathing, a sad-eyed Custer approached her and said he "wished Dad would stick around more on Saturdays. It's kind of lonely when he's not here."

"Do you want me to speak to him?" Nadine asked.

"Would you?" Custer said. "I would like that."

It is perfectly appropriate for a stepmother to act as a spokeswoman for her neglected stepchildren. Often she can present their case more articulately and forcefully than they can. But her involvement should be limited to representation. The stepmother should tell her husband how his children feel about his absences, then leave it for the man and the children to resolve the problem. Nadine's misstep was going beyond representation. She started to nag Earl; she told him he was being neglectful and hurtful to his children.

In our experience, this strategy usually backfires. After a while the content of the woman's message gets lost. All the man hears is nagging—and since nagging is annoying, the man gets angry. He tells the woman to mind her own business, to stop bothering him. If the complaints persist, a triangle usually develops. On one side is the unhappy husband, on the other, his unhappy children, and in the middle, unhappiest of all, is the stepmother.

Matriarchal men react particularly sharply to persistent complaints of child neglect. Their laid-back, undemanding style is posited on the belief that the benefits of family life can be enjoyed with a minimum of entangling and onerous family responsibilities. In the face of stepmother interventions—always perceived as threatening to this belief—the Matriarchal man can either shed his easygoing manner and lash back, or he can attempt to remove the source of the problem. In Earl's case, he stopped seeing Wendy and Custer.

Matriarchal women may, like other stepmothers, make an occasional misstep, but they are also ingenious about fixing mistakes. Take the gathering that greeted Earl in the Archers' living room one evening about two months after he stopped seeing his children. His daughter, Wendy, was there, as was his son, Custer, and sitting side by side on the couch, the two Mrs. Archers, Nadine and Earl's first wife, Beverly.

Over the years the two women had developed a pretty good working relationship. Often when Matriarchal Nadine, who was unofficially in charge of family scheduling, would call to arrange a Saturday morning pickup for Earl, she and Beverly would chat for a few minutes.

"I know you care about the kids too," Beverly said during the phone call that led to the confrontation in the Archers' living room. "They're real upset. They haven't heard from their dad in seven weeks. What's going on with Earl?"

Nadine said she thought Earl felt guilty about not spending enough time with Custer and Wendy, and, in typical Earl fashion, he was dealing with his guilt by avoiding the children entirely.

"Custer's so upset, he cries himself to sleep every night," Beverly said. "He misses his daddy so. I am sorry, Nadine, I know Earl is your husband now, but I would like to give that man a piece of my mind."

Nadine said she thought Earl deserved a piece of somebody's mind. "Why don't you and the kids come over next Monday night and talk to him?" she said.

However, this time Nadine did not make the mistake of putting herself in the middle. She told Earl why Beverly, Custer, and Wendy were at the house—"They have something they wanted to say to you"—then excused herself.

The following week Earl's weekend visits resumed. I cannot report that every weekend thereafter was full of rich, rewarding father-child interactions, but Earl did begin to make a real effort to be with his children when he was supposed to be with them.

WHEN A PART-TIME STEPCHILD
BECOMES A FULL-TIME STEPCHILD

In the late 1980s, Arlington and Nancy Weaver, and daughter Winnie, lived near the Archers. The Weavers' modest one-story brick house was only a few blocks from Nadine and Earl's modest two-story brick house. But after the project ended, the Weavers, like the Coles, moved. When I called Nancy to arrange a follow-up interview, she said the family now lived in Pasadena, another Houston suburb.

I could not remember my last conversation with Arlington, but I still recall my last talk with Nancy very vividly.

It was in December of 1991, a few weeks before Christmas. As soon as I was seated at the kitchen table, Nancy announced that she had something she wanted to show me, then excused herself. There was a frayed newspaper clipping in her hand when she reappeared a few minutes later.

Nancy looked around. "I thought I heard the front door," she said. "Did Arlington come home?"

The question puzzled me. The first thing Nancy told me when she greeted me at the door was that Arlington would not be joining us today. He was taking his son, Lane, to the Summit. The circus was in town.

"You heard the dog," I said. "He knocked over Winnie's bike when he leaped up to greet me."

"I don't know how Arlington would feel about me showing you this," Nancy explained, then she handed me the clipping.

It was dated March 14, 1985, and under the headline HUSBAND AR-RESTED IN ASSAULT was a photo of a long-haired man with a massive face, bushy beard, and a brawny pair of shoulders. The man was being escorted to a patrol car by two police officers. The photo was grainy, but I recognized him immediately. It was Nancy's ex-husband, David.

I looked up.

"Read it," Nancy insisted.

The article said that a David Cartwright had assaulted a Mr. Arlington Weaver outside his apartment building the previous evening. Mr. Cartwright claimed he had visited Mr. Weaver's apartment looking for his wife, Nancy. Mr. Cartwright told the arresting officers that Mr. Weaver was having an affair with his wife.

"Surprised?" Nancy said.

I was, but I decided not to admit it. "At the article?"

Nancy shook her head. "No. At Arlington and me. That we could have started out so messily and ended up so happily."

I had wondered why Nancy wanted to show me the clipping. Now I understood. It was an act of self-justification. If the Weavers' success as a stepfamily (like the Coles and Goldsmiths, they were in our Neotraditional group) did not completely atone for the events that led to the night of March 14, 1984, in Nancy's mind it justified them. The affair may have been unfortunate—more than unfortunate; but it had produced a good marriage and a happy family.

I wondered how the Weavers' marriage and family were faring now, in the late winter of 1997. On the phone, Nancy said that there had been a big change recently; three weeks ago Arlington's son, Lane, now thirteen, had moved in with them.

Twenty of the one hundred stepfamilies in our study had a similar experience. At one point or another the husband's child moved in with the stepfamily full time, thereby transforming the woman from a part-time to a full-time stepmother. The most frequent movers were boys in Lane's age group, early adolescence: twelve, thirteen, or fourteen. The success rate for moves was about 50 percent. Half of the stepfamilies thrived after a move, while half developed problems. One factor that determined the success of a move was the family's stage of development. Established stepfamilies often absorbed new members more easily. But new families, engaged in the principal business of cycle 1— bringing people in, bonding Insiders and Outsiders together—frequently found themselves at cross purposes with the child, who was engaged in the principal business of adolescence: moving away from the family to establish an identity of his or her own.

Also important was whether the move was voluntary. Voluntary moves usually went very well because they tended to be motivated by a desire for reconnection. The child wanted to get to know his father better. Often this desire grew out of a developmental task (one we will look at more closely in cycle 3). Before children can establish their own identity, they need to know where they came from. A move to Dad's house creates an opportunity for the biological father to play family historian.

Forced moves frequently produced problems. Most often the stepfather initiated these moves. Early adolescence is not the most peaceful or gracious period of life, and a significant number of stepfathers, about 10 to 15 percent of our sample, weary of the surly, rebellious teenage behavior, eventually issued an ultimatum: "Him/her or me." The ultimatum was rarely put this baldly, but everyone in the family, including the object of the ultimatum, knew that it was on the table.

I should say that no biological mother in the project was happy to see a child leave. Even when a move to the father's house was thought to be beneficial, it produced maternal unhappiness. In almost every case, the mother experienced deep sadness and depression after a child's departure.

Lane Weaver's move seemed to fall somewhere between voluntary and involuntary. Lane began to talk about moving in with Arlington and Nancy last year. After a few run-ins with the truancy office and a nasty fight with six-year-old half brother, Bartholomew, Lane's stepfather, Sam, began to actively encourage the move.

"It's a real big change for us, James," Nancy said. Then she apologized for Arlington's absence. He had to attend an emergency meeting at work, she said.

Nancy was still quite pretty, but at thirty-seven she was beginning the transition toward middle-age handsomeness; her face had a new weight and character to it. I also noticed a new self-assurance and authority. I thought this change might have something to do with her current job. At the door, Nancy, a nurse during the project, said that she managed the radiology department at a local hospital now.

"How is everyone adjusting?" I asked.

Nancy said she was not terribly happy about the way Lane talked to her. "He has a sharp tongue, and I'm not quite certain how to respond. I don't know where I stand in this family anymore. Sometimes I feel like a stranger in my own house."

"Have you talked to Arlington?" I asked.

"About Lane? Sort of."

I told Nancy that in my experience, "sort of" almost always led to chaos.

The definition conversation is essential for a full-time stepmother. A woman has to know before the child moves in how much parental authority she has. Also, unless the biological parent agrees to be the principal parent (and sticks to his promise), that authority should be substantial. Parents and baby-sitters have very different needs in regard to a child. Within the family, it should be clear that the stepmother has full parental authority and that her rules of conduct and good order govern along with the father's.

This statement may seem to conflict with project findings about full-time stepfathers, but women who become full-time stepmothers in midstream are in a different position from men like Jeffrey Goldsmith. They already have a relationship with a stepchild and an established family; and these parental bona fides give a stepmother's words, thoughts, and rules an emotional weight and authority that a new stepfather's lack.

One other point about the definition conversation. Decisions about who should exercise authority and how much should take into account the child's age and stage of development. Younger children—seven-, eight-, and nine-year-olds—do not need to be consulted in depth about family rules and who will exercise them, but the more independent adolescent does. Indeed, in the case of twelve-, thirteen-, or fourteen-year-olds, parents should signal a willingness to negotiate about rules and family lines of authority.

Parental authority always should be exercised in the language of empathy—in language that shows an understanding of the child's loneliness but that also reflects the stepparent's unhappiness about disrespectful or surly behaviors. In a case like Lane's, a statement such as "I know this is a difficult time for you, but it hurts when you talk to me like that. Is that your intention?" would achieve both purposes.

During the project, we discovered two other things that help to facilitate a child's move. The first is encouraging regular contact with the nonresidential parent. Many biological fathers can get by with one or two visits a month; but most biological mothers cannot. Before the move, most mothers are in almost hourly contact with a child, and, as I've noted, when contact ends, profound sadness follows. "The sense of loss was like a little death," said one bereft woman. "I felt a part of me died the day Glen went to live with his father."

Encouraging regular calls to the nonresidential mother is not only an act of compassion, it also is essential to a key stepfamily task: management of the nonresidential parent. Not uncommonly, infrequent contact produces paranoidlike fantasies in that parent. The child wants to call but the wicked stepmother won't let him; or the stepmother is undermining the biological mother's position. Fears like these can cause problems for a stepfamily.

The other thing we learned during the project is even less surprising. Children cannot be treated like loose change. They cannot be sent off to their father's family until they annoy someone there, then be packed up again and sent back to their mother's family until they annoy someone there (usually the stepfather).

Children, even adolescent children in search of an individual identity, need a sense of belonging. Being exchanged back and forth like a prisoner of war makes children feel they do not belong to anyone, and children who feel this way are only one train stop away from another, even more debilitating feeling: They quickly conclude that no one wants them because they are worthless.

Frequent moves are detrimental for another reason. Children in a state of perpetual motion are children who are not being monitored very closely by either set of parents, and that can create opportunites for misbehavior. An example was a project boy named Adam, who assured his new stepfamily that he was spending Saturday afternoons with his biological mother. Adam probably could have gotten away with this little ruse forever if he hadn't come home one Saturday afternoon with lipstick on his collar and grass stains on his chinos. Odd mementoes for a weekend visit with Mom, Adam's father thought, so he decided to call his former wife. She said she had not seen their son in three weeks. Adam, it turned out, was spending Saturday afternoons at a secluded local park with his girlfriend.

I asked Nancy if she and Arlington had discussed how long Lane would be staying.

She shook her head. "We haven't talked about that yet."

This oversight is common, probably because, with a new member coming, a family has a lot of other things to do. But it's important to establish a firm time frame—whether it is for a year or until the child graduates from high school—before the move and to stick to it. At times youngsters become so disruptive that stepfamily functioning is endangered, but even in these cases youngsters should not be summarily removed. Their departure from the family should be timed to a natural demarcation point, such as the end of the school year.

POINTS TO KEEP IN MIND

- Many of the issues part-time and full-time stepmothers face are similar to the ones stepfathers face, but there is one major difference. Because of a combination of social expectations, female socialization, and the male belief in the "mommy gene," women are under pressure to become involved with their stepchildren.
- It is imperative to come to an agreement about rules for visiting stepchildren.
- It is normal for visiting children to be possessive about their fathers, and this can make a stepmother jealous. This is another aspect of the Insiders vs. Outsiders phenomenon, and it needs to be discussed within the family.
- A child dumper is a man who expects his wife to take total—or nearly total—responsibility for the care, nurturance, and entertainment of his visiting children. Conflict about child dumping may lead a man to stop visiting his children, and stepmothers can help stepchildren talk with their fathers about these issues.
- About 20 percent of adolescents change residences and live with their fathers, usually during the early teen years. This is generally a developmentally appropriate change, but in order for a move to succeed the father and stepmother have to renegotiate their parenting roles and develop ways to integrate the new child into their family.

chapter seven

The Romantic Stepfamily:
Waking from the Dream

Cycle 2—years 3 to 5—is the golden period of stepfamily life. Almost all the major dividing points that made years 1 and 2 so tumultous are now resolved, almost resolved, or, for the time being, in abeyance. The Insider-Outsider gap is closed or almost closed. The lines of stepparent authority—whether that of the full-time stepfather or the part-time stepmother—have been established, and the family has had enough time to develop a stabilizing structure of household routines and family rituals.

The tranquility of cycle 2 provides families with an opportunity to enhance their cohesiveness and to add new rituals to the ones they have already established. From a family development perspective, years 3 through 5 serve as a period of consolidation. Families have an opportunity to build on cycle 1 solutions to unify themselves further. It is important to take full advantage of this opportunity because, in cycle 3, which begins in year 5, turbulence resumes. In this case though, the trigger has less to do with the stepfamily than with the turbulence of one of its members—the child who is passing through adolescence.

The relative quiescence of cycle 2 is available to all three stepfamily types. Unfortunately, however, only Matriarchals and Neotraditionals are able to take full advantage of the new opportunities this period creates for further consolidation and harmony. Things get better for Romantics too, but not as good as they could or should because Romantics are still in the thrall of some of their unrealistic expectations.

HAPPY ALL THE TIME

One major reason for the tranquility of cycle 2 is that it coincides with the child's passage into latency; years 8 through 11 are the calmest in childhood. And since marital pressure flows *upward* from the children to the couple in stepfamilies, instead of downward from the marriage to the child as it does in a nuclear family, happy stepchildren usually make for happy stepfamilies.

While the child's passage into latency is a major reason for cycle 2 contentment, other reasons also exist. For one thing, the stepfamily itself usually has achieved a new stability by the beginning of the third year. The children have adjusted to the stepfather—to his presence in their midst, his habits, and his taking up of their mother's attention and affection. In addition, by this point the stepfather and stepchild have established a relationship—one with its own language and behavioral codes. The stepfather has ceased to be an awkward, resented interloper and is now a comfortable part of the household. And if there was a move after the marriage—and a large majority of our newly formed stepfamilies changed residence shortly after formation—by year 3, 4, or 5 of the cycle, children have adjusted to their new home and school and developed a new circle of friends.

In addition, parenting arrangements finally have developed a mutually satisfying pattern. The raw animosity of the first postdivorce years has abated, and custody and visitation conflicts usually have been resolved in ways that everyone can live with. Not only has the form of visitation become routine—for example, the kids go to Dad every other weekend and every Wednesday night until 8 P.M.—but that form has been filled with substance: The kids now have real friends in their father's new neighborhood; they are used to seeing their father intermittently instead of daily; children and father have found a way to converse so that emotional intimacy and the parent-child bond is preserved despite the originally unsettling gaps in physical presence.

Then there's the issue of maturity. The children, three years older now, are cognitively advanced enough to see their parents in a more nuanced way. Six-, seven-, and eight-year-olds see only good guys and bad guys, guilt and innocence; more mature ten- and eleven-year-olds have developed a more sophisticated view of human behavior. They are old enough to understand that sometimes even good people do bad and stupid and hurtful things.

How much children improve in cycle 2 can be seen in one of the comparisons we did. In cycle 1 and again in cycle 2, the parents of our one hundred target children filled out a Child Behavior Checklist. One of the things the checklist measures is how much a child "externalizes" behavior: acts out in aggressive or disruptive ways. We found a marked decrease in such behavior among children measured six months after stepfamily formation (the beginning of cycle 1) and those measured in year 3 (the beginning of cycle 2).

Not surprisingly, since the children's stress levels so directly impact on the mother's and stepfather's, the quiescence resonated throughout the family. Between cycle 1 and cycle 2, the rates of stress in our stepfamilies dropped by an astonishing 200 percent.

THE ROMANTIC EXCEPTION

The failure of Romantic stepfamilies to improve as much as Neotraditionals and Matriarchals can be explained largely in terms of those last few unrealistic expectations they refused to surrender, which made them vulnerable to what might be called the Groundhog Day syndrome. Readers familiar with that 1993 movie will remember that the hero, Bill Murray, through some cosmic trick, got stuck in Groundhog Day. Every day Murray awoke, the calender said February 2, Groundhog Day, so every day Murray repeated the same set of experiences he had had yesterday (also February 2) and the day before yesterday (also February 2).

The Romantic stepfamily's version of Murray's plight, endlessly re-enacting cycle 1 conflicts, has its roots in the family's insistence on hanging on to a few of the unrealistic expectations that other families have discarded by the time they moved into cycle 2. To understand how a lingering unrealistic expectation can set a Romantic stepfamily up for the Groundhog Day phenomenon, let me tell you about two related incidents that happened to the McDougals early in cycle 2. These incidents—or rather the trauma they caused—originated in one of the unrealistic expectations that the McDougals, and Joanne in particular, refused to let go of; it was a variant of the nuclear-family myth called the Just Us. The adults in the family assume that eventually the supporting cast around the stepfamily—the former spouse, the former spouse's relatives, and the man's biological children—will quietly fade out of the picture and the stepfamily will come to look like a nuclear family.

The reason this myth—like a lot of other lingering nuclear-family myths—leads to an almost endless replay of cycle 1 conflicts is that it blinds people to one of the unalterable givens of stepfamily life: Stepfamilies have porous borders.

In nuclear families, common ties of blood, history, and genes create a thick, almost impenetrable wall around the family. But the complicated biological geography of a stepfamily makes its borders very permeable; anyone with a connection to a member of the family—former spouses, former spouses' girlfriends, parents, and so on—has a right to enter the family, no matter how inconvenient or annoying that right is to the adults in the family.

During cycle 1, everyone found this facet of stepfamily life hard to cope with. But in Neotraditional and Matriarchal families, two things usually happened once people began to discard their various nuclear-family myths. The porous nature of the stepfamily was accepted, and that usually produced a decline in stress because people are less inclined to worry about things they know they cannot control. The second thing happened at the beginning of cycle 2. Neotraditionals and Matriarchals began to realize that having porous borders was not an entirely bad thing. True, they sometimes made the family vulnerable to unwanted intrusions, but they also had certain advantages. One was a larger pool of baby-sitters. With four sets of grandparents to call on, people almost never had to miss a new movie. Porousness also was an advantage around the holidays because it usually meant more gifts for the children. Some of our more sensitive participants also noticed a third advantage to having porous family borders. While some involved nonresidential fathers tended to treat the stepfamily like a second home, on the plus side, their involvement with the children eased the kids' adjustment to stepfamily life.

The allegiance to the Just Us expectation in Romantic stepfamilies deprived a family of these advantages. But the most destructive aspect of hanging on to it and similar expectations is that the family becomes vulnerable to the Groundhog Day phenomenon. In cycle 2 Romantic couples were still going around in circles about former spouses—and many other things—that had become nonissues for Neotraditional and Matriarchal families.

Besides the unrealistic nature of their expectations and their tendency to get mired in cycle 1 issues, Romantic stepfamilies share one other unusual characteristic: There is more than one type of Romantic family.

THE THREE FACES OF
THE ROMANTIC STEPFAMILY

A single thread marks all Romantics, one that they wear like a scarlet R. Romantics see their marriage as a glorious and heroic enterprise; they also believe that, like Superman, it can do just about anything: fly faster than a speeding bullet, leap tall buildings in a single bound, heal any wound, however deep, and right any wrong, however egregious. But Romantics also differ from one another.

Destiny Romantics, the first type of Romantic couple, believe their union is ordained, not accidental; there is something special about it, and that specialness will help them vault past the usual hurdles of second-marriage-with-children problems. In the personal narrative Destiny Romantics create for themselves, first spouses are depicted as uninspired, arbitrary, or merely convenient choices: not bad people, but simply the men or women the Romantics were not suppose to marry. By contrast, Romantics think of their second marriages as emotionally, spiritually, or temperamentally destined. These couples think of themselves as soul mates whose union was preordained. Destiny Romantics believe the deeper connection that drives their second marriage imbues the marriage with a special emotional current—one that can nurture the children born of the first marriage. Destiny Romantics believe this special emotional current establishes a moral mandate to create an "instant family."

Other Romantic couples might be called Second-Stage Romantics. The husband, wife, or both view the first marriage as one that was made too early and eventually was outgrown by personal development: the college match that amicably dissolved as each young spouse realized his or her potential; the marriage made by the formerly traditional woman who became enmeshed in a political or cultural cause and realized she no longer had much in common with a husband who had not grown the way she had; the man who, once he moved up and out in the world, felt that his homemaker wife was no longer as exciting or interesting as the female lawyers or executives who were his work-a-day colleagues. Second-Stage couples believe that what gives the stepfamily its special capacity to vault over typical stepfamily problems is not a spiritual bond (which Destiny Romantics feel) but a sense of greater mate-appropriateness—appropriateness that is based on some kind of *advancement* (educational, intellectual, ideological, or professional)— which provides the new couple with the superior skills, status, and resources to steer their stepfamily past the typical problems and that will license their "instant familyness."

Both Destiny and Second-Stage Romantic couples feel they have achieved a new level of compatibility in their second marriages, but they do *not* feel that the second marriage exists to correct the pain and flaws of the first one. But a third kind of Romantic couple—what one of my researchers calls Antidote Romantics—*do* feel this way. In the couple narrative of Antidote Romantics, the husband and wife are in each other's lives to heal and cure one another from toxic first marriages.

This is a very seductive notion. Who wouldn't want to think of their marriage as a righter of passed wrongs? It is also one that tends to evoke sympathy in others. Indeed, Dwight and Joanne McDougal struck a personal chord with my research staff. "You want to root for them," one of my assistants declared while viewing their initial videotape. The image of these two "givers" (Joanne's favorite description of the McDougals) who had been previously married to two takers—the Gap assistant manager discarded by his upperwardly mobile first wife and Joanne who, after extricating herself from a bad marriage, spent nearly a year in a postdivorce purgatory of church socials—holding hands on that weathered living-room couch had been stirring. Even remarks that might otherwise seem cloying—such as Dwight's assertion that "we even hold hands when I'm driving"—seemed merely part of the McDougals' declaration of how lucky they felt to have found one another at last.

Couples like Dwight and Joanne are also distinguished by a second belief. They see the new stepfamily not only as an antidote to a bad first marriage but as an antidote to the bad parenting their children received in those marriages.

During the cycle 1 interview, Joanne said that Dwight had been too nice to fight his ex-wife, Pamela's, rules on child care. "He let a lot of stuff slide," she said. "So when he got together with me, I told him when Kendall and Dale visit, I want them to follow the same rules I make my sons follow." For example: "They had to wash their own dishes after dinner; they couldn't watch TV until half their homework was completed; if they hadn't gotten permission in advance to spend the night at a friend's, well, they could not make the last-minute decision to accept such an invitation." Joanne explained that her stand on rules was motivated by more than the need for consistency; Kendall and Dale were "wild kids"; the rules would help them. Thus, in the McDougals' view, they were performing corrective parenting with each other's children.

When Dwight and stepson Tray had had their contretemps in cycle 1—Dwight determining that Tray and his friend had stolen hubcaps and Tray then hurling angry and obscene words at his stepfather—Joanne said it broke her heart to see her husband and son at odds. But as she described the incident between her husband and son, I couldn't help noticing that she seemed rather pleased by the aggressive, let's-get-to-the-bottom-of-this stance Dwight had taken. To Antidote Romantics, stepfathers *are* fathers: period, over and out.

Antidote Romantics are highly judgmental. They see themselves as the good guys and their ex-mates as the bad guys. At the intake interview Joanne had said: "I was with a very selfish person, and Dwight was with a very manipulative person."

Antidote Romantics also stress their similarities, and they make these similarities part of a shining narrative of their togetherness. Listen to the McDougals' from their cycle 1 interview:

Joanne: "Dwight and I are both from big families, and we both grew up believing in discipline and structure, in working for your advantages."

Dwight: "When I grew up, the children went wherever they wanted. At other houses, it was 'Oh, don't touch that! Don't go in that room!' It's not that way at my parents' house. There you'll find sometimes six grandkids on my father's bed—and he may be on the bed too. So it's real warm, and everyone is welcome in."

But it is not enough for them to have an uplifting narrative; Antidote Romantics' ex-spouses have to provide the dark counternarrative—in this case, permissiveness and the inability to bond with a large family. According to Joanne, Pamela did not enjoy Dwight's big family. Her parents were two hippie professors with "very strange" ideas about family life. "That woman does not know how to say no to a child," Joanne said. "She's very permissive." According to Joanne, her first husband, Tray, Sr., was worse than permissive; he was a virtual nonparent. Joanne: "Unfortunately, the boys did not count on their dad for anything, because they knew they couldn't. They counted on me for absolutely everything."

Thus, when Antidote Romantics find one another, they are finding their true soul mate—the spouse who neatly (almost too neatly) corrects the first spouse's failings, the mate with whom he or she can bring that Technicolor narrative of family life to healing fruition. In the paradigms of such couples, the contrast between first and second spouse is not shaded; it is stark. Dwight: "Pamela was cold; Joanne is very warm." Joanne: "With Dwight [as opposed to Tray], my sons know they can count on him. They know he'll be fair. They know that he'll help them if he can. They know he's dependable. He's not going to zombie out and be asleep on the floor when they need him."

Antidote Romantics set out as a bonded team: good parents. It goes against their personal ideology—it is almost threatening—for them to recognize status disparities that other stepfamilies usually acknowledge: that the biological parent is *the* parent and the stepparent is the cautious interloper who slowly has to earn the child's trust and find a place in the authority structure. Instead, Antidote Romantics believe in instant parental authority—not out of power hunger or pushiness, but because a quick appropriation of authority is, as Joanne said to me, "in the best interests of both sets of children." Now, she declared, her sons were seeing what a relationship should be: "two people who are thoughtful and considerate and respectful of each other, who work together, who have the same goals and priorities." This bonded, virtuous front gives Antidote Romantics like the McDougals the license to be not just instant and unambiguous appropriators of the parenting role with one another's children but also to be judgmental and, if necessary, *strict*. Therefore, Joanne became very critical when she noticed that Dwight's daughter Kendall was "clingy" and "too dependent" on him—always running to his lap, wanting him all to herself. Such behavior, she told me, was not in the girl's best interest. "It wasn't good for Kendall to want constant adult attention, not to be autonomous."

Moreover, Joanne encouraged Dwight to be almost as authoritarian with her children as she was with his. She had nodded when Dwight had said, "Our policy is: 'Look, this is what the rules are. Your job is to sweep the floor; it's gonna be swept. And if I go in there and there's dirt on the floor, they're gonna sweep it *again*.'"

This pride in their united front, this instant sharing of parental authority, this fierce self-congratulation, and this disciplinary strictness, all of these traits came forth when the McDougals began to partake of something that is a mainstay of Romantic stepfamily life: the official blended-family outing. Theirs was to a place called Teacup Junction.

THE THREE STAGES OF GETTING STUCK

Teacup Junction in western Alabama is the seat of the large McDougal clan. Every year Dwight, his four siblings, their spouses, and children gathered in Teacup with Dwight's parents, aunts, uncles, and cousins for a weekend of dining and dancing. Dwight and Joanne had been to three of these reunions since their marriage. Joanne thought the first two were wonderful, but the third was different, I learned the moment I arrived to conduct the McDougals' cycle 2 interview.

"No more Teacup Junction, ever," she announced as she watched me walk toward the porch where she was standing.

I thought she looked different from the Joanne I met at the cycle 1 interview—wearier and, despite the smile, sad, not in some transient way but sad in the deep way—sad the way people look when they feel life has done them a great injustice.

"I thought you loved the reunions," I replied.

"Tray, Jr., walked out on us," Joanne said, ignoring my remark. "Right in the middle of the reunion, he just up and left."

I asked Joanne where Tray was now.

There was a long sigh, then she said, "San Antonio. He's with his daddy."

I was not entirely surprised by this news. As noted, besides Just Us, one other expectation that Romantics in general, and Antidote Romantics in particular, resist surrendering is the expectation for instant familyness.

I also was not surprised that Teacup Junction was the place where all of the hidden resentments in Tray, Jr., and Dwight's relationship finally exploded. It was at McDougal family reunions where Dwight pressed hardest on the most pernicious aspect of the instant family expectation, the right to exercise unquestioned parental authority over the other spouse's children. Thus, for Dwight, these reunions were almost patriarchal coronations. "I'm going to make sure that Joanne's boys are accepted just like they were mine," Dwight told me before he and his wife attended their first reunion together. Later, Joanne filled me in on what Dwight meant when he said "accepted like my own."

In Teacup Junction, surrounded by family and friends, Dwight behaved as if Tray, Jr., and Evan really were his sons, not Tray, Sr.'s. He criticized the boys—and especially Tray, Jr.—freely and openly. "Elbows off the table!" he barked during a backyard barbecue at his aunt's house. There were also some showy displays of intimacy that, I believe, upset Evan and even more young Tray—hugs and not very funny jokes about the boys' girlfriends and their personal foibles.

Dwight's behavior probably would not have produced the explosion it did if Dwight had, through a few years of supplication and sensitivity, earned the right to make dumb father jokes and to issue orders. (Although even years of supplication and sensitivity don't earn a man the right to humiliate a child—biological or step—in front of others—especially if most of the others are total strangers.) Jeffrey Goldsmith and other Neotraditional men understand this.

But Dwight never did. Indeed, just the opposite. His—and Joanne's—refusal to surrender the instant family myth had undermined his relationship with Tray from the beginning—from his confrontation with the boy about the hubcaps.

"That's when it all started going downhill for them, James," Joanne said.

We were inside now, seated on the same weathered couch where Dwight and Joanne had held hands. As she talked I looked around. The McDougal living room had changed almost as much as Joanne. Gone were the family group shots on the mantel, although individual pictures abounded. The neat-as-a-pin appearance had relaxed; the morning's *Chronicle* and an errant plate and saucer still lay on the coffee table; jackets and caps and shopping bags that had been out of sight in closets now hung on a clothes rack. The shag rug was in need of vacuuming. But the house was not messy or disheveled. On the contrary, it was lived in, and the sight of it in this state made me realize that, during my two prior visits, it had been almost desperately well kept. Still, given what we had already been finding about our Romantic stepfamilies at this juncture, the relaxed condition of the McDougal house suggested a state of mind more defeatist than merely comfortable. The house seemed to be expressing a sentiment for Joanne.

She stared off for a long moment, and both of us noticed the awkward silence that seemed to be leading to some kind of confession or concession. Then, tipping her head back and drawing a breath, she began to recap the sad history of Dwight and her son's relationship. It could have served as an object lesson.

"To me," Joanne says, "the beginning of the bad period is when Dwight called Tray's friend's parents and demanded to know if the boys were lying. I thought that was a good thing, but Tray felt betrayed. Betrayed and then some! Oh boy, did he get mad! And *stay* mad. He felt Dwight had crossed the line, overstepped his 'role' as a stepdad—that hurt Dwight; Dwight felt he was doing what a good father should do."

When I mentioned that the biological parent is the most appropriate person to handle serious transgressions by a biological child, Joanne said, "No, I think you're wrong. I was glad Dwight took the lead. I think it showed Tray how seriously Dwight took his role as father."

Stage 1

People, families, relationships, do not get stuck suddenly. The sticking process—the Groundhog Day phenomenon—occurs slowly over time and is characterized by certain warning signs of paralysis. As Joanne contined to describe Dwight and Tray's troubled history, I recognized several of these all-too-familiar signs. In the case of the stepfather-stepchild relationship, the first is usually rebelliousness; it often begins early in the first cycle, and it is triggered by a characteristically Romantic form of blindness.

As the child's *real* father, the Romantic man assumes he can can do what Dwight did through most of the McDougal family's first two years—criticize his flawed predecessor—at will and in front of the children.

"Your daddy has a lot of problems," Dwight would observe whenever Tray, Sr.'s, name came up at the McDougal dinner table. I must have looked surprised when Joanne told me this, because she quickly added that Dwight always qualified his criticism. "He wouldn't just criticize, James. He would say, 'Now, don't get me wrong, Tray. I don't think your daddy is a bad man; I just think he has a lot of problems, and I don't want you having problems too.' "

I would date Tray's rebelliousness to the hubcap incident, but Joanne dated it to something that occurred a few months later. For some reason, Tray, Sr.'s, name had come up at dinner one night, and Dwight, in the midst of making his usual observation about his predecessor, was interrupted by Tray, Jr., who threw down his napkin and shouted, "At least my daddy ain't no shithead like you"; then Tray stormed out of the dining room and house. He spent the next three days at the house of his accomplice in the hubcap incident, Will. The reason criticism of a parent foments this kind of ferocious rebellious behavior is that children perceive the criticism as an implicit criticism of them. Tray, Jr., was the son of this flawed father. Therefore, he, the son, must be flawed too. Worse still, if his father had serious problems, how could he, as his father's son, escape them? These are powerful anxieties for children, so powerful they require expression, an outlet. It may have almost been a *relief* for Tray, Jr., to go over the edge: to steal those hubcaps with his friend Will, to lash out at his stepfather and shocked mother at the dinner table.

Stage 2

Stage 2 is characterized by a move back toward the biological father. A kind of emotional exhaustion drives it. The child, tired of arguing with the stepfather about the extent of his parental authority, moves back toward the biological parent. And, indeed, not long after the eruption at the dinner table, Tray, Jr., started reaching out to his father. Since Joanne and Dwight had never encouraged Tray Honeycutt, whom they deemed an almost worthlessly irresponsible father, to set up visitation with his sons, Tray, Sr., had slipped out of the boys' lives while he was trying to reconstruct his life after his personal and financial downfall. Tray, Jr., rather touchingly, became a detective—calling his father's old business partner, then calling his father's sister in Phoenix. (When Joanne found the toll call to Phoenix on the phone bill, she was astonished.)

Tray's efforts to track down his father behind Joanne's and Dwight's backs greatly disturbed them. They saw the boy's behavior as a violation of the family ideal of closeness and honesty, although Tray didn't.

"You're not really my family! My family includes my dad!" he snapped when Dwight accused him of betraying the family.

Eventually, father and son made contact, and the McDougals reluctantly agreed to Tray's—and eventually Evan's—weekend visits with the man they had written off as a bad character. To make up for the boys' desultory weekends in a singles' apartment complex with someone "who could not cook more than a boiled egg for their supper if his life depended on it," the McDougals made their own family activities and ceremonies all the more lush and compensating. "We had the biggest, most beautifully decorated Christmas tree! We had the best vacations!" Joanne said. "I didn't realize that Tray had begun to resent our efforts." The boy had begun romanticizing the simple, stripped-down pleasures he shared with his father—the fold-out sofa bed with the creaky springs, the trips to the 7-Eleven in the morning for cellophaned coffee cakes instead of the full-dress homemade breakfasts that Mom and Dwight served. His father had stopped being the bad guy. To Tray, Jr., Tray, Sr., was now the misunderstood underdog.

Stage 3

Stage 3 usually is marked by a volcanic eruption that unsticks the relationship for good.

During the McDougals' next interview, Joanne said that she marked Tray's movement away from Dwight and from the McDougal stepfamily by his behavior during the three visits the family made to Teacup Junction. "The first trip, Tray hung back a little from all the family festivities," she said. "The second, he refused to play in the dads-and-sons baseball game. Said he had a cold. Even"—she smiles—"even coughed on the sidelines, so the other relatives would believe it.

"The third trip . . ." Joanne dug into her handbag and pulled out a wrinkled slip of paper. It was the stub of a Greyhound bus ticket. "The third family reunion, the night of the big dinner celebrating Dwight's father's seventy-fifth birthday, Tray announced to us that he'd saved three months' allowance to buy himself this: a bus ride, leaving that night, back to Texas." Something in Joanne's broken, whispery voice told me it was best to keep staring at the ticket stub, not to move my eyes to her face.

"But not to Houston," she continued. "To San Antonio. His dad had a new apartment and a new job there. He had already shipped his camp trunk—filled with enough T-shirts and jeans to last him a few months—the week before. He shipped it off secretly. He had decided to live with his father." Joanne began to cry.

An explosion like Tray, Jr.'s, is often how a stuck relationship finally gets unstuck. There are limits to how long two people can continue circling around each other, fighting the same old battles over and over again.

"It's terrible the way things have worked out," Joanne said, looking as if she were going to begin crying again.

I asked her how Tray and Dwight got along during Tray's weekend visits.

Joanne took a sip of ice tea then said that for now, Dwight was intentionally keeping a low profile during the visits.

She also said that if Tray ever decided to move back home, she would insist that the entire family—Dwight, Tray, Jr., Evan, and herself—enter therapy.

I considered this a great stride. Romantic families believe themselves to be problem-free; Joanne's acquiescence signaled that the Romantic haze that had shrouded the McDougal family was finally beginning to lift.

OTHER WAYS ROMANTIC
COUPLES GET STUCK

Besides the stepfather-stepchild relationship, other early stepfamily issues continue to cause contentiousness in Romantic families in cycle 2. And again, all these early issues linger into later stepfamily life for the same reason: because some of the Romantics' unrealistic expectations linger into later stepfamily life. The issues are porousness, change, and the former spouse.

Porousness

What do I mean by "porousness"?

If you were raised in a nuclear family, think of how you sum up your family of origin's allegiances and alliances. They are fixed and certain, aren't they? Sometimes it's as simple as saying "I was my mother's daughter and my sister was my father's." Or: "My father always thought Bobby could do no wrong and he always picked on Ricky." Indeed, plays and novels about families are often memorable because the characters' relationships to one another are so vividly etched in defined terms and boundaries.

With stepfamilies, however, those defined relationships—those interpersonal boundaries—are much more permeable and elastic. They often shift according to circumstance. Husband and wife may have one kind of dynamic when her children are around, a different one when they are alone, yet another one when his nonresidential children visit.

On a more fundamental level, stepfamilies are also porous because the large cast of supporting characters around the stepfamily, including former spouses and former spouses' relatives and a current spouse's nonresidential children, all have a right to penetrate those permeable borders. There are about one-third *more* people for each family member to deal with, on a regular basis, than there are in nuclear families— and half of the family members are now shouldering twice as many roles as they did before they entered the stepfamily. And most upsetting of all to the adults in the stepfamily, they have little or no control over who enters the stepfamily and when they enter it.

At the beginning of stepfamily life, the constant "traffic problems" (as one project mother called them)—"the how-come-all-the-stepkids-are-over-tonight-for-dinner?" stuff—is almost welcome: The large cast of characters distracts from bigger fears. As one project mother, a Neo-traditionalist named Susan McGinness, put it, "I'd rather have a dumb fight with [her husband] Gene about why his daughter and her boy-friend always come over to 'borrow' the car at the wrong time than talk honestly with Gene about how he doesn't seem interested enough in developing a loving relationship with [her younger son] Paul. I'd rather clench my teeth about Gene's ex-wife's mother's intrusiveness when we go to [his daughter] Liza's ballet recital than cry myself to sleep won-dering if I married the right man, after all."

The difference between Romantic stepfamilies on one hand and Neotraditional and Matriarchal stepfamilies on the other is not that Neotraditionals and Matriarchals feel different about intrusions. But as they begin editing out their most unrealistic expectations, Matriarchals and Neotraditionals begin to realize that certain features of stepfamily life are fixed and unalterable. And one is the access rights of the large cast of supporting characters around the family. A family can take certain steps to make that access less intrusive. One is not to make commitments to outsiders without checking with other family members first. In the case of the man, this means checking with a wife before inviting a child over or committing her to do something with the child. A second is to establish a regular visiting schedule for relatives (aunts, uncles, grandparents, etc.) of a former spouse. They have a right to see their nephews, nieces, and grandchildren but not anytime they want. Let them know they are welcome but only on certain days and at certain times.

However, intrusions cannot be curbed completely. And this knowl-edge, this realization brings a kind of peace of mind. The couple ac-cepts the fact that a certain degree of intrusiveness is an unavoidable part of stepfamily life, and since the stepfamily matters, they decide that they will find a way to live with it.

Because of their unswerving allegiance to the nuclear-family myth, Romantics often never get to accept this situation. Even deep into cycle 2, intrusions by former spouses and former spouses' relatives continue to be painful to Romantic stepfamilies, and because they are painful, the intrusions continue to cause conflict. The couple get stuck in conflicts like this one:

"Why can't you get your son to call before he comes over here?" the wife shouts.

"Why can't you get your ex-husband to stop calling all the time?" the husband shouts back.

Romantics also frequently have trouble with another issue that arises from porousness: constant change. In stepfamilies, nonresidential parents fail to show up when they are supposed to, and children show up when they are *not* supposed to.

I remember one project wife telling me with more than a little anger about an intimate candlelight anniversary dinner that was interrupted by her husband's teenage son and the son's friend. The two boys happened to be in the neighborhood and happened to be ravenously hungry. So the woman's stepson said to his friend, "Let's go over to my dad's house; we can get something to eat there."

In cycle 1, incidents like this one have a certain novelty value; sometimes they are almost "cute." But by cycle 2, they have lost whatever charm they possessed and some—like the chronically "no-show" nonresidential parent—did not have much to begin with, which is why dealing with change becomes a big issue in this cycle.

Successful managers of change like successful managers of porousness are characterized by two traits. First, they do what they can to work with change. For example, a back-up baby-sitter is kept on call, so Date Nights do not have to be canceled at the last moment because the nonresidential parent forgot he was supposed to pick up the kids. And as with porousness, good change managers also accept that change is an unalterable part of stepfamily life. You can soften its impact, but you cannot eliminate it.

Romantics make bad change managers for the same reason they make bad porousness managers. Imprisoned by the nuclear-family myth, they can neither accept nor manage change. So every unexpected change feels like a fresh outrage.

The Former Spouse

Among the people who can pour into the life of a stepfamily are former mates. But intrusive ex-spouses raise so many complex issues that they represent their own special case.

Perhaps because women are the relationship gatekeepers in a family, or perhaps because they take so much more care of the day-to-day aspects of domestic life, especially child care, project wives often report that, if there are unresolved issues with a husband's former spouse, those issues usually end up spilling over not just into the stepfamily, but directly into their lives.

Joanne McDougal was one of the women who reported this to be so. The friction between her and Pamela intensified during the first three years—nearly to the point of a showdown. No sooner had Joanne come to terms with the departure of her son, Tray, Jr., than war or near-war broke out between her and Pamela. Joanne decided that even if Dwight would still tolerate his ex-wife's manipulating him, she was no longer going to do so.

Joanne said she was tired of the way Pamela used Kendall, Dwight's daughter, "to jerk him around." But I think the combativeness on the part of the usually pacific Joanne also was fueled by class and income resentments. The McDougals lived in a modest ranch house in Pasadena and, at the time of the study, lived on a combined annual income of $42,000. They bought their clothes at WalMart and Sears. Glamorous Pamela had a six-figure income, lived in a large house with a swimming pool, and had a closet full of Armani and Ralph Lauren suits and dresses.

"When we were consumed with Tray's and Dwight's problem together, I could just sigh and roll my eyes up at Pamela—or *try* to," Joanne said to me one day. "She wasn't my worst problem. Anyway, I thought that her dropping the kids off and leaving *me* to find the addresses of their birthday parties was just part of a bitchy period she was going through: Sure, she had dropped Dwight, but I had picked him up and dusted him off—and didn't he suddenly look good, now that she didn't have him?

"Even though I wasn't on the big career track, like she is, I'm sure her competitive little nose was bent out of shape about that. So she was punishing me for finding the good things in Dwight that she had been too shallow to appreciate."

Joanne's analysis may have been astute, but it did not go far enough: Pamela's petulance and manipulation turned out to be more than a passing phase. As stepfamily years 1 and 2 turned into stepfamily years 3 and 4, Pamela and Joanne's relationship did not improve. By the time we met for the next interview, Joanne could recite Pamela's long list of intrusions from memory. And she recited that litany with color and wit. For example: "One Saturday morning, when we were expecting Kendall and Dale to be dropped off at ten, the doorbell rings at seven-thirty—rings *impatiently,* I might add—and as I shuttle to the door in my bathrobe, there's Pamela dressed to kill for a professional conference. In Dallas. She says—without apologizing, mind you—that no, she wasn't supposed to *drop* them at ten; the conference *started* at ten. And she was taking the plane. And here they were. No 'I'm sorry for the misunderstanding'—she just leaned down and kissed them with all that phony concern and turned on her high heels and clip-clopped down to her black Lexus and checked her makeup in the car mirror and was gone."

There were also tales of Kendall announcing, on the Sunday night of a weekend visit, that she had to have a costume for her school history play the next day and hadn't her mom told Joanne that she, Joanne, was supposed to make it? (Joanne then provided a gripping narrative of a ride around Houston, trying to find open novelty or fabric stores—then settling on a K-mart: buying feathers, leather scraps, colored beads, and moccasins and stitching together a passable Sakajawea, with the last stitch completed after midnight.) And there was the famous story of the elementary school graduation party that Pamela threw for Dale and his classmates at her house, during which Dwight and Joanne ended up running to the store to buy more hamburger buns and serving the cake and ice cream.

It was after this party that the McDougals had a big blow-up—about Pamela's role in their life. "Here I was, at *her* party, as a *guest*—and who ends up washing the dishes?" Joanne had screamed at her husband as soon as they were alone in the car. "*I* did!"

"She didn't ask you to! You *wanted* to," Dwight retorted (not, Joanne eventually would concede, untruthfully). "You like being the competent, giving one. Pamela's faults make you feel good about yourself."

"My God, Dwight!" This—Joanne recalled to me—is when she started to cry. "You act like you're on her side! Maybe she keeps reeling you back in her life because she knows you're still in love with her!"

Often poor communication contributes to the "stuckness" of Romantic families. But the problem isn't that Romantics resist relating to one another fully or lack communication skills (although some Romantic couples do have skills deficits). Again, because of their allegiance to the nuclear-family myth, it is impossible to deal with a problem like an intrusive former spouse unless you are willing to be candid with one another.

However, Romantics resist candor because it offends them ideologically. If you love the other person, that love automatically should tell him or her what to do. As one Romantic mother put it, "For me to give Alan, my husband, pointers on how to relate to my son would be insulting. I'd be telling him I don't trust him enough to be a good father."

Thus Joanne and Dwight almost never talked about the McDougal family issues with Pamela, Dale, and Kendall or with Tray, Jr., and Evan. So these issues festered and festered until they finally exploded during fights like the one that followed Pamela's party for Dale's class.

Two facts were clear from Joanne's outburst that night. One, she and Dwight communicated so rarely about Pamela that when they tried to, a burst of accusations and counteraccusations resulted; and, two,

Dwight's relationship with Pamela had become a miniobsession to Joanne.

The afternoon Joanne described this fight, I remembered that three other project women—all Neotraditionals—had found creative ways to free themselves from similarly contentious and obsessional relationships with their husbands' ex-wives by taking a "vacation" from the ex-wife, by becoming temporarily deskilled, and by resolving not to take parenting criticism personally and inviting the stepchild's mother's input.

Take a "Vacation" from His Ex-Wife

When Tina Balsam announced to her stockbroker husband, Neil, one day—in a fit of frustration and pique—that she "needed to take a vacation" from Neil's first wife, Gloria, she had a novel reaction to her own figurative statement: She decided to take it literally. Gloria was, Tina believed, a spoiled country club wife with Dallas-sized hair and jewelry and a shamefully outsized capacity to enrage and annoy. Tina's take-a-vacation remark had been occasioned by a typical Gloria ploy: Neil and Gloria's daughter, Lily, had spent the night over and that day was a friend's Sweet Sixteen party. "So Gloria, *of course,* makes Lily a hair-and-nails appointment at Neiman's—at 10 A.M. (Why it could not wait till 1 or 2 P.M., I have no idea.) That way Gloria gets to call Neil—at 8 A.M. Saturday morning, while he is of course in bed with *me*—and push him around: order him to get Lily up and drive her to Neiman's. In other words, Gloria pushes herself, and her stupid values, into my marriage bed!"

Since Lily saw her father once a week and every other weekend, taking a temporary vacation from all thoughts of the irritating Gloria might seem an unrealistic order, but Tina soon figured out a way. "I won't be home when she drops Lily off—I'll make it a point to be at a movie, or playing golf, or out shopping. I won't go to any events—PTA meetings, parties—that she goes to. I will resist the urge to ask questions of Lily that will solicit any information about her mother. And I will request that Neil make Lily-related plans with Gloria *before* she is dropped off at our house, so she does not have to call the house when Lily is here."

This policy was in place for two months. It was a simple plan, easy to stick to. At the end of the two months, certain patterns that Tina had been stuck in regarding defining, relating to, and competing with Gloria had dissolved from sheer disuse.

Become Temporarily Deskilled

The relationship Neotraditional Jackie Kane had with Melinda, the first wife of her husband Arthur, was not unlike Joanne's relationship to Pamela. In the Kanes' paradigm, Jackie was the doer, the problem-solver—the one who helped her stepchildren do their homework, plan parties, and shop for science-project materials. As the boys had become teenagers—able to come over to their father's house on their own, on a whim—Jackie (whose daughter from her first marriage lived with her and Arthur) felt that porous stepfamily life ate into her time and energy at every turn.

Jackie often wondered: Why did the boys lean on her so? She didn't think she pushed herself into their lives. She realized that, especially next to their shy and quiet mother, she was perceived as skilled at solving problems and that she naturally volunteered help whenever she got cues from the boys that they needed it. "So I deskilled myself for a month," she said. "When one of them asked if I'd proofread his term paper, I made myself say I was too busy doing something else. When the other asked me an Internet question, I pled ignorance." In the vacuum that was created, the boys' self-reliance grew. At the end of the month, Jackie had two self-reliant stepsons and more time for herself during their increasing—and increasingly spontaneous—visits.

Resolve Not to Take Parenting Criticism Personally and Invite Your Stepchild's Mother's Input

Louise Coplan was rankled by her husband, Jeff's, first wife, Sally, for a familiar reason: "Sally could never appreciate what I did for her daughter, Nicole. She just wouldn't let me have one bit of credit or acknowledgment. If I'd spent an hour helping Nicole make her birthday party invitations, Sally would throw mine away and make her own. If Sally called when Nicole was over and I happened to mention I was making a beef stew, she had to find a way of making it clear that she did not approve of fatty meats in Nicole's diet. When we took Nicole and my son and daughter on a trip to historic Civil War battlefields, I wondered: How is she going to make something this obviously educational seem bad? But she did. She disapproved of the emphasis on war."

Louise soon realized that Sally's disapproval of everything she did for Nicole was Sally's way of asserting her motherhood within a stepfamily matrix that was threatening to her. Louise also realized that as long as she secretly wanted Sally's approval, the woman's remarks would ruin her whole day. Louise recognized that she could either let Sally's attitude get to her every time it was displayed or she could "tune it out, make myself not take it personally, and go from there." This forced tough-hidedness made Louise feel less vulnerable. In time, she added a second part to the managing-Sally program: "Before weekends that Nicole was coming over, I started asking Sally if she had suggestions for the weekend. I would say 'Sally, we were going to rent videos, but I invite your input.' At first, I was afraid Sally would take advantage and get bossy. But the opposite happened: All Sally wanted was to be deferred to, affirmed as Nicole's real mother and a *good* mother. Like Rodney Dangerfield, she wanted *respect*. And my inviting her input was a way of giving her that."

I thought that these three strategies could help Joanne manage her stepchildren more effectively, but I didn't believe they would be of much use against what I suspected was at the heart of her unhappiness. She was angry at Dwight—very angry—for being so vulnerable to his first wife's whims. What Joanne wanted to hear Dwight say to Pamela is "Damn it, you don't control me anymore! I'm married to *Joanne,* not to you. I'm not going to be sucked in by your requests, your manipulation, or your neediness." But Joanne could not bring herself to *tell* her husband. "Expressing that thought would be as good as telling Dwight I was jealous of Pamela," Joanne told me one day. "And I'm not. How can you be jealous of someone you don't admire? Or someone who made your husband—with whom you have happiness—unhappy?" In short: To Joanne, expressing anger at Pamela's lingering control over Dwight was an admission that the McDougal marriage was less than perfect, and the nuclear-family myth does not allow for less-than-perfect marriages. So problems like manipulative former spouses linger on and on, and the more they linger, the more conflict they produce.

But the McDougals' fights never resolved anything because, like a lot of Romantics, they fought about the wrong things. All Joanne's unhappiness about Pamela got displaced onto issues like undisciplined stepchildren and all of Dwight's about Tray, Jr., into complaints about his father.

The following eight steps can help to correct communication problems like the ones the McDougals were having.

1. Make an appointment to talk things over.

Having a conversation about problems in the marriage and family is too important to be left to a spontaneous dialogue. Honor that importance by making an appointment. Do not schedule a talk when you are in a bad mood or are under pressure. Choose the time and place so that you will have time to explore your concerns freely (not late at night, not before work in the morning, not when the kids and stepkids are around).

2. Bring a list of what you want to talk about to that appointment.

Too often, the agreed-upon time for The Talk comes, and one or both persons forget what seemed so important earlier in the day. In such "cases," the person pressing for the conversation (usually the woman) feels embarrassed while the other person feels annoyed—and the opportunity to get at key issues in the marriage vanishes.

But if you have a written agenda—just as you would for a

board meeting—you cannot let the issues that brought you to this moment dissipate.

3. Bring a notepad and pen, have a clock clearly visible, and employ standard debate rules.

As you may recall from high school debate teams, each speaker gets to talk, uninterrupted. The goal is to *listen,* rather than thinking about what you are going to say or how you are going to defend yourself. "Uninterrupted" is the operative word. While one of you is speaking, the other can jot down demurrals and retorts but *may not interrupt* the speaker.

4. Speak in "I" sentences. Avoid "you" directives and generalizations.

Establish an accusation-free zone. State complaints, fears, resentments, dreams, and goals in terms of "I want," "I wish," "I need," "I'm afraid," and the like. Do not start sentences with "You should," "You said," "You promised," "You always," or "You never." The point is to get your mate to hear your narrative, your version, your experience—not to feel belittled, attacked, or criticized.

5. Determine that it is more important to understand what the other is feeling than it is to win the argument.

You are going on a fact-finding expedition, and the facts to be found are what the other person is experiencing and feeling. Do not attempt to alter the course of your mate's narrative by making "corrections" in his or her perceptions. Attempting to be right will only interfere with getting along. Do not require the other person to be consistent or unhypocritical. (Nobody is.)

6. Reward yourselves afterward with a—nonverbal—Date Night.

Whenever I recommend Date Nights, couples sigh and dismiss the notion as cliché, but over the years I have learned that they are important. After the talk, go to a movie, go jogging, go to a church dance, play tennis, get a massage, go bowling, shoot pool. Do something pleasurable together that does not involve facing one another over a table and talking. *That* you have already done.

> *7. If you are still having trouble, join a stepfamily group.*

You can find one by consulting the Stepfamily Association of America.

> *8. If you are still having trouble communicating, find a good psychologist or family therapist who is knowledgeable about stepfamily issues.*

(Those not knowledgeable can do more harm than good.) Your local church, synagogue, or psychological association is a good place to start.

For Neotraditionalists, Matriarchalists, and those Romantics who have worked through the aforementioned struggles and have gotten themselves successfully past cycle 1 issues, the relatively peaceful years of cycle 2 present the opportunity for family consolidation and family ritual-making. It is an opportunity that should not be lost.

Now is the time to take that family vacation, to start building a home-video library of stepfamily moments, to host a party. Now is also the time to build up those personal rituals unique to your situation. Some stepfamilies have found Thursday night dinners and stepparent-stepchild projects especially appropriate.

Since weekends are the time when the stepfamily expands and contracts—when the children go (to visit their father), when the stepfather's children come, or when the stepfather leaves to take his children out for the day—the last preweekend family dinner has a "togetherness" value unique to stepfamily households. It's a last evening to be together before the weekend permutations hit. One of our families chose to highlight this significance by making it a rule that everyone had to be home for dinner on Thursday night. Another went further and declared the Thursday night meal a special meal: either jointly prepared by the whole family or (when workloads and schoolwork got busy, since this is a workday) a special order-in meal from a favorite restaurant.

Also, by cycle 2, everyone knows one another's interests and skills. This is a good time to let similar interests flow together and novel activity partnerships to evolve. Reflecting their resilience, vitality, and variety, our project families came up with a plethora of bonding activities. Stepfathers coach stepchildren's softball, basketball, and soccer teams. One salesman stepfather took it upon himself to (aggressively) sell his stepdaughter's school-drive cookies at his office. There were stepfather-stepkid jogging, stamp-collecting, and Dungeons and Dragons bondings. One stepfather took a Red Cross CPR course with his stepdaughter. Stepmothers and stepdaughters started ragdoll collections, tap-dancing lessons, and yard-sale browsing. One stepmother and stepson went on a workout plan together. Another pair worked together on a political campaign. One stepmother and her stepsons (sixties music fanatics, all) turned a toolshed into a shrine to Woodstock Nation.

As one of my researchers put it, "With talent, energy and originality like this, how can these stepfamilies *not* succeed?"

POINTS TO KEEP IN MIND

- Because the settling-in process is now complete or almost complete and the youngster is in latency, the quietest period of childhood, cycle 2 is usually characterized by less stress, greater family cohesiveness, and better child adjustment.

- Neotraditional and Matriarchal stepfamilies experience the most calm and adjustment during this cycle. Having surrendered their unrealistic expectations, they have resolved the major issues of cycle 1. Romantic families are more likely to have continuing problems in this cycle because lingering illusions about the nature of stepfamily life prevent them from working through cycle 1 issues.

- About 20 percent of children move and live with their fathers in early adolescence. This is usually a developmentally appropriate change, as it helps the adolescent deal with autonomy and identity issues. However, in some cases the adolescent moves because of problems in the stepfamily. If this is the case, it may leave the adolescent vulnerable to more behavior and developmental problems.

- Porousness is a characteristic of stepfamily life that refers to the more permeable boundaries and outside influences, such as the nonresidential parent.

- Stepfamilies have to learn to cope with constant change. Often these changes are outside their control, including those inspired by the nonresidential parent and his family (parents, aunts, uncles, etc.).

- Remarried women can cope with the stress and strains of problems with their husband's ex-wives by learning to "take a vacation" from their usual pattern of behavior, by becoming temporarily "deskilled" at solving family problems, which allows other members to take care of issues, and by not personalizing criticism from the child's biological mother and inviting her to provide input on issues.

- Using good communications skills and scheduling time for discussing issues is essential for resolving problems and concerns.

- Developing family rituals that promote positive interactions and fun among family members is also important. Scheduling a special dinner night and developing stepparent-stepchild activities or projects also helps to promote better relations among family members.

chapter eight

The Nonresidential Parent:

The Changing Father

When he was married to his wife Natalie, Robert Rust had been one of those fathers you see in life-insurance commercials. He pushed his kids on playground swings. He stood behind them with his arms out wide and his smile half bright, half nervous, as they pedaled off on bicycles newly shorn of training wheels. Natalie assumed it would always be that way, even after they split up, which they did when Ben was seven and Nina was five. Robert may have assumed it too.

But then came the divorce, and, three years later, Natalie's remarriage, and Robert became a different person. Baffling so many who had known him—Natalie, not least of all—he virtually dropped out of his children's lives. Over the course of the first year of Natalie's remarriage, Robert rented a small apartment and changed his work schedule as a television station media salesman so that he was out of town half of each month. By the end of that year, it was her new husband, Artie Lewis, who was biking and Rollerblading with Nina and Ben.

Natalie thought that Robert's being on his own might have thrown him—that all he needed was a good woman to get him reattached to his domestic side. Yet when Robert became involved with a coworker named Gabriella—a warm Hispanic woman who came from a large family (just the kind of woman Natalie expected would guide him back to fatherhood)—the opposite happened. "He was totally wrapped up in her. He got a motorcycle, he was always vacationing in Mexico," Natalie told me with a quizzical look on her face. "It's as if he had never left the single life. It's as if he didn't have kids."

This is a fairly common male reaction. According to research by Mavis Hetherington of the University of Virginia, men who have been very active fathers sometimes drop out of their children's lives after divorce. Dr. Hetherington described this behavior as an avoidance mechanism. These men were coping with pain as men sometimes do— by simply pretending that the source of pain was not present. At the beginning of the separation, they might have tried to keep up a strong relationship with their kids: gamely taking them to movies and plying them with popcorn and sweets, trying not to feel their hearts break when that easy, wisecracking familiarity—with dinner habits, home-work quirks, sibling squabbles—gave way to slightly more stilted, obligatory conversation. After weeks or months of this loosening bond—"this slow demotion," one such man said bitterly, "from Daddy to *Uncle* Daddy"—the men began dealing with their heartache as they would a heartache of the romantic kind: by forcing an out-of-sight/out-of-mind equation. They sought to stanch the unbearable pain by emotionally letting go of their children. It was that simple.

My researchers and I encountered this heartbroken/defensively avoidant man with enough frequency to coin a name for him: the Suddenly Vanishing Father. About 10 to 15 percent of the nonresidential fathers in our study fit into this category.

During the course of the project we also met two other kinds of nonresidential father. One of these types I call the Divorce-Activated

Father, because it is the dissolution of the marriage that awakens his zeal—sometimes panic-driven—to be an involved parent. Just as a mild heart attack serves as a wake-up call for a man with sloppy eating and exercise habits, the divorce can be a wake-up call for this careless father who has regarded his closeness to his son and his daughter with that same cavalier inattention.

"The divorce was an eye-opener," said one such project father. "I realized, right off the bat, that I had to shape up and get my act together or I'd lose my kids. I decided to stop working on weekends—since weekends were the only time I could see them. And I cut down on golf and on hanging out with my buddies." Some of these men found that the removal of the "crutch" (as one called it) of their wives' presence forced their emergency-driven attention to fatherhood. "Betsy always did *everything*," project father Wade Gibbons marveled. "All the meals, all the carpooling, all the entertainment. I was just a couch potato who had my kids handed to me on a silver platter: prewashed, prefed, preentertained." Gibbons, a trucking company foreman, guffaws and shakes his head. "Man, I was clueless." Now he's stopped laughing. "Having Kelsey and Wade, Jr., with me that first weekend in my little furnished two-bedroom was really depressing. They near 'bout cried 'Get us out of here! You can't do anything for us. We want to be home with Mom!' " Wade's born-again fathering was rooted in that touched-bottom moment.

The ex-wives of some Divorce-Activated Fathers encountered a true irony: The fact that these men had not been attentive fathers *during* the marriage—they had preferred watching *Monday Night Football* to quizzing the kids on grammar—had been among their wives' key complaints about them. Yet here they were, *after* the divorce—just at the time when so many men get wild and crazy—doting on their children. One project mother noted her ex-husband's shepherding their dyslexic son to a three-times-a-week tutor and said dryly: "If he'd done that before, I wouldn't have divorced him."

The third type of changing father can be called the Remarriage-Activated Father. Like the Divorce-Activated Father, he changes from an inattentive to an involved father, and he does so after the end of the marriage. But he is activated by a different set of emotions. He is jealous and upset at the prospect of another man—a stepfather—supplanting him in his children's lives. He is their father, and he does not want another man stealing that role away from him.

The changes these nonresidential fathers experience after the divorce create a ripple effect. If the man has remarried, the ripples spread to his new wife. They also spread to the stepfamilies that these men's ex-wives make with their children and their new husbands.

Let us take these fathers one by one, to see the challenges, the problems—and, in some cases, the benefits—that occur, to them and to their children and their ex-wives' new marriages, when a radical change in fathering occurs.

THE SUDDENLY VANISHING FATHER

When a man essentially drops out of the lives of his children because it is too painful for him to continue as a part-time parent, the pain has to root somewhere, and the lack of resolution is transferred from A to B, B usually being the man's new marriage and, if he is part of one, his new stepfamily. Many arguments Suddenly Vanishing Fathers have when they enter a stepfamily are really a form of displacement. The man who complains about the sloppy state of his stepchild's room or the child's awful taste in music is really complaining about something else: the loss of his own biological children and how much pain that causes him. The stepchild's room and musical tastes are diversionary issues—decoy issues.

Some men became involved with women who pressed them to reestablish close ties with their children; but other Vanishing Fathers see their second marriages founder either because their new wives want a child and they do not, or sometimes, where the woman had a child, because the man resisted the stepfather role. They felt guilty becoming close to other children, since they had let go of their own. It made sense that such men felt most comfortable being part of Matriarchal stepfamilies. Carrying on the pattern they established with their own divorce, these men eschewed involvement with the children.

Since avoidance—not just of their own children but of so many issues—is a leitmotif of Suddenly Vanishing Fathers' remarriages, tensions are pitched high from the start. The baggage these men bring into their new marriages is substantial—and tightly wrapped. One of the tensest and most inflexible of such fathers and stepfathers was a man named Ed Coakes. Ed was a tall, steel-jawed, handsome man. He looked in control. A former naval officer and now a successful small-business owner, he had been a highly authoritarian parent in his first marriage. After the divorce, he had tried to keep up that tough-dad persona with his children, and he had expected to enjoy the same predivorce power with them. He soon realized, however, that a visiting daddy is, perforce, an accommodator—the wooer, not the wooed. Ed did not take very well to the new role of weekend father; both the loss of his daily closeness with his children and his diminishment as an authority figure crumpled his ego and heart. His relationship with his children atrophied, and when his ex-wife moved them to Memphis to be closer to her parents, he neither fought the move in court nor visited them more than once a year.

Ed was five years into his second marriage, to a boutique owner named Judith, who had an adolescent daughter, when we visited the family. Theirs was a Matriarchal stepfamily mainly because Judith, an elegant and charming woman who knew how to position people with one another at dinner parties and in life, kept Ed from exerting his natural authority-figure role over the willful teenage Merilee. Headstrong Merilee let it be known that she was not taking orders from a former sailor, and, while tolerating her mother's marriage to the man, the girl closed the door on any but the most perfunctory stepfather-stepdaughter relationship. When Ed's feathers were ruffled by Merilee's brusqueness toward him, Judith compensated by soothing and attending to her husband with a single-mindedness that melted his anger and distracted his complaint.

In fact, Judith Coakes was a prime example of the kind of Matriarchal wife we saw a good deal of: the Ambassador. She skillfully served as a liaison between her husband and her children—so skillfully that neither of them knew she was managing things and keeping them at arm's distance from one another, as much for their own good as for hers. A sanguine, pragmatic woman with a classic Southern woman's ability to pull strings carefully and tactfully, Judith realized that her emotional daughter and her power-interested husband were a potential powder keg. "Soon Merilee will be away in college," Judith whispered, leaning in and touching my arm. "I'm just keepin' things in balance till then." That way she could have her husband *and* her daughter, without explosiveness.

To Ed, coexisting with a teenager he did not have authority over was cause for grumbling. Our videotape showed him as a befuddled, defensive patriarch-without-portfolio. "I'm always made to feel like I'm the bad guy!" he complained. He was unbending on his values. "I learned, growing up and in the navy: 'There are rules, and you follow those rules,'" he said. "These are my values." Despite his stern words, Ed's eyes telegraphed sadness and confusion—almost, in fact, defeat.

What saved Ed from utter discouragement was his work. As the owner of an office-security-systems company with twelve people working for him, he had a daily outlet for playing the role of the boss. Authoritarianism was acceptable in his work-a-day milieu, and if he could not be a respected and somewhat feared father, well, at least he *could* be a respected and feared employer. This role clearly gave expression to his personality and utilized a good deal of his energy. Judith, who liked to have her husband on her arm at the rodeo, at benefits, and at art gallery openings, complained that he often worked until 8 P.M. Still, when pressed, she said she preferred his occupational absorption to the alternative scenario: fights and tension at home.

In the Suddenly Vanishing Father scenario, the man himself is not the only one who suffers. There is also pain for the children of such men—

and that pain often gets pushed from child to mother, in the child's desperate attempt to dispel blame for the father's mysterious disappearance. When this displacement occurs, both the child and the mother end up confused and unhappy. But if that is the bad news, the good news is this: Sometimes something as simple as overdue honesty can go a long way toward rectifying the misunderstanding and ameliorating the double heartache.

The Newleys, a Neotraditionalist family in the project, are an example of this situation. During our initial interview, Karen Newley had described why her former marriage had failed. Her then-husband, Willis Pratt, had reacted to her going back to school for her master's degree and seeking work as a nurse with fear and disapproval. When the chasm this created in their already fragile marriage became too great to be bridged, they separated, then divorced. Clearly, then, the divorce was mutual. Karen knew this. Willis knew this. *I* knew this. But, as we would all later find out, one important person in the equation did not have access to this knowledge.

And that person was then six-year-old Noah Pratt.

Karen had tried to encourage Willis to stay close to their son, who was six when the divorce was final and eight when Karen married Jim Newley; but Willis had, in Karen's words, "slunk away, him and his wounded pride." When Willis remarried—to a decent woman whom Karen approved of—she was hopeful, as are many ex-wives of Suddenly Vanishing Fathers, that he would be domesticated back into his proper fatherly role. Jim, supportive of Karen and instinctively cognizant of the limits of his stepfather role, was hopeful also. In this regard, Karen and Jim were typical of Neotraditional couples. Neotraditionals *want* the nonresidential father to be appropriately involved in the child's life. (By contrast, Romantic couples want nonresidential fathers to stay away, thus leaving them free to indulge their just-like-a-nuclear-family myth. In Matriarchal stepfamilies—given the nature of the woman in the couple—the nonresidential father may well have been as vestigial a character in the child's life during the former marriage as the stepfather becomes in the subsequent marriage. Still, Matriarchals, like

Neotraditionals, appreciate parenting help from outside, since it helps the Matriarchal stepfather get what he's come to the marriage to obtain: responsibility-free marital companionship.)

Like many such Neotraditional wives of Suddenly Vanishing Fathers, Karen's hopes were in vain. Willis Pratt saw Noah only intermittently over the next four years. By the time Karen, Jim, and Noah appeared for their follow-up interview, Noah had changed. The boy I remembered as a bright, eager eight-year-old was now an angry, sullen twelve-year-old whose grades had dropped from B's to C's and D's and who was being disrespectful and disobedient at home and at school. The Newleys, who had had a good marriage during Noah's latency, were feeling the stress of the boy's problems acutely: Karen pressed her new husband, Jim, to be a more active, involved stepfather; Jim told Karen he was trying but that *Noah* was now rejecting *him*. Why was Jim blaming her son, an angry Karen demanded to know.

Still, more disturbing than the mother-stepfather arguments, was Noah's recent cruelty toward his mother. He would bark at Karen at the least provocation. Although she understood that bristling over maternal help is a normal earmark of adolescence, Noah's anger clearly went beyond the normal. His insults were plainly mean and intentionally hurtful. "The other day," reported the unlithe Karen with dismay, "he called me Fatso." As for Jim, he was now resigned to being permanently, annoyedly, baffled by Noah's double messages. "James, it's the damndest thing," Jim said. "One minute Noah will ask me to throw the baseball around; then when we go out back with the gloves and the ball, he'll go all aloof and nasty on me, as if *I* were the one who'd suggested playing together. I have to hold my temper now whenever I'm with him."

Both Newleys were almost desperately eager for me to talk to Noah. So, on the summer day of our follow-up interview, as Karen went out on the back deck with a pitcher of lemonade, two glasses, and one of my research assistants, I sat in the den with Noah and Jim Newley. Noah ignored both of us. He sat, aggressively punching the buttons on his video game clicker while the Nirvana song he'd put on the CD player filled the silence with the unnerving reminder of terminal young male misery.

I opened the conversation by asking him if he had seen his dad lately.

Noah's face turned from hostile to sad in an instant. He replied: "I don't have a dad anymore."

"You don't?" I asked. "I seem to remember a conversation where you told me your dad's name was Willis."

Noah shook his head. "He's not my dad anymore. He left after my mom divorced him. I used to be really close to him, but then after Mom divorced him, he stopped coming around." I noted the noun-verb sequence: Mom did the divorcing. *It was Mom's fault.*

It was clear that Noah blamed his mother for the divorce; Willis Pratt was out of his life because Karen had driven him out of the marriage. I was also pretty sure that this construct of his parents' divorce was at the root of Noah's problems with his stepfather. Noah was keeping his distance out of self-protection. He had lost one father; he did not want to go through the wrenching pain of losing a second.

Behavior like Noah's is fairly common in homes where the reasons for the parental divorce have never been explained to the child. Left in the dark, the child makes up his own scenarios. Even more debilitating, not talking about the divorce prevents closure. The destruction of his family of origin remains an unresolved issue for the child and, as such, it continues to affect stepfamily life.

The Divorce Conversation

Children want to know why their parents dissolved their marriage. Indeed, they *need* to know. The act of speaking truthfully to a child about divorce serves three functions: (1) It puts closure on the marriage for them; (2) it lets them know that their parents care enough about them to carefully articulate a difficult truth without hedging or avoiding; and—illustrated in the reverse by Noah Pratt, (3) it keeps them from having to resort to imagining reasons that the divorce took place: reasons that can cause pain to their parents.

One reason parents often avoid divorce conversations is that they feel their children will not be able to understand the complex emotions that cause a marriage to be dissolved. Adult feelings, especially those aroused in the hothouse of a bad marriage, are too subtle—and too revelatory of adult secrets and behavior—for children to understand.

While it is true that young children's comprehension of adult feelings and behavior is limited, five- and six-year-olds can grasp broad-stroke explanations such as "Mommy and Daddy couldn't get along." Older children, particularly adolescents like Noah, will want and need a more detailed account of divorce.

A story Karen told me illustrates how egregiously the reasons for a divorce can be misinterpreted by a child, even a fairly mature one like Noah.

One afternoon, a few days after my visit, Karen and Noah had a very surprising talk about the end of her marriage to Willis Pratt. What made it surprising for Karen was that Noah told her what he had told me: The divorce was her fault. Karen had stopped loving his dad, Willis, and drove him off.

"Is that what you think?" a shocked Karen exclaimed. "That I ran your father off? No, no! That's not what happened!" Then, in emotional words, Karen explained the reasons for the Pratts' divorce. She and Willis had had some financial problems, she was not happy in the marriage, and she wanted to go back to school and then go back to work. He wanted neither. "We had grown too far apart," Karen told her son. "Sometimes that happens with people. We had a real difference of opinion. We decided to divorce. The divorce was a mutual decision."

That emotional session made a big difference to Noah Pratt. His behavior did not change overnight, of course, and the pain of divorce did not entirely lose its grip. But now he understood one important piece of his parents' divorce—that his mother was not to blame for his father's disappearance from his life and that neither parent acted unilaterally.

The slow dissipation of Noah's anger after this mother-son conversation illustrates how emotionally liberating a divorce conversation can be for children, especially when the parent patiently answers any and all questions the children have about the divorce. To facilitate understanding, a parent should explain the divorce in simple, nonjudgmental words that do not apportion blame. It is also important for the parent to explain her or his perception of the breakup without embellishment or apology.

Many parents believe that children in general, and adolescents in particular, do not want to hear intimate personal details about a parent's life. And, indeed, some teens do not. In those cases, the best policy is to avoid turning the divorce discussion into a confessional. Do not become maudlin or sentimental; do not act as if you want your kids feel closer to you; do not act as if you want them to understand you or bond with you. Just get the facts out, simply, economically, with dignity. Even if they act put-upon, you are giving them information that will help them far more than they will ever admit to you.

The Sons and Daughters of Divorce

Willis Pratt was not spurred by Noah's academic and behavior problems to make a reappearance in his son's life, but many formerly Suddenly Vanishing Fathers do go that route. Research indicates that standoffish nonresidential fathers are more likely to get pulled back into a boy's life if the boy acquires behavior problems. Why is this? In a crisis, the father whom pain drove away now has a powerful emotional incentive to reenter his son's life, his head held high. That incentive is the role of the Rescuer. As the mother and stepfather have tried and failed to help the boy over his problems, here is the opportunity for the father to come riding in on the metaphorical white charger.

Many formerly distant nonresidential fathers of troubled boys take that opportunity. Project results show that nonresidential fathers have better relationships and more visitation with sons who have behavior problems—and with daughters who do not have them.

The response of men to their sons may seem contradictory. Why are boys who *deserve* a father's proud support unable to obtain it? This paradox may be rooted in evolutionary necessity: Troubled boys *need* male help. Untroubled boys can make it on their own more easily, without the emergency reentry of their Vanishing Fathers. Psychological health and behavioral resources make untroubled boys more self-sufficient and more able to have good relationships with their stepfathers.

Troubled girls are likely to have less contact with their nonresidential fathers (while high-functioning girls tend to get more attention from their fathers). But, again, in the natural course of parental protectiveness, girls are usually not in harm's way: We have found that the mothers of these girls generally expend a great deal of care and nurturance—as well as dismay and worry—on their troubled daughters.

So safety nets exist for many of the children whose Vanishing Fathers refuse to come back and attend to them. However, for *really* troubled kids, that safety net is thinner. Indeed, it can be alarmingly thin. Boys and girls whose mothers and stepfathers have thrown in the towel and whose nonresidential fathers do not want them either wind up with a grandparent, aunt, or some other relative or end up on the street.

The Stepfamily Marriage and the Suddenly Vanishing Father

Children almost always do better when they continue to see their biological fathers. But the reemergence of a Suddenly Vanishing Father can cause two problems for a stepfamily and for the marriage at its foundation.

First, the man becomes an ongoing reminder of something the stepfamily did not really have to think about before—that the family is not a nuclear family. Before they could forget or pretend; now they can't. The reactivated father brings them face-to-face with the fact that they cannot live the nuclear-family myth.

Second, if there are unresolved emotional issues between this figure and his newly married ex-spouse, they may reignite when he reappears. Often, when conflict erupts between the divorced parents, especially after the remarriage, these rumblings are not fresh battles—or even child-related battles—but leftover tensions from the divorce or from the marriage.

THE DIVORCE-ACTIVATED FATHER

The Divorce-Activated Father is the formerly indifferent man who springs back into his children's lives because he is afraid he might lose them. And, on the face of it, he is a sympathetic, indeed, a heart-tugging figure. He wants to protect and preserve his place in their lives.

But positive motives sometimes can impact negatively on other people's lives. One of the potential adverse effects is on the woman the Divorce-Activated Father is dating. The man, eager to reestablish his paternal preeminence, often takes the child anywhere and everywhere, including on dates. Some Divorce-Activated Fathers present themselves and their children as package deals. After a single date, the woman gets the man *and* his kids—she's essentially being auditioned as a prospective stepmother. Some women find this presumptuous, inappropriate, and intrusive. But other women, women who are intrigued by the stepmother role, do not mind the audition. Often they become such active stepmothers that the man's ex-wife may feel threatened by the encroachment. Who is this woman who is suddenly so eager to look after my children?

The Divorce-Activated Father
and the Romantic Stepfamily

The Divorce-Activated Father's good intentions are a problem for a Romantic stepfamily—indeed, more than a problem. He is often a nightmare for a Romantic stepfamily. Couples invested in the we're-just-like-a-nuclear-family myth don't want anyone else in the family. One Romantic mother, Vicki Leeds, represented an extreme version of this attitude. At our first interview, she actually took me aside and said, of her ex-husband, Pete, "Everything would be fine if Pete would just leave us alone. Paul and Suzi get along fine with their stepfather, but Pete's always getting in the way."

Vicki actually had valued her ex-husband's divorce-stimulated involvement with Paul and Suzi. But after her remarriage, Pete, threatened by the sudden presence of another man in his children's lives, became uncooperative. Instead of bringing the kids home at five, as she requested, he would take them out to dinner and not get them home until seven. He also ignored Vicki's remonstrances about stuffing the kids with sweets and fast food. After one outing, Suzi and Paul came home with wads of Hershey's Crackles paper crumpled in all their pockets. After several weeks of such provoking behavior, Pete and Vicki had a big blow-up—and the already imperfect relationship crumbled.

Families—and they are almost always Romantic families—that find themselves in situations like that of the Leeds need to keep several points in mind.

The first is that the Divorce-Activated Father is here to stay. He cannot be made to go away. The court has assigned him legal rights vis-à-vis the child, and those rights have to be respected. Denying or challenging them opens the door to an emotionally and financially draining lawsuit. One way for a Romantic woman to make this thought more palatable is to remind herself that the presence of the Divorce-Activated Father is *good* for the children.

The second essential point to keep in mind is that no one should try to turn the children against their eager father. Criticism or either/or choices can create terrible loyalty conflicts for a child—and that is as true for a child of sixteen or seventeen as for one of six or seven.

The third important point to remember is that reassurance can go a long way. The former wife or her new husband—or both, together—should reassure the man that they recognize his unique place in his children's lives and will respect it. No one plans to supplant him.

However, as a quid pro quo for that respect and recognition, the Divorce-Activated Father should be told that the stepfamily expects him to respect its rules about what the children can eat, where they can go, and the time they should be returned home. It is also a good idea to let the Divorce-Activated Father know that he is never spoken about negatively in front of the children and that the adults in the stepfamily expect that courtesy to be returned.

The Divorce-Activated Father and His Children

In most stepfamilies, the biological father's reappearance is welcomed by the children, who usually benefit. But sometimes his reappearance can trigger terrible loyalty conflicts in children, who may feel that in reconnecting with their father, they are somehow betraying their mother. One of the most poignant conversations I had during the project was with Nicky Fitchings, the son in a Romantic stepfamily—a son whose biological father was beginning to show interest in coming back into his life.

Nicky's father, Warren Ed ("W.E.") Fitchings, a building-trades apprentice and would-be country-western studio musician, initially had been unstable. Nicky's schoolteacher mother, Ruth, briskly initiated the divorce when Warren's hours on his electric guitar began to exceed his union-protected time on the scaffolding of local construction sites. She married a widowed assistant principal—an educated, responsible man: everything dreamy and mercurial W.E. was not—and, with Nicky, the two set up a Romantic stepfamily.

For the first two years, W.E. was completely unthreatening to Ruth's new nuclear-family dream. His occasional stabs at seeing Nicky again were easily dismissed by virtue of his hapless life: Claiming to be going back to engineering trade school (a claim Ruth judged to be a wish dream), W.E. moved to Lubbock shortly after the divorce; every eight or ten weeks he would show up in Houston on a Friday night with big plans to take Nicky for the weekend, only to return him later that evening because the friends with whom he was houseguesting had mysteriously rescinded their invitation.

Ruth and her new husband, Richard O'Banlon, had a baby daughter. There was ginger talk—by Ruth and Richard—of Richard's eventually adopting Nicky so that the whole family could have the same last name.

Then W.E. started to come back.

Much to Ruth's amazement, her ex-husband had finished his trade-school course. He got a job in an engineering firm and moved back to Houston. He began making more serious bids for his son's time. He even started paying child support. (Ruth and Richard, shrewdly, never took W.E. to court, understanding that if they wanted to have Nicky to themselves, attempting to extract support payments from the rather impecunious W.E. would just defeat their purpose.)

When I visited the O'Banlons for a follow-up interview, Nicky Fitching (who now called Richard "Daddy Rick") spent about half an hour demonstrating for me, while his mother smiled happily on, how his various bird-whistle imitations and toe-tickling incited his baby sister, Rebecca, to gales of infant glee. But when his mother exited the room, baby sister in tow, and I asked Nicky how he was doing, his little face turned worried and guilty.

"Are you gonna tell my mom what I say?" he asked.

"No," I told him. "Whatever you tell me is private."

He regarded me a long time, then asked, "You *sure*?"

"Yes. Everything you tell me is private, unless it's dangerous to you."

His eyes began tearing. He whispered, "I want to see my dad."

When I asked Nicky why he was crying, it became clear that he felt guilty for that desire; he knew it would not please his mother that, despite all the love "Daddy Rick" had given him, it was W.E. he wanted to bond with.

I told him that I really thought his mother would want to know how he felt.

"No, she wouldn't," he said. "It would hurt her feelings."

I wanted to hug this wonderful eleven-year-old boy, who was empathetic enough not to want to hurt his mother. But, even more than that, I wanted him to be able to tell his mother how he felt. That proved unnecessary.

A few minutes later, when Nicky joined Ruth and Richard for a videotape interview, Ruth sensed that her son was upset, but, since I had promised Nicky confidentiality, I could not tell her why.

Eventually Nicky did tell Ruth how he felt. Ruth was surprised at first and perhaps, indeed, a little hurt. And Richard was taken aback. Otherwise so reasonable, both O'Banlons had stubbornly held a commonly mistaken assumption: that if they did not receive much—or legally press for—child support, the errant father had no claim on his son. (In Texas, as in many other states, payment of child support is not directly linked to visitation. The right to the former is not, strictly speaking, dependent on full compliance with the latter.) But the O'Banlons soon realized the same thing Vicki Leeds had to realize: The nonresidential father was *in* the child's life. The man could not be wished away. The child was a part of him—50 percent of him. And his longings to see and know and bond with his father were simply there, no matter how virtuous and generous and decent his stepfather happened to be.

Matriarchal and Neotraditional Stepfamilies

Unlike Romantics such as Ruth and Richard O'Banlon, Neotraditional and some Matriarchal stepfamilies often view the Divorce-Activated Father as a convenience and an asset. These couples understand that the children should have a healthy, involved relationship with their fathers, and they support such arrangements. They also see the advantages for their stepfamily: Dad's involvement with the kids gives Mom and her new husband extra "couple time," which ultimately benefits the whole household.

Still, even with good intentions, logistics—situational and emotional—do not proceed flawlessly. If both ex-spouses are remarried to people who are themselves parents, each spouse's attachment to his or her children has a domino effect on the other parents' children. And when a Divorce-Activated Father marries a women who herself has children, and if he is an avid enough family man to become an active Neotraditional stepfather (as well as a guilty nonresidential father)— well, sometimes he finds himself divided against himself.

One project father, a pipe fitter named George Severin, is a prime example. Although able to bond well with his stepchildren, George was keenly—painfully—aware that his primary fatherly loyalty lay with his biological children, the ones he no longer lived with. George felt so guilty about this new living arrangement, and he was so anxious about sending his biological children the message that he wanted them with him, that he displaced his stepchildren to make this point: Every other weekend, when his kids came to visit, he made his stepchildren move out of their bedroom (the house had only two bedrooms) and onto living-room couches so his children would feel welcome. His viewpoint was: "My kids are just visitors, so when they come over, they should be treated special."

The first couple of times, it was actually fun for the six- and eight-year-old stepsons who got displaced for the weekend—they acted as if they were camping out (brandishing flashlights, even). Then the novelty wore off, and the boys quietly, then vocally, resented being displaced to make room for George's seven-year-old son and five-year-old daughter. Why were George's children using *their* toys and rifling through *their* drawers? It wasn't fair!

His stepchildren had a third complaint for George. Not only were they uprooted from their beds, and not only were their rooms occasionally ransacked by George's children, but, they felt, they were also being held to a different—and higher—standard of behavior than George's children were. *They* had to be the saintly hosts if George's kids spilled Coke on their Houston Oilers mouse pads or doodled on the edge of their math homework; George's kids were always "the guests" who could do no wrong!

George was heartbroken. "I don't know why the kids can't love each other," he said to me. Big-hearted George, while not Super-Dad, was idealistic enough to want his two roles—nonresidential father who sees his own kids every other weekend and involved stepfather in a Neo-traditional stepfamily—to mesh seamlessly. He wanted his children and his stepchildren to be best friends. Yet his zeal as a Divorce-Activated Father and his guilt as a nonresidential father who was also a stepfather had led him to sabotage his dreams.

His stepkids resented his biological kids, and, of course, his wife took his stepkids' side.

Within six months, the Severin family was embroiled in a not atypical father/stepfather divided against himself crisis.

To his credit, George took immediate steps to alleviate the crisis. Here is what he did:

1. He listened to his stepchildren's complaint to him: "You say 'Everyone's got the same rules,' but it's not true." He saw their point of view—that there was a double standard—and he apologized to them.

2. He listened to his children's complaint to him: "Whenever we're with you, you're always with *them*. Why can't we have any time alone with you?" He made plans to spend one of his visitation weekends per month alone with his children—at Six Flags over Texas, at a cousin's house, or out camping.

3. He gave his children their own drawers and their own shelves in his house. That way they could leave their things there, and if their things just happened to be "borrowed" (and dirtied or broken) by his stepchildren . . . well, then, both sets of kids were, indeed, living by the same rules.

4. He got bunk beds, so that all of the kids could have a bed during visits—no one had to camp out on living-room couches.

5. After a year he rented a larger house. His own children now had their own bedrooms, just as his stepchildren did.

THE REMARRIAGE-ACTIVATED FATHER

Actually there are two very different kinds of Remarriage-Activated Fathers.

The first type, like the Divorce-Activated Father, is motivated by the desire to protect his paternal role, which he fears will be usurped by the new stepfather. While his former wife remains unmarried, this man is a fairly typical nonresidential parent in terms of his relationship with his children and the frequency of his visits. The new stepfather acts as a kind of catalyst. Only when he enters the picture does the Remarriage-Activated Father realize fully how important the parent-child relationship is to him and how badly he wants to preserve it.

The second type of Remarriage-Activated Father comes back to his children *not* on his own accord. Rather, he is pulled back in by court papers demanding payment for delinquent child support. And not uncommonly, if he accedes to the court's demands, he will demand a quid pro quo from his former wife and her new husband: a greater voice in the children's lives. The man not only wants to see the children more, he wants more parental authority.

Ironically, often it is not the woman but her new husband who activates this second form of father who regains an interest in the lives of his children. Most men are happy to contribute to the support of a stepchild, but understandably, they also feel the child's biological father should do so as well. But since going after delinquent child support can backfire, before initiating legal action against a deadbeat dad, a stepfamily, particularly a Romantic stepfamily, should ponder the following question: If life in the stepfamily is already happy, do you want to risk that happiness by opening the door to a third party who, in return for his support payments, will demand more visitation rights and other forms of control?

Since the reappearance of a Remarriage-Activated Father is often not a source of great joy to the adults in the stepfamily, particularly the man's former wife, it is not in the best interests of the children to fight old fights, to play old games, to settle scores from ten years ago. It is not in the best interests of the children to relive the past. In dealing with Remarriage-Activated Fathers, mothers must draw an imaginary line in the sand—between the old marriage (unresolved as its ending may have been) and the new mutual duty: to see that the children are happy and stable. It is not in the best interests of the children to deny such men fair access to their children just because you think they were not fair to *you* during your marriage, or even if you think their reasons for springing back into the children's lives are opportunistic, possessive, or anything other than purely motivated. (Nobody has perfectly pure motives.)

A few couples, finding themselves stuck in an unresolved divorce (even when both have remarried), have gone in for couple's counseling. The goal of this kind of therapy is to work out the emotional issues that continue to trouble the man and woman. (A sign of this is continuing or renewed fighting about old issues.) But the vast majority of ex-spouses with unresolved divorces would never entertain this step. In such cases, the best thing to do is simply cut with the past as cleanly as possible. Here are some ways to do that.

1. Have a formal information session.

Have your ex-spouse over when your new husband is there. Use the first-person plural in clearly describing your expectations and routine. ("We don't allow TV watching until homework is done." "We visit [her new husband] Jim's mother every other Sunday night.") Make clear that your ex-husband must deal with you and your husband in a present-forward, not past-inclusive way.

2. Remember—and reiterate—"It's not about us."

Arguments will be inevitable, but refuse to participate in arguments about the two of you as ex-marrieds. With each difference of opinion concerning the child, ask: Is the difference truly about the child—or is it old business from the former marriage? Only issues relating to the child are relevant now.

3. Avoid "you" sentences that include generalizations.

"You never . . ." "You always . . ." "You seem to assume . . .": Such sentences are accusatory and presume a history. Your aim now is not to provoke or accuse, and not to go back into that history. Your aim is to keep things in the present, moving forward.

WORKING TOGETHER

The most frequent result of the steps I've outlined is an arrangement we call the "typical standard," and it is one of several ways the stepfamily and the nonresidential parent resolve the parenting issue. Those ways include cooperative coparenting, parallel parenting, fiery foes, fathers who never visit, and cases where the fathers' rights are terminated.

Cooperative Coparenting

Coparenting is the best arrangement, when a couple can make it work. And to make it work, the man and woman have to have a friendly and cooperative postdivorce relationship and a mutual commitment to working together—which means working on their relationship to keep it civil and harmonious and sharing the same ultimate goal: the well-being of their child or children.

One other characteristic of couples who make coparenting work is that they live relatively close to each other. Proximity facilitates more visits and allows fathers to participate actively in their children's school and extracurricular events. In addition, visits to Dad are less likely to disrupt the children's social lives, which is a key issue for adolescents particularly.

Often when coparenting works, the former husband and wife achieve something like a real friendship. During the project, one nonresidential parent took the "ours baby," the half sibling from the remarriage, on weekend visits with the other children. His explanation was that this gave his former spouse and her husband some time without the children and that his children wanted their new sibling to be with them during visits.

Parallel Parenting

A more realistic model for many divorced parents is "parallel parenting." A term first coined by University of Pennsylvania sociologist Frank Furstenberg in the mid-1980s, parallel parenting just means that, the divorced mother parents in a way that is comfortable to her, and the divorced father in a way that is comfortable to him—and they do not talk about it. Most of the time this arrangement works. The exception is in cases where one parent is invitingly permissive and the other offputtingly authoritarian. Then, the children prefer being with one parent over the other. When this happens, talks between the divorced parents, or sessions with a psychologist, counselor, or stepfamily specialist are merited.

Parallel parenting is often used in what is known as the "standard visitation" arrangement. In the majority of stepfamilies, children visit with their nonresidential fathers on alternate weekends and holidays. In these cases, the fathers appear to be involved with their children in limited ways, although most children like to see their dads and enjoy time with them. There is some variability for kids in their relationships with their fathers, with most children wanting more access to their biological fathers. One child said, "I want to see my dad every day." A few kids want less access, mainly because Dad, unused to parenting alone, doesn't know how to engage or entertain a child. Said one girl, "I love Daddy. But when we visit, he just puts us in front of the TV or drops us off at Grandmother's house."

Fiery Foes

A small group of couples never resolve their differences. Connie Ahrons, a well-known divorce researcher, labeled these couples "fiery foes" because of their intense antagonistic relationships. Among these couples differences about parenting can be expressed in low-level chronic sniping or high-decibel shouting and yelling. Court battles are common among fiery foes, as are problems with child support payments, visitation, and custody.

One fourteen-year-old girl described what it was like to be the child of fiery foes this way: "It makes my stomach turn upside down and hurt when I see my parents fighting all the time. I can't eat and all I want to do is run and hide. I wish they would grow up and get over it." The best way for fiery foes to handle the normal logistics of the child's visits is to avoid face-to-face encounters. One way to do this is to have the father pick up and return the children at school rather than the mother's house.

Fathers Who Never Visit

A substantial number of fathers have no contact with their children following divorce and remarriage. Reasons for no contact vary from hostility and conflict between ex-spouses, to fathers having personal problems that prevent visitation, to long-distance parenting. The absence of the father, however, does not mean he has no impact on the family. Many children continue to feel close to their absent fathers and may idealize them. During a first interview a nine-year-old boy talked on and on about his father, describing all kinds of things they did together and plans they had for the future. When we talked with the mother, she said that her son had not seen his father in over two years and rarely talked with him on the telephone. Thus these fathers are present psychologically for the children and may influence the family and parent-child relationships. Custodial parents also keep the absent parent alive in the family through projective identification of the nonresidential parent onto a particular child. Statements such as "You act just like your father," or "Your father used to do that to me" keep the nonresidential parent part of the family, even when there is no contact with that parent. Alternatively, some mothers help the child develop a more empathic understanding of the father's absence and do not necessarily denigrate the absent parent.

Interestingly, many fathers who have very limited or no contact with their biological children often are highly involved with their stepchildren and provide both economic and emotional support for them. This was a most perplexing situation. Several fathers indicated their pain and confusion about being called a "deadbeat dad" when they were taking care of their stepchildren and providing for them. One man stated, "You can't win for losing. I am here with my stepkids and I provide all the things that their dad doesn't do, and all I get is, 'You're no good because you don't do it for your own kids.' Heck, my ex-wife doesn't want me in her life, and she makes it near impossible for me to see my kids. That's not fair." These fathers reported that they had difficult relationships with their exes or felt pressure from their new spouses not to see their children.

Termination of Parental Rights and Adoption by the Stepparent

In a small number of cases, the nonresidential dad's parental rights are legally terminated. This usually occurs in two cases. First, the nonresidential parent voluntarily gives up parental rights due to lack of involvement with the children. Second, the nonresidential parent's rights may be terminated in absentia or because it is judged to be in the children's best interests (for example, if the nonresidential father has psychiatric problems or if there has been sexual or physical abuse). In these cases, children usually have no relationship with the parent and consent to the termination.

The desire of the custodial parent and stepparent to have the stepparent adopt the stepchildren is another, infrequent cause of termination of the nonresidential parent's rights. Adoption of children by the stepparent is an infrequent arrangement.

THE RAREST KIND OF NONRESIDENTIAL PARENT

A couple of years ago, I was invited to speak to a Houston support group. "We would love to have you address our group, Dr. Bray," the organization's president said on the phone. "We have heard that you are positive and inclusive in your attitudes about family definitions today."

I thanked the woman for the compliment, and as we spoke a bit about when and where the meeting of her group was to be held, I caught a wisp of uncertainty in her voice. This was striking, because I knew she was a very successful business executive. Yet the undertone of her voice was insecure and sad.

When I addressed her support group, I found the room filled with people like her. Accomplished, successful, high-powered women who were that rarest kind of nonresidential parent: the mother who has chosen to cede custody to her ex-husband because she honestly feels that he will make a better primary parent than she.

These women, like all minorities, struggled mightily against a society that looked askance at them. People asked them all the time, "Why don't you have your children?" "Why don't you want your children?" They struggled with their loss of femininity—one, because they did not have their children, and two, because they were further alienated from their feminine sides through their male-oriented careers. In fact, part of the reason they were in the support group was because it gave them the opportunity to reconnect with other women.

What they wanted from me was to say it was okay that they did not have custody of their kids. And I did say that, because I felt it was true. All of these women had thought long and hard before making their unconventional decision to become nonresidential parents. It was much easier for those who had sons to make their decision, because sons often wanted to be with their fathers. Those with daughters worried that their daughters were not getting enough mothering. Still, almost all of these women were much more involved nonresidential parents than men usually are, and the ex-husbands they left their sons and daughters with were notably nurturing fathers.

I gave my talk, I answered their questions, and I had warm conversations with several of these women over coffee and cookies. As I left, I realized I was moved—very moved—by their vulnerability in the face of their professional success. And in their extreme act of going against the grain, I saw a personal integrity that seemed familiar.

Driving back to my office, I realized that almost every single one of our project families, struggling gamely against expectations and with unbidden challenges to live the life that was best for their families, embodied that same integrity.

POINTS TO KEEP IN MIND

- Nonresidential parents, who are mostly fathers, have changing relationships with their children and former spouses over the course of the stepfamily life cycle. Fathers develop a number of different types of relationships after the divorce and after the creation of the stepfamily.

  The Suddenly Vanishing Father was active in his children's lives prior to the divorce but drops out afterward to avoid the pain of not seeing his children on a regular basis.

  The Divorce-Activated Father was minimally involved with his children prior to the divorce but springs into action when he realizes that he might lose his children after the divorce. This is often perplexing to the mother and children and requires some adjustment in including the father as an active parent.

The Remarriage-Activated Father had a limited or a marginal relationship with his children but gets involved with them after his former wife remarries, usually out of competition about being replaced by the stepfather or due to being sued for child support payments. Remarried couples often do not realize that their legal actions will bring the father back into the picture.

- Children often are not told why their parents divorced. In the absence of information, they make up reasons or "stories" about the divorce that may impact them negatively. Parents need to provide their children with some basic information about the divorce and realize that as the children mature, they may ask for more details of what happened. It is important to present the basic facts, but children do not have to be given the graphic details of the divorce.

- Some men who have very limited or no contact with their own biological children are very active and supportive stepfathers. These men feel caught in between because they are labeled "deadbeat dads" when they are providing support for their stepchildren.

chapter nine

The Passage to Adolescence

"James, how are you?" Ellen Lawton's voice, loud and enthusiastic, crackled through the phone line. This morning I had left a message on her answering machine. Our cycle 3 interviews were beginning, and I wanted to know whether Ellen and Andrew would be available for an at-home interview. Efficient Ellen returned my call within an hour. "Of course, we have time for you, James," she said. "But it's a long drive, you know."

Ellen had finally got her house in Austin. At the end of cycle 2, a large hospital in the city had recruited her as an oncology nurse and Andrew as counselor. The day she told me about the "twofer" (the Lawtons' nickname for the joint recruitment), Ellen had sounded absolutely sure that life in Austin would be wonderful. And in many ways it seems to have turned out that way. She sounds very happy as she describes her new house and job and the Lawtons' summer visits to Lake Travis.

Andrew, apparently, is also thriving. Ellen tells me that he was recently promoted to deputy director of social services at the hospital and received a sizable raise. I think, in the early days of the Lawtons' marriage, Ellen sometimes worried that Andrew would turn out to be a more polished version of her rudderless first husband, Tom, but that fear seems to have dissipated. She says that since the move, Andrew has come into his own.

There is also good news about Caroline.

Ellen says that her daughter has grown into a wonderful student. "She gets straight A's and she loves to read."

"That must please, Andrew," I say. I remember Andrew was a reader.

"It does," Ellen says. "The two of them have gotten real close. I have two real readers on my hands."

When I ask about Todd, however, the music goes out of Ellen's voice. I get a dissatisfied grunt, then a sour "Oh, God, that boy!"

One of my sweetest project memories is of eight-year-old Todd standing in the front yard of Ellen's Melton Street house with a Tonka truck tucked under his arm. But apparently that lovely little boy has been replaced by an uncommunicative, churlish, surly teenager.

"I don't know what's going on in his mind anymore," Ellen complains. "He hardly speaks to me and he is always so rude—rude, rude. Remember how he used to be?"

I mention my memory of the summer day.

"Ohhh," Ellen purrs, "wasn't he just the sweetest thing then?" However, according to his mother, the current Todd is doing poorly in school, lacks direction or interests. Ellen also is unhappy with Todd's new Austin friends. "There are so many wonderful young people down here. The sons and daughters of professors and doctors and government people; and who does Todd pal around with? A bunch of raga-muffins and bums."

Ellen's voice suddenly drops to a conspiratorial whisper. "He's drifting, James. I worry that he's going to turn out just like Tom. Todd needs to pay attention to his schoolwork and get some direction. I always had plenty of direction. I do not understand what's wrong with him."

CYCLE 3: SINGING IN THE RAIN

I am not entirely surprised by the mixture of concern and happiness in Ellen's voice. Our early cycle 3 interviews already had suggested that years 5 through 9 are a paradoxical time for stepfamilies. Most aspects of stepfamily life are good and getting better, but a few aspects begin to get difficult again.

When we analyzed our data for this period, we found that a gap had reopened between our step- and nuclear families on markers like stress and parental conflict. There was also an increase in acting out and social problems among the target children in our stepfamilies. But all of these negative changes were related to the same—mercifully—transitory phenomenon. The stepfamily had a teenager in it now.

The most important—and heartening—positive changes in cycle 3 involved marital satisfaction and family identity. Our data show that the marriage at the heart of the stepfamily strengthens in years 5 through 9. But our data show this in a subtle way. When we saw the increases in stress among project couples, we thought that we would see a corresponding dip in marital satisfaction. But to our astonishment, no correlation materialized. Cycle 3 saw an increase in marital satisfaction among project men and women.

One reason for this apparent paradox was the effects of time: By cycle 3 our couples had been together for five, six, seven, eight, and nine years; they had shared a great deal and weathered a great deal together. Their marriages had deep, deep roots now, roots that wound around a thousand common experiences and were nurtured by a common well-spring of joys and sorrows and triumphs—and a few defeats. The young adolescent's behavior might be stressful and sometimes exasperating, but having been through so much together, our couples never lost hope or heart.

A second reason why marital satisfaction remained remarkably high was the almost palpable sense of achievement, of pride that began to develop in our stepfamily couples toward the end of cycle 3. Its source? The way that once-intolerable young adolescent had turned out. At the end of the study, the vast majority of our target children were doing well—in school, in their social lives, on all the indices social scientists use to measure healthy functioning. These now almost young men and women were headed toward productive, useful lives; and understandably, their parents and stepparents took great pride in that achievement—a pride that enriched their lives and their marriages.

Family identity was a third area where we saw positive change in cycle 3. Project participants told us that they had stopped thinking of themselves as stepfamilies and just thought of themselves as families. This was partly a matter of time-bred familiarity—everyone in the family knew everyone else very well by now—and partly a matter of feeling; in the third cycle, family members described even the annoying idiosyncrasies of others with a kind of rueful affection. I think that this now-firm family identity, this almost organic sense of being a family, is why our stepfamilies stood up so well to the cyclone—the emerging teenager—that swept through project homes during cycle 3.

THE TRANSITION TO ADOLESCENCE

Ellen has gotten her Austin house on a hill. The stucco, southwestern-style house I park in front of the day of the interview sits on the rise of a hill about three miles from downtown Austin. Getting out of the car, I can see the dome of the capitol building gleaming in the warm April sun.

Todd, who is twelve now, greets me at the door. He still has a boy's face, apple cheeked, but there is a man's body underneath the face now. Todd is almost my height—five ten—and he has inherited his mother's build; he is lean and muscular in the way that gymnasts and track-and-field athletes are. His blond hair, cut short in a military-style crew cut, emphasizes his babyish features.

Never effusive, Todd's introduction in the Lawton living room is a model of economy.

"Dr. Bray," he says to Ellen as the two of us stand in the doorway. Todd, I notice, is staring at the floor.

Ellen frowns. "Mr. Manners himself." She looks at me. "James, I hope Toddy's been polite to you."

"Very polite," I say.

"Lucky you."

When I turn around Todd has vanished already. Ellen notices my surprise.

"Zorro's gone already," she says. "That boy cannot stand to be around people for one second, at least not grown-up people."

Ellen is still staring at the doorway as I take out my tape recorder. She seems a bit miffed at the sullen introduction I was given.

"That's not the way *he* was brought up," she says. "I want you to know that." Still slim and athletic, Ellen has a tomboy attractiveness to her.

"Todd was very polite," I say again.

Ellen frowns and informs me she is still in turmoil over "this morning." Apparently, at breakfast, Todd was lobbying her very vigorously for a postponement of his weekend interview with me. Andrew came to her defense and Todd told him to "butt out. This is between me and my mother."

"I don't know who Andrew was madder at," Ellen says, "me or Todd. He stormed out of the house this morning shouting about how 'I was losing control of my child' and how he couldn't start his day like this any more. It was *too* nerve racking."

Finding a Self of One's Own

The disruptive behavior associated with early adolescence—the surliness, the rebelliousness, the provocative behavior—arises from *the* primary developmental issue of the teenage years: separation and individuation. In the early teen years, children take the first major step in the journey that will carry them out of the family and into adult life.

What makes disruptive behavior an element in this process is that, first, it facilitates separation—it helps maturing children to establish clear boundaries between themselves and their parents, boundaries that, as they sharpen and deepen, will mark the youngsters off as distinctive individuals; not as "so and so's children" but as "Mr. or Ms. So and So."

Disruptive adolescent behavior also helps to define who Mr. or Ms. So and So is because as children bounce off their parents, they begin to learn how "I" am like and unlike Mom and Dad. And from this knowledge young adolescents will begin to fashion a unique "I." It really is not too much of an exaggeration to say that rudeness and surliness are to young teenagers what a chisel is to a sculptor, a paintbrush to a painter—a tool of creation.

However, adolescence also foments stepfamily disruption for another reason.

Somewhere between the ages of twelve and fourteen, children suddenly become very interested in their family of origin. What was their life like before their biological parents divorced? And what were their parents like when they were together? And what *really* caused the divorce?

These difficult questions seem to be an element in Ellen's unhappiness with Todd.

Last week, she tells me, Todd was rummaging around in the garage when he came across a scrapbook Ellen had kept during her first marriage. "He took the book up to his room and spent the whole night looking through it. You should have heard him the next morning, James!" Ellen whoops. " 'Who was that man in the picture with Daddy on Grandma's porch? Who was that lady with you and me at Herman Park? What year did Daddy buy that '78 Lincoln?' "

Ellen stops on the '78 Lincoln. "Tom and I had one of our biggest fights over that car," she says. "Did I ever tell you the story, James?"

I tell her no.

"Well, it *is* a story," Ellen says. "One evening I pull into the driveway and there's a man standing there. He says hi, I say hi back. Then he asks me to get out of the car and give him the keys. Turns out he's the repo man." Ellen snaps her fingers. "Just like that we have no car. The repo man drives it off. Naturally Tom could care less.

"When I went inside and told him the car was gone, he says, 'Too bad, I'll call the finance company in the morning,' then he goes back to watching *Family Feud*."

I try to redirect the conversation back to Todd.

"It must have been interesting for him," I say. "Hearing you talk about the people in the pictures. Learning what his life was like when he was little."

The small muscle above Ellen's nose knots up in consternation. "Why would I want to talk to Todd about the people in the pictures?" she asks. "They were all Tom's friends. I spent five years digging out from that life. I don't want to be reminded of it now."

Ellen stands up. "You want an ice tea, James? I'm thirsty all of a sudden." This conversation is making her uncomfortable.

"Please."

"I told Todd he could keep the album as long as he wanted," Ellen says over her shoulder, then disappears into the kitchen.

Todd's questions about the photo album were legitimate. But they ran into a parental emotion that inhibits not only many divorce conversations but also many family-of-origin conversations as well: embarrassment. Ellen, with some justification, considers the marriage to Tom the biggest mistake of her life; but, in this instance, her embarrassment kept her from providing Todd with information he needed to complete an important developmental task.

Guilt is another common parental silencer. A parent ignores questions about the child's family of origin because the parent played a role in that family's collapse. The nuclear-family myth also silences adults, particularly in mature stepfamilies. The family has been living together happily for four, five, or six years; now suddenly the teenager wants to dredge up a lot of memories the adults would just as soon forget.

Parental silence typically invites two responses, both of which the silence was intended to avoid. Children may shift allegiance from their stepfamily to their nonresidential parent or, if that option is unavailable, children may become frustrated, which leads to acting out.

I think it significant that in cycle 3 the greatest difference between project children and the control families was acting out (there was also a great gap in the stress index); in stepfamilies the incidence soared again. Most of the acting out was what you would expect from preteens and young teens: surliness and rebelliousness. However, in a few cases it went beyond the normal teenage misbehavior.

Nancy Weaver was in an awkward position when her daughter, Winnie, began asking questions about her family of origin because that family was ended by an affair between Nancy and Winnie's current stepfather, Arlington Weaver.

"I don't know what to tell Winnie," Nancy told me one day during an at-home interview. "I don't want to lie, but I'm afraid to tell the truth."

In my experience, teenagers like Winnie are able to deal with candid parental disclosures because they are old enough to understand emotional complexity. However, the affair has to be put into context. The child needs to understand that the parent's unhappiness is what ended the marriage, not the affair; the affair was simply a by-product of that unhappiness.

Nancy, however, could not bring herself to tell Winnie the truth. "Later, maybe," she said during my visit, "but not now. I feel . . ." Nancy said she wasn't sure what she felt, but some instinct told her that this was not the right time to say anything to Winnie about the affair with Arlington. For a time she managed to fend Winnie off with statements such as "We just didn't get along." But that dodge only made things worse when Winnie came across the newspaper clipping Nancy had shown me several years earlier. Winnie found it one day while she was rummaging through her mother's bureau for a scarf.

" 'We just didn't get along!' Tell me another one," Winnie shouted when she confronted Nancy at the front door that night.

Nancy had no idea what Winnie was talking about. She hadn't even had a chance to take her coat off. "What are you yelling about?"

"I'm yelling about this," Winnie said, waving the newspaper clipping in front of her mother's face. *"This."* Then she read the first paragraph of the clipping out loud. " 'Mr. David Cartwright was arrested last night for assaulting Mr. Arlington Weaver, who he alleged is having an affair with his wife, Nancy.' Is it true?" Winnie shouted. "Is it true?"

Nancy said it was true.

A few days after this confrontation, Winnie ran away to Los Angeles to find her biological father. At my next visit, Nancy told me that the Los Angeles police picked Winnie up a week later in front of a package store on Hollywood Boulevard.

The Matriarchal Woman and Adolescence

Ellen is still talking about Todd. But now we have moved on to his sloppiness. Ellen says his room defies description. "It is the Chernobyl of Central Texas," she says; it is a toxic waste dump of old pizza boxes, CDs, dirty underwear, and candy wrappers. Ellen, who seems incredulous about every aspect of the teenage Todd, is particularly incredulous about his sloppiness. "I don't know how he can live in that room," she exclaims. "I do not know how any human being could."

Ellen's upset is genuine. But I think there is another factor at work in her complaint about Todd—a factor that, in Matriarchal homes, often exacerbates normal cycle 3 conflicts: the Matriarchal woman's need for control.

Believe it or not, that cultural cliché, the teenager's sloppy room, really does have a developmental purpose. The unpicked-up clothes and unput-away CDs represent first steps in the separation process; adolescents are creating their own individual space away from the family. Many other steps will be necessary to carry them fully into the world. But this creation of *my* sloppy room, along with its accomplices, *my* outlandish clothes and *my* crazy hairstyles, are among the first steps in that long journey—and if the other steps are to go smoothly, the first must be respected.

In practical terms, this means allowing teenagers a certain latitude in areas like neatness and dress. If the latitude taken is more than the latitude offered, a formal parent-child negotiation can and should be conducted to iron out differences. This tactic not only gives each party a little of what is wanted, the negotiation serves an important developmental purpose; it tells a teenager, "I support your journey toward independence."

The reason this journey exacerbates cycle 3 conflicts in Matriarchal stepfamilies is that it runs head-on into the woman's control impulse. The Matriarchal mother tends to support the domino theory of parenting: Give a little on the state of the room, and the child will immediately turn around and demand a lot, and not just about the room. Before you know it, the room will lead to a funny haircut, and the funny haircut to strange clothes. And as each cherished domino falls, the woman will lose that much more control over the child.

The domino theory, however, often overlooks the effects of the Matriarchal woman's own often superb parenting, which provides children with an innate sense of limits. The theory also overlooks something most parents are unaware of: Overcontrol can harm not only a child, it also can harm the parent who tries to exercise it.

Exhibit A is the experience of Bess Redgrave; pretty, blue-eyed, strong-willed Bess was not a project participant; I saw her and husband, quiet, self-effacing John Redgrave, in my capacity as a clinical psychologist. Bess and John's visit to me was prompted by an unprecedented development in the Redgrave family. Strong-willed Bess, used to getting her own way with other family members, suddenly was not getting her way with her fifteen-year-old daughter, Halley. According to Bess, who did most of the talking during my first meeting with the

Redgraves, she and Halley had been engaged in low-level guerrilla warfare for the past two years—mostly over the usual teenage issues, clothing, friends, and curfews. But lately the warfare had erupted into something much more heated, and the source of the conflagration seemed to be Bess's rule on phone calls.

John Redgrave interrupted at this point, to say that the rule required Halley to call in whenever she was away from home. "Halley hates the rule," John said. "It makes her feel like a baby."

"I don't care," Bess snapped. Then she looked at me. "The phone calls are perfectly appropriate, Dr. Bray. I want to know where my daughter is, what she is doing, and who she is doing it with. I don't see anything wrong with that."

I didn't either—initially. But the more I learned about Bess's telephone rule—essentially, Halley was required to check in with her every two hours, even if the girl was at a movie—the more inclined I was to side with John. Bess seemed to be using the telephone more as a leash than as a monitoring device.

"Halley's embarrassed," John said. "None of her friends have to check in constantly with their parents."

"I don't care," Bess shot back. "It's for her own good."

While the activities of young teens should be monitored, the monitoring should allow some room for autonomy, and Bess's telephone rule did not. At the end of the first session, I resolved that I would urge her to sit down and negotiate a new set of phone rules with Halley. But at our next meeting, strong-willed, Matriarchal Bess dug in her heels. "No," she said. "I think the rules are a good idea, and I'm going to keep them." However, her intransigence quickly backfired on her.

Halley turned rebellious. She refused to go out for cheerleading as Bess wished, she developed a sudden taste for provocative clothes, and most upsetting of all, Halley announced that she was going to go to college out of state.

"I hope you have someone to pay your tuition," Bess snapped when Halley made the announcement.

"I do," Halley said. "Dad." According to Halley, her biological father, William Moore, had offered to underwrite her tuition to his alma mater, Bates College, in faraway Maine.

Perhaps more surprising were the changes I saw in Bess. Halley's growing independence was making her mother feel powerless. And parental powerlessness, unlike parental negotiation, does produce a domino effect of sorts. In time the powerlessness gives rise to feelings of worthlessness (if I were a more competent parent, I'd find ways to make my daughter obey me), hopelessness (I've lost my daughter forever), and resignation (I am helpless to change things). Over time these feelings turn into one of two even more troubling things. The first is illness. The parent somatizes her feelings of hopelessness and worthlessness into headaches or stomach ailments. The second consequence is depression.

During the first two months I worked with the Redgraves, Bess's mood changed visibly. Assertive Bess suddenly became passive, then almost affectless. The animated woman who had commanded the spotlight during the Redgraves' first visit now was stone-faced and spoke in a murmer. One day, when I mentioned this change, she sighed and explained, not very convincingly, that the Houston housing market was in a slump and she was not moving many houses these days.

A few weeks later, when John half complained about Bess's "gloomy mood," she offered another explanation. She was feeling "blue" because her sister, Ann, was moving to California. "I'll miss Ann," Bess said.

John looked incredulous. "Why?" he said. "You and Ann barely talk now and she only lives a few miles away."

Finally, one day, in the middle of a session, Bess broke down and began to cry. "I'm losing Halley," she said in between sobs. "I don't want to lose her. But I am, I am."

Bess's unusual intransigence was rooted in the way Matriarchal women define motherhood, a role they hold in very high regard. They view it in terms of control; a good mother oversees every aspect of her child's life. Thus, the separation and individuation process becomes not a sad but inevitable part of the life cycle, as it is for other parents, but something more traumatic, a threat to the woman's identity. If she cannot control her child, maybe she is not such a wonderful mother. And, typically, people who feel threatened at a core level resist ferociously.

Redefining the parenting role in a way that reflects adolescents' changing needs—which are now more for wise counsel and advice and less for close oversight and control—not only helps the adolescents, it fosters parental success, because counsel and advice are things teenagers welcome. (Even if they sometimes act otherwise.) And as Bess Redgrave discovered, that welcome can provide the opportunity to heal a wounded parent-child relationship.

Halley never did go to Bates. She wanted to stay near her family. She's at Rice University, right across the street from my office.

The Matriarchal Man and the Adolescent

I am pressing the STOP button on my tape recorder when the front door opens and an Ellen-like whoop rumbles down the hall into the living room. "We're home," shouts Caroline, Ellen's seventeen-year-old daughter. The "we" refers to Ellen's husband, Andrew, who was at the library with Caroline when I arrived.

Andrew, the family intellectual, has found a companion in seventeen-year-old Caroline, who has developed into something of an intellectual herself. According to Ellen, her daughter has an unquenchable passion for nineteenth-century English literature in general and for Jane Austen in particular. Ellen, while appropriately respectful of this exotic new development, seems a little perplexed by it too. Books are a mark of intelligence to her, so, from that perspective, Caroline's interest in things literary is a definite plus; Ellen also is pleased that Caroline and Andrew have a new bonding point; I gather that the two have grown quite close during the weekly library visits. But practical-minded Ellen also seems bit worried about the impracticality of Caroline's new love.

"Those books are all right for now," she said at the start of the interview before she got sidetracked on Todd. "But all that Jane Austen stuff is not going to do Caroline much good later. I hope it's just a stage."

Andrew, however, is very enthusiastic about the literary Caroline. "I think it's wonderful," he says, "absolutely wonderful." Caroline has Ellen's energy and intelligence, Andrew says, but with an overlay of intellectuality. "Sometimes I have to remind myself that I'm talking to a kid." Then Andrew also mentions her grades. He is inclined to give Caroline sole credit for that straight-A average, but he deserves some credit as well.

The children who did best on indices of academic achievement and healthy psychological adjustment at the end of the project shared one thing: a stepfather who remained involved throughout the stepfamily life cycle.

The stepfather did not have to have a close emotional relationship with the stepchild—indeed, Caroline and Andrew's friendship developed only as she entered late adolescence. But the stepfather did have to be involved with the child. When we looked at this finding more carefully, we found that involvement translated into several concrete characteristics. One was a trait Matriarchal men like Andrew are adept at: monitoring the child's behavior. The other stepfather traits associated with an unusually good outcome for a stepchild define a parenting style called authoritative.

Authoritative parents are warm and engaged and provide appropriate control, which means they monitor and guide the child's behavior; they also employ reasoning in their discipline. In other words, authoritative parents explain *why* the child should not do what he or she did. They also criticize behaviors as "bad," but never children.

While our data on child outcomes—on how well children do—represent a powerful argument for stepfather involvement, often during cycle 3 involvement falters because the young adolescent (as opposed to a more mature teenager like Caroline) willfully ignores the rules of civility and good manners in ways that can try the stepparent's patience to the limit. Andrew seems to be approaching that limit now with

Todd. When I ask him how he and Todd are getting along, his voice becomes as sour as Ellen's was on the phone.

"Todd's a very confused kid," Andrew says. "And rude, Jesus, is that kid rude. I'm tired of being told 'You're not my father' every time I ask him to do something. Like this morning . . ."

I tell Andrew that I already know about "this morning." Ellen told me about it.

"You should've heard the way Todd talked to her," Andrew says. "I told him don't you dare speak to your mother like that, mister. Show some respect."

"And Todd told you to butt out," I say.

"That's what Ellen told you?" Andrew asks.

I nod.

Andrew smiles. "She cleaned up the story for you, James. Todd told me to butt out . . . asshole."

In most project homes, as in the Lawton home, the stepfather became as much an object of surly and rude adolescent behavior as the biological parent. And while our Neotraditional and formerly Romantic men—project families that continued into cycle 3 had lost all their Romantic illusions—generally held up well under the firestorm because these men wanted a "family experience," often our Matriarchal men did not. They entered stepfamily life to be with the woman they loved, not to be tormented by a teenager. So, frequently, the torment became a source of alienation from the child, and in time this disaffection begins to spill over into the marriage.

This observation touches on one of our most paradoxical findings about cycle 3, one that encompasses not just our Matriarchal families but all our families. While our couples reported being happy in their marriages, our cycle 3 videotapes of husband-wife interactions actually show an increase in negative interpersonal behaviors. People were more likely to whine and complain about each other; we also saw more brusque, short-tempered exchanges between our couples. For the most part, these displays of negativity were a reflection of stress, not marital dissatisfaction. The teenager behaved the way Todd did at breakfast, and the parents, rattled by the youngster's behavior, began to get short-tempered and snippity with one another.

While this kind of negative behavior between the spouses usually is benign, a husband and wife should recognize that, over time, it can take its toll on a marriage.

The Neotraditional Man and the Young Adolescent

In Neotraditional and formerly Romantic stepfamilies, cycle 3 stepparent-stepchild conflicts took a different form. Paternal insecurity, rare among Matriarchal men, for example, was a common trigger in other families. The persistence of this insecurity surprised me. At the beginning of the study, I assumed that by year 6 or 7, the man's role in the stepchild's life would be clearly defined; a close parent-child relationship would have developed, the two would be friends; or they would have agreed, more or less, to go their separate ways. But even in mature stepfamilies, ambiguity remained. The insecurity this created was a frequent contributor to cycle 3 conflicts because it led stepfathers to *personalize* a lot of annoying but normal teenage behavior.

A story Doris Clark, a project mother, told me provides a case in point. One evening during dinner, husband John was expounding on his principal passion, the Houston Oilers, when stepson Mark interrupted to observe: "The Oilers were retards." Then he offered a further observation; Oilers' fans were even bigger retards for supporting such a bunch of losers.

"I don't know why John just didn't ignore him," Doris said. "These days, every other word out of Mark's mouth is 'retard.'" But John did not. According to Doris, he shouted, "How dare you call me retarded!" Also according to Doris, the dinner ended with Mark running to his room and she and her younger daughter, Melody, in tears.

Ironically, John was actually very fond of Mark; his temper tantrum was rooted in his stepson's edgy, unpredictable responses to that affection. When Mark introduced him to a camp friend as "my dad," John was thrilled. But a week later at a meeting with Mark's teacher, John found himself demoted to "my mother's husband." Not coincidentally, I think, John's explosion about the "retard" crack came two days after this second introduction.

Paternal insecurity also can produce a serious misreading of the separation portion of the separation and individuation process. A growing involvement with the world and lessening involvement with the family is a normal part of adolescence. But stepparents, their judgment clouded by insecurity, see children's growing involvement with friends not as a normal and necessary part of the journey to adulthood but as a rejection of the stepfamily in general and of them, the stepparents, in particular.

A family conference where teenage motives can be explored and explained is the best way to deal with such misreadings. It also is important for step- and biological parents to understand the whys and wherefores of the developmental tasks of adolescence; this knowledge can help provide a context for a lot of annoying behavior.

One bit of information that is particularly critical to keep in mind is the developmental purpose of provoking and baiting adolescent behavior. Children are not being rude for the sheer joy of being rude (although it often seems that way to the beleagered parent), they are being rude and antagonistic in order to draw boundaries between themselves and the family (and parents), which has provided them with an identity up until now. All those annoying behaviors help teens to mark themselves off as separate, unique people, part of a family but not subsumed by its identity.

Lingering paternal illusions also can contribute to the charged cycle 3 atmosphere in stepfamilies, particularly Neotraditional stepfamilies where the paternal role is important to the man. A study by Lawrence Ganong and Marilyn Coleman of the University of Missouri provides a good context for a discussion of these expectations. Recently Drs. Ganong and Coleman asked a group of adolescents in mature stepfamilies (very much like our cycle 3 families) two questions. The first was

"What do you call your stepparent?" A large minority, 37 percent, said "Dad"; the majority, 57 percent, said that they used the stepparent's first name; 6 percent used a nickname. Next the teenagers were asked what they called their stepfather at the start of stepfamily life. The percentages were almost exactly the same: 32 percent said "Dad"; 62 percent said "first name"; and 7 percent, a nickname.

The researchers were so puzzled by the constancy—didn't five years of common family life change attitudes?—that they decided to sit down and talk to the teenagers. Why the reluctance? they asked. Was the term "Dad" too intimate to use in the stepparent-stepchild context? Most of the adolescents said no, there was another explanation. If you called a stepfather Dad, what did you call a biological father? You only could have one dad in your life, and custom, sentiment, and tradition dictated that a biological father, even an infrequently seen one, be given the title. Thus the only alternative form of address for a stepfather—even one you felt close to—was a first name or a nickname.

However, in formerly Romantic, and even to a surprising degree in Neotraditional, homes, "Dad" was a term many stepfathers coveted; for many men it represented a kind of Holy Grail of stepfamily life, the prize of prizes. However, except for a handful of radical Romantics, most men were realistic about the need to earn the title. So, in cycles 1 and 2 paternal expectations were kept in check. But in cycle 3 patience began to run out. Stepfathers and stepchildren had been living together for five, six, seven years, time enough for the child to feel comfortable with the term "Dad." Moreover, over those years, many men had invested an enormous amount of emotional energy and money in their stepchildren, so they felt that they had a material claim on the title. Yet here they were still being called Larry or Joe or Sam or, what really galled many project men, "my mother's husband."

At this point, sourness and disillusionment set in. Sometimes it led to withdrawal; metaphorically, the man threw in the towel. Unable to get what he wanted, he stopped trying and started to pull away from the stepson or stepdaughter; often this withdrawal was accompanied by the development of a more exacting paternal standard of behavior. Previously tolerated or ignored behaviors now became a frequent source of complaint. It was almost as if on some subconscious level, the man had concluded, "Okay, if you don't think I'm good enough to be your father, I don't think you're good enough to be my child."

Another frequent result of paternal retreat was a withdrawal of material support. Jeffrey Goldsmith told me that during Naomi's senior year in high school, he came very close to reneging on his promise to pay her college tuition. During his reinterview, Jeffrey reminded me of the many investments he had made in pursuit of the "Dad" title. In the first cycle, there was his (mostly) good-natured tolerance of Naomi's rudeness; in the second, his deep involvement in Naomi's gymnastics career and also his financial support. After Naomi's father was killed in an auto accident and Sarah decided to work part, not full, time, Jeffrey had assumed financial responsibility for his stepdaughter.

However, he said, none of this made any difference to Naomi, who continued to call him Jeffrey, except when she wanted to annoy him; then she called him Jeff.

"I notice she still calls you Jeffrey," I said at the reinterview.

Jeffrey smiled ruefully. "After we had a little talk, I decided 'Jeffrey' wasn't so bad after all."

The talk was suggested by Sarah. "One day," Jeffrey said, "I told her that I wished Naomi would call me Dad sometimes; Sarah said what Naomi called me was up to Naomi, but if it bothered me that much, I should talk to her."

It turned out that like many of Drs. Ganong and Coleman's teenagers, Naomi wanted to reserve the term "Dad" for her late father. "She felt it was a way of honoring poor Dan's memory," Jeffrey said. "I couldn't argue with that."

OTHER IMPORTANT CYCLE 3 ISSUES

While the transition to adolescence was the major reason for cycle 3 turmoil, it was not the only reason. Other factors also contributed to the renewal of distress in our stepfamilies; two of these—sexuality and visitation—deserve special mention.

Sexuality

This issue can express itself in many ways in a stepfamily with adolescents. One is by intensifying the stepfather wariness I mentioned earlier. Many men are afraid that their friendliness will be misinterpreted by the stepdaughter or by her mother. This concern, evident even in stepfamilies with ten- or eleven-year-old girls, often deepens into real worry when a stepdaughter is fifteen or sixteen.

Overt displays of parental affection also can raise the issue of sexuality in a stepfamily, though usually not in a mature one. Teenagers in our stepfamilies were no more annoyed by parental hugging and kissing than boys and girls in our control group. The hugging and kissing produced a certain amount of disdainful "oohhing" and "ahhhing," but these reactions are normal because teenagers are uncomfortable thinking of their parents as sexual beings. However, recent research shows that in *new* stepfamilies parental hugging and kissing can be disturbing to adolescents, and, interestingly, adolescent girls tend to be most upset. This may seem counterintuitive. One would think a boy more likely to view a stepfather as a rival. However, the mother-and-daughter bond in single-parent families tends to be much closer than the mother-and-son bond, so it is the teenage girls who feel most threatened by semipublic displays of affection.

A third way sexuality becomes an issue is if the stepparent has teenage children of the opposite sex. During weekend visits and joint vacations, the commingling can create awkward situations for the entire stepfamily.

Some strategies that are effective in dealing with the sexuality issue include:

- Dress codes. Bathrobes are a good way to avoid awkward encounters in the morning when people are walking to the bathroom to get dressed. And as a general rule, all family members should avoid suggestive clothing.

- Pillow talk. Sexually suggestive conversation upsets teenagers, particularly teenage girls, so parental pillow talk should be confined to the bedroom. The same is true for displays of affection that could be construed as sexual rather than friendly.
- Visits by the stepfather's teenagers. Enforcement of dress codes is particularly important on such occasions. Also one parent or the other should be charged with unobtrusively monitoring the teenagers.

Visitation

Visitation also added to cycle 3 turmoil in some stepfamilies. Many of our project stepfathers, who in their other lives were nonresidential parents, complained bitterly about canceled visits and less frequent visits from their biological children. Was the teenager's ball game or school trip or party really more important than seeing Dad? Most project men doubted it, and most were pretty sure who was behind the cancellations—not the child but a vindictive former wife.

However, more often than not, our men were wrong on both scores. One consequence of a growing involvement with the world is that outside interests engage teenagers in ways that they had not before, and, since their time is limited, teens frequently ignore family obligations, including obligations to nonresidential parents. Furthermore, this set of priorities—my interests first, Dad second—is developmentally appropriate. Engaging in interests beyond the family is an important part of the journey to adulthood.

The best way to prevent visitation issues from becoming a source of conflict between the stepfamily and the nonresidential parent is to have the teenagers speak to the nonresidential parent about canceled dates. The teens can make a much more convincing case for their time-consuming new life than a former wife. However, the mother might remind the nonresidential parent that his sadness is shared. She is also finding it painful to let the children go.

POINTS TO KEEP IN MIND

- The renewed stress and conflict in cycle 3 arise, not from problems within the stepfamily, but from the child who is making the transition to adolescence, a stormy period for all families.
- Marital satisfaction increases during the cycle 3. But so does the incidence of marital bickering. And it is important to be mindful of it, because while often stress-related—the teenager is behaving impossibly again—unchecked, the bickering can harm the marriage.
- Parents, particularly step- and nonresidential parents, should avoid personalizing the teenager's behavior. Canceled visits, rudeness, and other annoying teenage habits are normal by-products of the adolescent developmental process.
- Active stepparenting can have long-term benefits for a teenager. But too often, stepfathers allow themselves to be driven away by provocative and surly adolescent behavior.
- Adolescence is easier for the child and for the family if parents "let go" a little. Allowing a teenager a few personal idiosyncrasies, like a messy room or a funny haircut, not only help to reduce the incidence of family conflict, such measures also facilitate an important developmental task—the establishment of an independent identity.
- Dress codes and behavioral rules (including ones for adult behavior) can prevent sex from becoming an issue in a stepfamily with an adolescent.

SUCCESS, FAILURE, AND JUST GETTING BY

Looking back over the course of the DIS project, we've concluded that our families responded to the challenges of marital transitions and family life in three distinct ways: successes, failures, and those who just got by. The three groups more or less overlapped with our three archetypes, Neotraditional, Matriarchal, and Romantic, but exceptions were common. The first group of families were hugely and unabashedly successful and were largely made up of Neotraditional families, but it also included some Matriarchal and a few formerly Romantic families. The families in this group developed happy, loving marriages and family relationships that promoted positive growth and development for the children and adults. These families traversed paths filled with the adversities and problems of divorce and remarriage by developing loving and supportive relationships and creating successful coping mechanisms to carry them through the rough times, allowing them to live safe, secure, and prosperous lives.

The second group of families who failed to make it through these challenges ended in another divorce. This group was largely made up of Romantic families. The third group consisted of families who seemed to just get by—they stuck it out, but they seemed more focused on surviving than on flourishing. These families included some from all of the groups.

I think there are important lessons to learn from each of these groups of families.

FAILURE AGAIN

For some project families, marriage and family life the second time around was no better than the first, and for a few families it was much worse. These families told us that there was too much stress, too much conflict, and not enough commitment to carry them through the difficult times. While it was acknowledged that divorce was never easy, in the second relationship the man and/or woman were less willing to tolerate unhappiness and turmoil because they knew what they did not know the first time: divorce is survivable.

There were three things these couples said that might have helped them persevere through the difficult times. The first was knowing that cycle 1 stresses would end when the first cycle ended. The second was knowing what to *realistically* expect from stepfamily life, especially around the stepparent-child relationships. The third was having a road map, a knowledge of what might happen during the process of forming a stepfamily.

It might be impolitic to say it, but we also found a few people who were just not good at marriage. They were good parents, good friends, good coworkers, and good people. But they were not good at doing the kinds of things a man or woman needs to do to make a marriage succeed.

Marilyn Combs, one of our Matriarchal mothers, is an example. When we contacted her for the follow-up interview she said, "Well, James, you can come out to see me and the kids, but my second husband is long gone." When we arrived for the interview we learned that Ms. Combs's second marriage hadn't even lasted a year. Since that time, she had remarried for a *third* time and was now separated from *this* husband. Marilyn told us, "You know, James, what I have decided is that me and marriage just don't mix. I am just not the marrying kind of woman."

She continued, "I like my job, I like my house, I like my kids, but I don't like having any man interfering with those things. I like having a man around, until he starts telling me how to raise my kids and what I can and can't do around my house. I just don't need the grief." Marilyn stopped and smiled ruefully. "Believe me, James, it will be a long time before I invite another man to live in *my* house."

JUST GETTING BY

Some of the stepfamilies in our project managed to stay together, but they seemed only to survive and not to thrive. At the close of the study, life seemed to lack the luster and potential displayed at the start of the family relationship. Children and adults scored reasonably well on many of the social and psychological indicators, and sometimes even better than average, but if you scratched the surface a little, you could see a fog hanging over their heads. The adults in these families seemed to be just going through the motions. While on the outside life looked good—they were making it through the rough parts, they were handling the curve balls that life threw them—they seemed to be caught in a rut. They were persevering, but at quite a price.

Part of the problem was closedmindedness and habitual interacting.

The husband and wife were so sure that they knew everything there was to know about each other that they had lost the capacity to excite and surprise one another. In our videotapes of the couples, they responded to each other in the same, predictable ways—even when one partner did or said something surprising. There was a lot of low-level bickering and nattering in the relationships, which seemed to hold a reward for them. However, while the payoff was a feeling that they were right and life was predictable, the price seemed to be their vitality and zest for life.

They also seemed to be caught up in success. However, more success did not seem to bring them satisfaction—it became simply more obligations, more demands. In some cases, it seemed that although they had "made it," achieved their dreams and desires, they weren't drawn to or excited by the future. It was just more of the same, more just getting by.

These men and women not only lost the capacity to see and hear each other, but, just as critical, they lost the capacity to enjoy the small pleasures of domestic life. Indeed, the ultimate lesson to be learned from these families is that in order to thrive rather than simply survive, you need to have a future that excites and enlivens you, refuse to give in to resignation, and value and enjoy the day-to-day opportunities and pleasures of life.

SUCCESS AND HAPPY ENDINGS ALL AROUND

In the cases of the successful stepfamilies, the final years of the project turned out to have all the elements of great drama: turmoil (courtesy of the impossible teenager), sorrow (the impossible teen's impending departure from home), and finally, triumph. At the end of the project, couples could finally see the past taking on a pattern, adding up. As project husbands and wives looked back at the three cycles, the chaos of the first cycle, the quiet of the second, and the frazzledness of the third, they could see what their sacrifice, their steadfastness, and love had wrought.

We asked these families what had kept them together through all of this, what made it worth it. The consistent answer was *commitment*. Commitment to a life together, not just getting by but living and loving fully, communicating about issues, building a stable family, and enjoying a great life together. The end of cycle 3, especially, was rich in satisfactions for our successful stepfamilies, and these satisfactions were of a very deep and lasting kind. People had achieved a real sense of accomplishment. They had overcome hardship and setback, they had created enduring marriages and families. And they had raised happy, well-adjusted children.

All those almost-adults, with stories yet to be told, are now standing on the cusp of the future, standing there with the confidence, the optimism, the knowledge, the capacity for love and human connection that only the very best kind of family can give a child. If that isn't success, I don't know what is.

Amato, P. R., and B. Keith. (1991). "Parental Divorce and Adult Well-Being: A Meta-Analysis." *Journal of Marriage and the Family, 53,* 43–58.

———. (1991). "Parental Divorce and the Well-Being of Children: A Meta-Analysis." *Psychological Bulletin, 110,* 26–46.

Belsky, J., and J. Kelly. (1993). *The Transition to Parenthood.* New York: Delacorte.

Bernstein, A. (1989). *Yours, Mine, and Ours: How Families Change When Remarried Parents Have a Child Together.* New York: Macmillan.

Blau, M. (1994). *Families Apart: Ten Keys to Successful Co-Parenting.* New York: Putnam.

Bray, J. H. (1988). "Children's Development During Early Remarriage." In E. M. Hetherington and J. Arasteh (Eds.), *The Impact of*

Divorce, Single-Parenting and Step-Parenting on Children (pp. 279–298). Hillsdale, NJ: Lawrence Erlbaum.

———. (1988). *Developmental Issues in StepFamilies Research Project: Final Report* (Grant Number R01 HD 18025). Bethesda, MD: National Institute of Child Health and Human Development.

———. (1991). "Psychosocial Factors Affecting Custodial and Visitation Arrangements." *Behavioral Science and the Law, 9,* 419–437.

———. (1992). "Family Relationships and Children's Adjustment in Clinical and Nonclinical Stepfather Families." *Journal of Family Psychology, 6,* 60–68.

———. (1995). "Family Oriented Treatment of Stepfamilies." In R. Mikesell, D. D. Lusterman, and S. McDaniel (Eds.), *Integrating Family Therapy: Handbook of Family Psychology and Systems Therapy* (pp. 125–140). Washington, DC: American Psychological Association.

———. (forthcoming). "From Marriage to Remarriage and Beyond: Findings from the Developmental Issues in StepFamilies Research Project." In E. M. Hetherington (Ed.), *Coping with Divorce, Single-Parenting and Remarriage: A Risk and Resiliency Perspective.* Hillsdale, NJ: Lawrence Erlbaum.

Bray, J. H., and S. H. Berger. (1990). "Noncustodial Parent and Grandparent Relationships in Stepfamilies." *Family Relations, 39,* 414–419.

———. (1993). "Developmental Issues in StepFamilies Research Project: Family Relationships and Parent-Child Interactions." *Journal of Family Psychology, 7,* 76–90.

———. (1993). "Nonresidential Family-Child Relationships Following Divorce and Remarriage." In C. E. Depner and J. H. Bray (Eds.), *Noncustodial Parents: New Vistas in Family Living* (pp. 156–181). Newbury Park, CA: Sage Publications.

Bray, J. H., and D. M. Harvey. (1995). "Adolescents in Stepfamilies: Developmental and Family Interventions." *Psychotherapy, 32,* 122–130.

Bray, J. H., and E. M. Hetherington. (1993). "Families in Transition: Introduction and Overview." *Journal of Family Psychology, 7,* 3–8.

Brown, A. C., R. J. Green, and J. Druckman. (1990). "A Comparison of Stepfamilies With and Without Child-Focused Problems." *American Journal of Orthopsychiatry, 60,* 556–566.

Coleman, M., and L. H. Ganong. (1990). "Remarriage and Stepfamily Research in the 1980s: Increased Interest in an Old Family Form." *Journal of Marriage and the Family, 52,* 925–940.

Depner, C. E., and J. H. Bray (Eds.), (1993). *Nonresidential Parenting: New Vistas in Family Living.* Newbury Park, CA: Sage Publications.

Furstenberg, F. F., Jr. (1987). "The New Extended Family: The Experience of Parents and Children After Remarriage." In K. Pasley and M. Ihinger-Tallman (Eds.), *Remarriage and Stepparenting: Current Research and Theory* (pp. 42–61). New York: Guilford Press.

Ganong, L. H., and M. Coleman. (1994). "Adolescent Stepchild-Stepparent Relationships: Changes Over Time." In K. Pasley and M. Ihinger-Tallman (Eds.), *Stepparenting Issues in Theory, Research, and Practice* (pp. 87–104). Westport, CT.: Greenwood Press.

Gottman, J. M. (1994). *Why Marriages Succeed or Fail: What You Can Learn from the Breakthrough Research to Make Your Marriage Last.* New York: Simon & Schuster.

Hetherington, E. M. (1993). "An Overview of the Virginia Longitudinal Study of Divorce and Remarriage." *Journal of Family Psychology, 7.*

Hetherington, E. M., and W. G. Clingempeel. (1992). "Coping with Marital Transitions: A Family Systems Perspective." *Monographs of the Society for Research in Child Development, 57,* nos. 2–3, Serial No. 227.

Johnston, J. R., M. Kline, and J. M. Tschann. (1989). "Ongoing Postdivorce Conflict: Effects on Children of Joint Custody and Frequent Access." *American Journal of Orthopsychiatry, 59,* 1–17.

Kelly, J. B. (1988). "Longer-Term Adjustment in Children of Divorce: Converging Findings and Implications for Practice." *Journal of Family Psychology, 2,* 119–140.

Rosen, M. B. (1987). *Stepfathering.* New York: Simon & Schuster.

Sarason, I. G., J. H. Johnson, and J. M. Siegal. (1978). "Assessing the Impact of Changes: Development of the Life Event Survey." *Journal of Consulting and Clinical Psychology, 46,* 932–946.

Visher, E. B., and J. S. Visher. (1988). *Old Loyalties, New Ties: Therapeutic Strategies with Stepfamilies.* New York: Brunner/Mazel.

———. (1991). *How to Win as a Stepfamily,* 2nd ed. New York: Brunner/Mazel.

Wallerstein, J. S., S. B. Corbin, and J. M. Lewis. (1988). "Children of Divorce: A Ten-Year Study." In E. M. Hetherington and J. Arasteh (Eds.), *The Impact of Divorce, Single-Parenting and Step-Parenting on Children* (pp. 198–214). Hillsdale, NJ: Lawrence Erlbaum.

Wallerstein, J. S., and J. Kelly. (1980). *Surviving the Break-Up: How Children and Parents Cope with Divorce.* New York: Basic Books.